MAX WEBER CLASSIC MONOGRAPHS

Selected and with new introductions by Bryan S. Turner

MAX WEBER CLASSIC MONOGRAPHS

VOLUME I
From History to Sociology
C. Antoni

VOLUME II
Max Weber: An Intellectual Portrait
R. Bendix

VOLUME III
The Sociology of Max Weber
J. Freund

VOLUME IV
Max Weber and German Politics
J. P. Mayer

VOLUME V
Max Weber and Modern Sociology
A. Sahay

VOLUME VI
Weber and the Marxist World
J. Weiss

VOLUME VII
Weber and Islam
B. S. Turner

MAX WEBER CLASSIC MONOGRAPHS

Volume VI: Weber and the Marxist World

J. Weiss

With an introduction by Bryan S. Turner

London and New York

First published in 1981 in German as *Das Werk Max Webers in der Marxistischen Rezeption und Kritik* by Westdeutscher Verlag Gmbh

Reprinted in 1998
by Routledge
2 Park Square, Milton Park, Abingdon, Oxfordshire OX14 4RN

Simultaneously published in the USA and Canada
by Routledge
711 Third Avenue, New York, NY 10017

Transferred to Digital Printing 2006

First issued in paperback 2014

Routledge is an imprint of the Taylor and Francis Group, an informa company

7-volume set
Volume VI ISBN 13: 978-0-415-17457-2 (hbk)
Volume VI ISBN 13: 978-0-415-75732-4 (pbk)

© 1981 J Weiss; Introduction © 1998 Bryan S. Turner

Introduction typeset in Times by Routledge

All rights reserved. No part of this book may be reprinted or reproduced or utilised in any form or by any electronic, mechanical, or other means, now known or hereafter invented, including photocopying and recording, or in any information storage or retrieval system, without permission in writing from the publishers.

British Library Cataloguing in Publication Data
A catalogue record for this book is available from the British Library

Library of Congress Cataloging in Publication Data
A catalogue record for this book has been requested

Publisher's note: These reprints are taken from original copies of each book In many cases the condition of these originals is not perfect. The paper, often acidic and having suffered over time, and the copy from such things as inconsistent printing pressure resulting in faint text, show-through from one side of a leaf to the other, the filling in of some characters, and the break-up of type. The publisher has gone to great lengths to ensure the quality of these reprints, but wishes to point out that certain characteristics of the original copies will, of necessity, be apparent in reprints thereof.

INTRODUCTION

Bryan S. Turner

This study of the critical reception and rejection of Max Weber's sociology by Marxist scholars and more generally by communist academic authorities is Volume VII of the Routledge and Thoemmes Press *Max Weber Classic Monographs* series. Weiss's study was first published in 1981 as *The Marxist Reception and Critique of the Work of Max Weber* in Germany and published in English translation by Routledge in 1986. Following the fall of communism and the collapse of the Soviet system around 1989–92, this reprint of Weiss's study is a timely and significant intellectual event. Weiss's volume provides the student of Weber with the only comprehensive account of the communist critique of Weber. In the post-Wall political world, it is a fascinating contribution to the history of ideas.

The relationship between Marx and Weber has been the topic of considerable debate and research (Antonio and Glassman, 1985). We need to distinguish carefully between three somewhat separate issues: Weber's relationship to the social theories of Karl Marx, his relation to Marxism as an intellectual movement and his relation to communism as a revolutionary movement. It is clear that, while Weber was impressed by Marx as a social analyst, he did not know the entire corpus of Marx's work, he did not fully understand Marx and finally Marx did not make a lasting or systematic impact on Weber. There is no sense in which Weber was involved in a debate with 'the ghost of Marx' (Salomon, 1935). Many supporters and critics of Weber of course welcomed *The Protestant Ethic and the Spirit of Capitalism* as a refutation of Marx's analysis of industrial capitalism. In the 1960s and 1970s, in a similar fashion academic sociologists treated Weber's *Economy and Society* as the principal alternative to Marx's *Capital*. In fact, there is relatively little discussion of or reference to the work of Marx in Weber's sociology.

As many commentators have noted, Weber would have had access to such crucial texts of Marx as *Economic and Philosophical Manuscripts, Theses on Feuerbach* or *Grundrisse*. For Weber, Marx's work represented a mono-causal explanation of history in terms of economic conditions and therefore Weber believed that Marxist sociology had not adequately confronted the problems raised by neo-Kantianism and in particular by the methodological debates of Wilhelm Dilthey, Heinrich Rickert and Wilhelm Windelband (Sahay, 1971). To some extent, it was left to Austro-Marxism to undertake this confrontation with neo-Kantian epistemology (Bottomore and Goode, 1978).

Although in the formulation of his sociology Weber was not systematically influenced by Marx, this observation does not imply that there is no relationship. For example, it is very appropriate to note that there is an important similarity and connection between Marx's concept of alienation and Weber's concept of rationalisation (Löwith, 1993). It is also true that Marx and Weber shared similar ambiguities towards and understanding of bureaucracy, markets and science as crucial components of capitalist society and as forces of modernisation (Sayer, 1991). However, we cannot say that during his lifetime an engagement with the work of Marx was constitutive of Weber's sociological arguments.

Weber was of course very much concerned with the issue of the impact of Marxism as a social ideology on the German working class through the Social Democratic movement. Although Marx developed a revolutionary politics of capitalism, by the 1890s it was obvious that German capitalism would not collapse as a consequence of revolution. If anything, the real incomes and the standard of living of the working class had risen. There had been as a result no polarisation or pauperisation of society. Weber was critical of the German Social Democratic Party (SPD) which attempted to combine a reformist approach to electoral politics with a faith in the final triumph of socialism. Under the leadership of intellectuals like Eduard Bernstein, the SPD had adopted reformism, namely the theory that there would be a gradual transformation of capitalism through the electoral participation of the working class. Bernstein and his followers abandoned any commitment to practical revolutionary strategies and tactics, such as the general strike. Weber tended therefore either to despise reformism (because it combined political conservatism with revolutionary rhetoric), or to regard it as no longer a significant dimension of German politics, and yet paradoxically he was often in agreement with Bernstein who rejected, for example, Marx's doctrine of economic determinism (Breuilly, 1987).

While Weber was interested in the fortunes of the SPD and not entirely hostile to working-class politics, he was fearful of any destabilisation of the German state, especially after the defeat in 1918–19. Weber was closely involved with other scholars in political debates about Germany after the War. For example, in the debates in 1917 at Lauenstein Castle about the future, radical students, including Georg Lukács, had anticipated that Weber would announce a new world (Kadarkay, 1991: 187). Instead Weber welcomed the fact that Russian interference in Germany had been averted, and recognised the inevitability of American hegemony in the new world order. At a personal level, he was withdrawn from political life, and spent his time reading the prophets of the Old Testament.

Weber's lack of engagement with the radical politics of the student movement was also a function of the fact that he remained consistently anxious about the 'Russian danger'. As a nationalist, Weber was concerned to protect the cohesion of Germany as a strong nation state. In his essays on the Russian Revolutions (Weber, 1995), he attempted to analyse the failures of liberal–bourgeois democracy. The constitutional reforms had been frustrated by the failure of local and provincial governments to gain autonomy, the social and political weakness of the bourgeoisie as a class and the permanent authoritarianism of the Tsarist regime. Weber remained fearful over the persistent threat of eastern authoritarianism, and therefore rejected the views of the radical youth of Munich who sought an end to war through a Russian-style revolution.

Weber, influenced by the work of Robert Michels on 'the iron law of oligarchy', believed that a revolution could not succeed without a loyal bureaucratic staff, but bureaucratisation would also limit the scope of revolution (Mommsen, 1989). It was over these issues that he departed company with Lukács whose views he treated as romantic and utopian. In an important but incomplete passage on revolution in *Economy and Society*, Weber argued that the German bureaucracy had survived the War and thereby demonstrated the durability of modern bureaucracies. He also attributed some of the success of the Russian Revolution to the fact that workers and soldiers were able to take up bureaucratic tasks successfully. He concluded that 'every revolution which has been attempted under modern conditions has failed completely because of the indispensability of trained officials and of the lack of its own organized staff' (Weber, 1978: 266). Lukács and other radicals who regarded revolution as a *spiritual* transformation of society found it difficult to accept Weber's realism when it came to the assessment of political conditions.

After Weber's death, there was little discussion of his sociology in the English-speaking world and obviously intellectual exchange between Germany and the Allies was very limited. However, from the 1950s until the end of the 1970s, there was a steady stream of translations of Weber's major works, which illustrated the scope of his intellectual achievement. Weber's reception into North American sociology was, however, through the interpretation and perspective of Talcott Parsons, who did not pay much attention to Weber's economic and political sociology. Parsons was primarily concerned with Weber's relationship to the voluntaristic theory of action and to the sociology of religion (Holton and Turner, 1986). Against this perspective, a number of sociologists emphasised the importance of so-called 'conflict sociology' and interpreted Weber as a social theorist whose major contribution has been to the analysis of material interests, group struggle and social conflict (Rex, 1961).

During the Cold War period, there was also a huge expansion of undergraduate studies in sociology in European universities. In this context, there emerged a considerable ideological battle around the works of Marx and Weber. With the growth in popularity of so-called structural Marxism, Weber was increasingly, as Weiss so clearly demonstrates, defined as a 'bourgeois sociologist', whose commitment to methodological individualism and political liberalism confirmed his membership of the bourgeois class. There were a number of important translations of Marxist works into English which fuelled the debate such as *For Marx* (Althusser, 1966) and *Political Power and Social Classes* (Poulantzas, 1973). In England, sociology became polarised around those who supported Poulantzas's criticisms of individualistic and 'unscientific' sociology and those who by contrast supported the view of Marxism as a scientific theory of social formations.

In both America and continental Europe, these Marxist debates made less impact on the curriculum of sociology in the universities. The May events of 1968 passed without any permanent damage to the governments of western Europe. In the United States, despite the Vietnam War, Marxism made little serious progress and debates about social theory were more likely to be organised around pro-Parsons and anti-Parsons factions (Alexander, 1987), while actual empirical research was quantitative in the tradition of P.F.

Lazarsfeld. Radical and critical appraisals of Parsons drew on both Marx and Weber, because in the American context Weber often appeared as a radical social theorist (Gouldner, 1970; Mills, 1959). We therefore have the paradox, as outlined by Weiss, that in the communist bloc social theorists took Weber very seriously, but regarded him as a bourgeois sociologist. In western sociology, Weber was often neglected in favour of structural Marxism or because he appeared as a Machiavellian theorist of power politics.

By the time Parsons died in 1979, functionalism was moribund and has remained so, despite attempts to revive it in the shape of neofunctionalism (Alexander, 1985). A decade later organised communism eventually collapsed and there has been throughout the eastern bloc a significant revival of sociology which has ironically often involved a renewal of interest in Weberian sociology. Althusser committed suicide in 1990, by which time structural Marxism had ceased to be influential. During this period, however, there was also a general decline in sociology within western universities and a new interest in cultural studies with the result that the notion of 'culture' has somewhat replaced 'society' as the key topic of sociological discussion. The sociological reasons for these changes are to be sought in the growth of cultural consumerism, tourism, the aestheticisation of everyday life and the postmodernisation of culture (Connor, 1996). As one might expect, therefore, the contemporary interest in Weber tends to emphasise the importance of culture in Weber's sociology, to associate Weber with Nietzsche as a cultural critic and to relate Weber's dispute over values to postmodernism as a cultural theory. The relationship between Marx and Weber in western sociology is understated and other relationships (Weber and Nietzsche, Weber and Simmel) are emphasised (Turner, 1992). The future of Weber in the East, the subject of part of Weiss's investigation, remains an issue of fascinating speculation.

References

Alexander, J. C. (ed.) (1985) *Neofunctionalism*. Beverly Hills: Sage.
—— (1987) *Twenty Lectures: Sociological theory since World War II*. New York: Columbia University Press.
Althusser, L. (1966) *For Marx*. London: Allen Lane The Penguin Press.
Antonio, R. J. and Glassman, R. M. (eds) (1985) *A Weber–Marx Dialogue*. Lawrence: University Press of Kansas.
Bottomore, T. and Goode, P. (eds) (1978) *Austro-Marxism*. Oxford: Oxford University Press.

Breuilly, J. (1987) 'Eduard Bernstein and Max Weber' in W. J. Mommsen and J. Osterhammel (eds) *Max Weber and his Contemporaries*. London: Allen & Unwin, pp. 345–54.

Connor, O. (1996) 'Cultural sociology and cultural sciences' in B. S. Turner (ed.) *The Blackwell Companion to Social Theory*. Oxford: Blackwell, pp. 340–68.

Gouldner, A. W. (1970) *The Coming Crisis of Western Sociology*. New York: Basic Books.

Holton, R. J. and Turner, B. S. (1986) *Talcott Parsons on Economy and Society*. London: Routledge & Kegan Paul.

Kadarkay, A. (1991) *Georg Lukács: Life, thought and politics*. Oxford: Blackwell.

Löwith, K. (1993) *Max Weber and Karl Marx*. London and New York: Routledge.

Mills, C. W. (1959) *The Sociological Imagination*. New York: Oxford University Press.

Mommsen, W. J. (1989) *The Political and Social Theory of Max Weber*. Cambridge: Polity Press.

Poulantzas, N. (1973) *Political Power and Social Classes*. London: New Left Books.

Rex, J. (1961) *Key Problems of Sociological Theory*. London: Routledge & Kegan Paul.

Sahay, A. (ed.) (1971) *Max Weber and Modern Sociology*. London: Routledge & Kegan Paul.

Salomon, A. (1935) 'Max Weber's sociology', *Social Research*, 2: 60–73.

Sayer, D. (1991) *Capitalism and Modernity: An excursus on Marx and Weber*. London: Routledge.

Turner, B. S. (1992) *Max Weber: From history to modernity*. London and New York: Routledge.

—— (1996) *For Weber: Essays on the sociology of fate*. London: Sage (2nd edition).

Weber, M. (1978) *Economy and Society: An outline of interpretive sociology*. Berkeley: University of California Press, 2 volumes.

—— (1995) *The Russian Revolutions*. Cambridge: Polity Press.

Weber and the Marxist world

Johannes Weiss

Translated by Elizabeth King-Utz and Michael J. King

Routledge & Kegan Paul
London and New York

It can only be regretted that the works of the sociologist Weber are not yet illuminated with sufficient depth in Marxist literature.

I. S. Kon, 1973, 149

Contents

	Preface	ix
1	Introduction: the origins, purposes and outline of the discussion	1
2	The political and ideological 'ban'	9
	2.1 Historical materialism, Stalinism and sociology	9
	2.2 The history of the reception of Weber	15
3	Epistemological and methodological problems	19
	3.1 Subjectivism or reflection? The fundamental critique of Weber's epistemological position	19
	3.2 Objectivity and partisanship, ethical neutrality and value relevance	28
	3.3 Ideal types, laws, theories	43
	3.4 Explanation and interpretative understanding, materiality and meaning	63
4	The fundamental theoretical perspective: social action or material relations?	72
5	Special problems of the theoretical and empirical work	84
	5.1 Religion and the material base	84
	5.2 Class and status	90
	5.3 The city	94
	5.4 Problems of culture (science and art)	98
	5.5 Rationality, authority, bureaucracy	108
	5.6 Blank areas: economy, state, law	116

6	Social science and political commitment	123
	Notes	143
	Bibliography	175
	Name index	200
	Subject index	204

Preface

In the course of numerous discussions with students and colleagues I have encountered considerable interest in the relationship between Max Weber's sociology and the Marxist theoretical tradition. This interest is also demonstrated by the growing number of studies conducted by Marxist scientists (including those from socialist countries) examining the work of Max Weber. At the same time, however, the Marxist reception and critique of his work, in both its general and particular aspects, was until recently often determined by assumptions that have gravely impeded a fruitful confrontation between these two very important foundation stones of social science. To prepare the ground for and promote systematic discussions in the future it seems useful to me, therefore, to provide a reasonably comprehensive, structured and critical overview on the present concern with Weber's work from a Marxist perspective and, simultaneously, to draw attention to several authors and studies whose comparatively productive contributions deserve more attention that they received to date.

Some of the traditional premisses of interpretation, which so adversely influenced the Marxist critique of Weber (or the systematic comparison between Marxian and Weberian ideas of social science), are increasingly challenged by Marxist theorists themselves, even within the confines of an 'orthodox' self-definition of Marxism. The present study should thus be seen as an attempt to incorporate and counteract these approaches from, as it were, the other side. The fact that this takes the form of an extensive and thorough enquiry into the history of the Marxist reception and critique of Weber should not be seen as a waste of resources. We pay dearly for neglecting a thorough 'anamnesis' even in the history of science, in that previous knowledge is forgotten (and only laboriously retraced) while previous misapprehensions constantly regain ground.

This systematic perspective at various stages gave rise to the questioning of some well-established interpretations of the Marxian basis of social science. It goes without saying, however, that these fragmented and undeveloped regressions neither represent nor replace a well-explained and consistent interpretation of Marx. It is more likely that the anti-critical comments on the Marxist critique of Weber add up to a portrayal of the Weberian basis of sociology, which may serve the purpose of a special introduction as well.

My introductory remarks will provide further detailed information on the object and very limited aim of this critical enquiry. Moreover, in that context I shall also explain the concentration on (but not restriction to) a fairly limited range of Marxist literature. Beyond that I can only hope that a bibliographical and critical survey of this kind is of interest and use even to those who address themselves to the more concrete problems of social science research or, indeed, the construction of sophisticated theoretical syntheses.

My thanks both to those who strengthened my good faith in the worthwhile nature of this undertaking and those who cast doubt upon it. I hope that both have proved beneficial to my work. I express my gratitude to my ever-helpful colleagues at the university libraries of Duisburg and Cologne, as well as Mrs Christel Quasigroh, Mrs Renate Voigt, Mr Ulrich Schallwig and Mr Wilhelm Bükers for their patient support in the preparation of this manuscript.

1 Introduction: the origins, purposes and outline of the discussion

The latest developments in the philosophy of science need not have been necessary to demonstrate how little the history of scientific knowledge corresponds with progress in any 'research logic'. On the other hand, the history of several sciences, particularly that of the 'exact' natural sciences and mathematics, may at least seem to permit a later reconstruction along the lines of such a model. In comparison, such reconstruction in the humanities, in general, and sociology, in particular, may be faced with serious problems. This certainly applies to sociology when we refer to the relationship between various theoretical tendencies, or paradigms, rather than each of their separate developments. A historical sequence of these paradigms, in the sense that transitions are conveyed through an intensive 'critical examination' of each preceding paradigm, can obviously only be constructed here if we proceed from their own highly dogmatic presuppositions (e.g. in that a particular theory is assumed to be an *a priori* essential and, in the long term, inevitable result of development).

At this stage I am not engaging in a general discussion on what real and logical reasons inhibited and still inhibit such rational 'progress of knowledge' within sociology. The aim is rather to discuss critically the long-standing and fierce, as well as inconclusive, debate between two specific theoretical tendencies – namely, the one originating in Marx and the one founded by Weber. An analysis of this specific case of unsuccessful 'competition between theories' may possibly lead to some insights of general significance. Despite all the disagreements among the sociological 'scientific community', this expectation seems warranted since there is a far-reaching consensus that these two theoretical tendencies are of key importance, both with a view to their historical impact and within contemporary theoretical discussion.

Moreover, more recent theoretical discussion is not so much characterised by an isolated revival of the one or the other 'position', or an updating of the typological dichotomy of either tradition, as by endeavours to subject the relative strengths and weaknesses of the two paradigms to an objective and intensive examination. This applies particularly to the way Weberian sociology is perceived and discussed by authors who underwent their primary academic socialisation on the horizon of the materialist paradigm.

It is the principal intention of this book to contribute to these systematic endeavours. An answer to the question – in what respect and why was the Marxist reception and critique of Weber to date so remarkably inadequate and fruitless? – should prove most useful for the current controversies. The aim is to clarify traditional misapprehensions and deep-rooted tensions in order to channel and concentrate the controversy on those points which in fact constitute fundamental obstacles to both an objective communication among theorists and – even more importantly – the combination or integration of the theories. Thus the intention is certainly not to steer away from the existing conflicts, but rather to make the real conflicts and problems more apparent and so facilitate their discussion.

An undertaking of this nature may at first seem exceedingly naive. This uncertainty can ultimately be resolved only by the discussion below. At any rate we can draw encouragement from the fact that there are definitely some examples of productive critical treatment of Weber's sociology from a materialist perspective. The most important of the older contributions is that by Alexander Neusychin, which is laid down in a series of his earlier works of the years 1923–7.[1] These works by Neusychin have only more recently attracted attention and praise from other Marxist theorists and will receive due consideration in the discussion.

It would be naive or presumptuous indeed if the author of this book were to claim to be above the 'parties' in question or even science in general. To be sure, his understanding of empirical science is influenced to a particularly large degree by Weberian thinking. In his case he would, however, reject the label 'Weberian', not just to distance himself (convincingly or not) from Weberian thinking, but in fact to do justice to it. It is no accident that the enormous impact of Weber's work has not been transmitted over the decades in the form of the building up of a school by way of a system of doctrines (a so-called 'canon') developed in a logical way.[2] This is due not only to the experimental and fragmentary nature of the Weberian work, but it is bound up with his fundamental ideas on the importance and status of theory as well as the relationship between theory and empirical research in historical sociology. In terms of research practice the relatively great openness and flexibility of these conceptions expresses itself probably most strikingly in the very extensive usage of 'materialist' categories and theorems (in the broader sense) in Weber's empirical analyses.

The present discussion (at least in this form) would probably be superfluous if the Marxist reception and critique of Weber had taken up Weber's discussion on the Marxist scientific tradition. The consequences of restricting the reception to the *Protestant Ethic*, while neglecting Weber's own evaluation of the implications of his analysis, have obviously been very detrimental. With a small number of exceptions, Weber's preliminary works directed not at an abstract, but problem-related, confrontation with and partial combination of theoretical writings of diverse origin were, however, completely ignored.

Despite this situation the discussion below will not proceed from Weber's reception and critique of Marxism, although it seems to lend itself to such treatment. This is inadvisable, firstly, on account of workload economy, since there are hardly any precise references to this argumentation in the Marxist literature on Weber. Secondly, an independent, reasonably exhaustive and systematic (as well as, ultimately, critical) description of this aspect of Weber's work would be outside the bounds of the intended discussion.[3] Thirdly, and finally, there is the possible danger that questions of interpretation themselves would assume too much importance.

In the discussion below I shall therefore proceed by dealing with problems, which are constantly thematised in the Marxist critique of Weber, in the most systematic and sequential way possible. So far as it is necessary the Weberian reception and critique of Marxist concepts will be brought into play in the discussion of these problems. Further, at appropriate junctures, I shall consider some of those questions that have been almost entirely neglected in the Marxist literature on Weber to date, but which, in my opinion, have to be discussed within the framework of a critical treatment with systematic pretensions.

In what follows I shall provide a brief overview on the questions under consideration and their context. Before embarking on this venture, however, it seems appropriate to make a comment on the Marxist literature I selected. By 'Marxist literature' I understand that which was written by authors who explicitly claim to be representing Marxist theory as it was validly developed in basic outlines by Marx and Engels.[4] In other words, the criterion of selection was authors' own classification as representatives of the theoretical tendency that is as a rule denoted as 'historical materialism', regardless of whether they mutually dispute the validity of each other's claim.

This criterion at the same time largely excludes those theorists who explicitly define their relationship with the tradition of historical materialism in terms of a simultaneous continuation and critique (i.e. 'reconstruction'). This applies chiefly to critical theory (itself multifaceted). Its highly interesting and, at the very least, ambivalent relationship with Weberian sociology (although only inadequately explicated) will not be the object of a separate and adequate discussion. This limitation is not only due to the matching distribution of emphasis within the cited 'materialist' literature on Weber's work and the constraints imposed by workload economy, but also because it has a methodological advantage. The representatives of the 'orthodox' theoretical tendency (and here again, particularly the Marxist-*Leninist*) consistently formulate their objections in, as it were, ideal-typical purity and determination. The same applies to their portrayal of Weberian thinking, namely its anti-Marxist nature on all essential points. We can find the setting of one type against another among many other authors (Marxists as well as non-Marxist), and this has undoubted methodological and heuristic advantages if it is taken as the *point of departure* of a discussion. The fact that this kind of ideal-typical exaggeration and absolutising of particular characteristics is no simple fiction for reasons of methodological convenience, but occurs in historical reality (and this nearly exclusively in specific socio-political and intellectual contexts), frees the choice of this method from the suspicion that it only serves to facilitate the anti-critical enterprise. In fact it is, of course, entirely in keeping with the spirit of the present work if those schematisations are definitively overcome in the course of further discussion. Where necessary I shall therefore provide at least some brief references to those modifications and developments within the materialist theoretical tendency (in broader terms) which appear particularly interesting and productive for a future systematic discussion.

Within the framework of these limitations, I shall endeavour completeness only with regard to the most important argumentations. In my view, I should be able to achieve this without a comprehensive knowledge of publications of materialist origin that appeared after Weber's death. It is regrettable though that, due to a lack of linguistic expertise, the works by Polish, Czech, Serbocroat and Hungarian authors could be considered only in so far as they were submitted in German, English or French.[5] (In some individual cases translations were prepared on a private basis.) In comparison, the Russian literature on Weber is perhaps more adequately represented.[6]

Chapter 2 proceeds from some more general comments on the political-ideological conditions, which subdued the reception and critique of non-Marxist sociology in Soviet Marxism, in post-revolutionary history (particularly during the phase of Stalinist authority). The changes in general conditions are well exemplified by the varied treatment the work of Max Weber underwent over the decades.

Within the sphere of substantive critique, that which operates at the epistemological level most closely approximates a global defence, which is argued solely at the political-ideological level. The first two sections of Chapter 3 therefore deal with the discussion of Weber's epistemological premises and the thesis of ethical neutrality which directly follows from this. Subsequently the discussion turns on two central methodological problem areas. The Marxist critique of the ideal-type concept, which is dealt with first, gives rise to a more detailed consideration of the relationship between historical analysis and conceptual-theoretical generalisation in Weber and Marx. This should demonstrate that the two authors by no means contradict each other on this important question, so long as Marxian theses are kept free from metaphysical interpretations. I shall conclude this chapter with some very tentative considerations on the relationship between explanation and understanding. The conventional Marxist lack of interest in this problem has here and there given way to a decided interest in more recent times.

Chapter 4 will deal with those arguments that object to the conceptual-theoretical 'social action' approach. This problem area should prove particularly important because the Marxist critique of Weber seems to ignore consistently a constitutive shortcoming in its own position. Even in the most recent publications Weber's focus on social action and the 'subjectively intended meaning' of his approach have been contrasted with the necessity for a theoretical conception which thematises objective conditions, systems, structures, etc. But an alternative (possibly superior) theoretical position is evidently given only if it can be shown that those 'objective conditions' do *not* owe their emergence, persistence and effectiveness to interrelated human action. This has by no means been shown so far and it also contradicts some very decisive comments on this problem by Karl Marx. Besides, the thesis that conditions, which determine human action like an 'invisible hand', are continuously reproduced by the same action is by no means paradoxical – least of all for dialectical thinking.

The Marxist critique of two specific characteristics of the

Weberian concept of social action appears better grounded: namely, the central determination of the 'subjectively intended meaning' and the 'individualistic' character of this concept. The discussion attempts to explain to what extent the critique directed at these two characteristics is based upon a defensible interpretation. Here I shall place emphasis on 'interpretation', since Weber's own arguments on this point are in fact very fragmentary and may well be comparatively misleading. The primary issue to be discussed with reference to the definition of 'subjectively intended meaning' is whether this is balanced by an adequate treatment of the problem of alienation. I shall present a few arguments for the thesis that this problem can only be grasped with a concept of social action that is based on 'subjectively intended meaning'.

The discussion of the 'individualistic' character of the Weberian concept of action is not limited to methodological considerations. On the contrary, it is necessary to examine whether this fundamental individualistic feature of social theory construction is made essential by contemporary social conditions and whether this applies *a fortiori* if the theory of social science is supposed to be capable of guiding political action towards change by means of democratic channels.

Chapter 5 examines Weber's special theorems that can in fact be compared with actual or alleged materialist theorems due to their sphere of explanation and these were therefore a popular object of Marxist critique. The discussion in this sphere was determined by an overwhelming consideration for *The Protestant Ethic*. My aim is to clarify generally the explanatory intention of the Weberian and Marxist theorems, which can actually be related to each other, by starting out from the most important arguments presented in this context. This should at least show that the contrast between the 'idealist' mode of explanation, on the one hand, and the 'materialist' mode of explanation, on the other (found not only amongst Marxist authors) is definitively untenable and fundamentally unworkable. Beyond that it should become apparent that an adequate examination of the relative explanatory power inherent in both the Weberian and Marxist scientific methods requires a much more comprehensive and thorough study of Weber's theoretical and empirical endeavours than has hitherto been the norm amongst Marxist critics. It is precisely the heavy emphasis on socio-economic and, more particularly, class-theoretical explanatory approaches that make Weber's analyses both attractive to and difficult for a critical discussion from the Marxist perspective. Weber's development and modification of nineteenth-century class-theoretical conceptions (primarily the Marxist ones) have recently attracted increasing interest among materialist theorists. The beginnings of a critical analysis and the definition of the relations are discussed in Section 5.2.

The rank order value of socio-economic and class-theoretical assumptions in the context of Weber's broad historical-sociological research programme is exemplified, indeed within the narrower confines of his enquiry into Protestantism, by his essay on *The City*. Section 5.3 is concerned with the dominant role this essay played (for good reasons) in the early Marxist reception of Weber's work and in the important works by Neusychin in particular.

The critical treatment given to Weber's analyses by some Marxist authors concerning the position of science, on the one hand, and art, on the other, with the growth of rationalisation in modern European history is comparatively substantial, although perhaps contrary to initial expectations. These critical contributions seem suitable to encourage future discussion precisely because this field of Weberian research is both relatively undeveloped and very much neglected in the general reception of his work.

The critique of Weber's thesis of a trend towards the increasing bureaucratisation of socio-economic and political relations under both capitalist and socialist conditions deserves special attention in Section 5.5. The critique of this thesis has dimensions in the empirical field and the philosophy of science: on the one hand, it deals with the question of whether Weber's approach stands up to empirical scrutiny. In this respect, of course, it is necessary to take the intervening development in socialist countries into consideration. On the other hand, another issue to be discussed is the assertion that Weber's (supposed) resignation in the face of this process is rooted in the fundamental affirmative feature of his action theory approach.

The final section of Chapter 5 refers to fields of research that are dealt with only peripherally in the reception of Weber's work to date, although they coincide with the central sphere of explanation of historical materialism and would therefore be particularly worthy of a systematic discussion from this perspective. This applies not least to the overlapping general and social-historical framework of reference within which Weber explores the interrelationship between the economy, political (especially state) authority and the law. The revival of the discussion on the precise status of this framework of reference opens up new avenues for a comparative critical examination of those claims concerning the philosophy or 'logic' of history that represent a central problem for the most recent attempts to 'reconstruct' historical materialism.

INTRODUCTION

The final part of this book (Chapter 6) discusses a question of fundamental importance to the entire discussion and critique of Weberian thinking by Marxist theorists and has therefore been repeatedly addressed in the preceding sections of this work – particularly in Chapters 2 and 3. The question is posed as to how scientific and political-ethical conceptions relate to each other. In order to clarify this question I shall at the outset refer to and discuss the most important arguments asserting a relationship between Weber's political (and class) position and the specific (systematic) weaknesses of his sociological work. In their subject matter, arguments of this kind belong primarily to the genuinely Marxist critique of science, but they were expressed with special emphasis by some non-Marxist authors. The discussion of their implications leads to some general concluding considerations on the relationship between political and scientific orientations. I shall advocate and expand on the thesis that the specific prerequisites for rationality of the *two* spheres of argumentation call for a divorce in principle.

At the same time, however, I shall endeavour to show that, given this divorce, it is possible to think in terms of and achieve a close and fruitful reciprocal relationship between the two spheres. Neither Weberian rigour nor the idea of a 'dialectical' mediation, distinctive of the Marxist tradition of thought, present any solutions to the problem that can still manage to convince today.

2 The political and ideological 'ban'

2.1 Historical materialism, Stalinism and sociology

As a general rule there is little chance for any real scientific discussion if scientific controversies are primarily interpreted in political terms and, what is more, if politics is understood in terms of a 'friend-enemy' model. A scientific theory or position is thus not perceived and evaluated according to its truth content and logical stringency, but purely in terms of its function in the political struggle. At the very least efforts will be made to determine the scientific quality of a theory as a function of the political status attributed to its author. The successful refutation of a competing theory thus consists of establishing that its author belongs to the camp of the political enemy or that this theory objectively serves the political interests of an enemy (i.e. even without the author's knowledge and intention).

This substitution (or functionalisation) of scientific theory with political argumentation undoubtedly corresponds to neither the ideas of scientific critique held by the Marxist classics (Marx and Engels)[1] nor the method actually practised by them. Rather, their method consisted in showing the scientific superiority of their own conceptions and therefore also the necessity for socialist politics (an imperative derivation from these scientific conceptions) by means of an intensive, rational and empirical critique of competing theories. It is, of course, an entirely different question, and one worthwhile pursuing, whether certain 'classical' fundamental assumptions about the status and possibilities of a sufficiently thorough ('radical') empirical theory and analysis of society could not also be employed to defend that obversion of the relationship between scientific and political (ideological) critique. Implied are those fundamental assumptions that presuppose a logically imperative interrelationship between the (empirically) true theory of bourgeois society, on the one hand, and the essential goals of political practice, on the other.[2] Of course, in Marx and Engels this interrelationship was clearly meant to portray that genuine analysis was the prerequisite, while the correct theoretical and practical critique should be the consequence. Here nonetheless resided the possibility for simplifying and vulgarising conceptions to draw the obverse conclusion of the untenability of an author's scientific ideas if his/her political orientation was asserted to be misguided, the critic thus being able to dispense with a substantive analysis of these ideas with a good conscience.

This discussion proceeds on the assumption that this type of method cannot be based on convincing epistemological or logical scientific reasoning, indeed not even within the framework of a Marxist conception of science, and that there is therefore no possibility for a rational discussion of such arguments.[3] In comparison, the stated fundamental assumption held by the Marxist classics is very easily accessible to, as well as in need of, a critical examination. Beyond that this assumption marks, or so it seems, a genuine contrast to Weber's conceptions concerning the relationship between science and critique, and I shall therefore return to it at an appropriate juncture.

The political functionalisation of the reception and critique of scientific conceptions with Marxist premises is particularly characteristic of the Stalinist rule. Whereas the absurdity and perniciousness of this method in the field of the more or less stringent and economically important natural sciences was difficult to ignore after a while (to some extent even before Stalin's death), leading to a matching reserve (although only reluctantly to an explicit revision in logic),[4] it is possible to observe a progressive intensification in its application in the fields of philosophy and sociology (as well as the remaining cultural and social sciences).[5] This process was helped by the fact that these sciences, at least in the short or medium term, are of no empirically examinable or important economic and technological use value. This aspect is of course all the more important if material and technological progress is clearly seen to be and pursued as the highest or even single political goal, as indeed was the case during this phase of Soviet-Russian history.[6]

Above all the social sciences evidently possessed (and possess) comparatively weak *endogeneous* powers of resistance against their use as an ideology. In the face of profound disagreement among not only non-Marxist, but also self-conceived Marxist theorists, such dogmatic regulation and alignment could be almost interpreted as a great exoneration and necessary solid foundation for a consistent and undisturbed development of the social sciences. This, to a large extent, may explain the feelings of superiority evidently felt by a number of Marxist theorists even today when they contrast the plurality and divisions amongst competing approaches with the unanimity and ideological protection of their own system. In this vein, for example, the editorial 'Foreword' to the first volume of the journal *Unter dem Banner des Marxismus*, after a description of the predominant 'feeling of general insecurity and uncertainty' in 'official bourgeois science' (as a whole) argues that: 'In contrast the *hegemony of Marxism* has been consolidated in the Soviet states.'[7]

In fact, orthodox Marxist authors, even in their most recent analyses of competing interpretations within the social sciences (including Weber's conception), see the mere classification of a position as 'pluralist' in terms of being a grave critique. Indeed, the development of Marxist empirical sociology is correspondingly accompanied and safeguarded by the observation that its reference back to historical materialism, containing the definitive solution of all fundamental questions (Hahn, 1974, 37), reliably protects such sociology from irritation, insecurity and, thus, 'pluralism'. This interpretation of historical materialism consistently appeals to Lenin in particular (perhaps justifiably): '*At best*, pre-Marxist "sociology" and historiography brought forth an accumulation of raw facts, collected at random, and a description of individual aspects of the historical process.' In contrast, 'the Marxist doctrine is omnipotent because it is true. It is comprehensive and harmonious, and provides men with an integral outlook . . .' (V. I. Lenin, 1973, 24, 7).[8]

In the field of the social sciences (but also, for example, in philosophy) it is frequently difficult to discern whether such pronounced interest in an all-encompassing and enduring synthesis is really built on a love for truth or rather on the will for power. It is particularly hard to decide on this with Marxist theories if and in so far as they are convinced that there is no contradiction between the interest in gaining/maintaining political power and the one and 'absolute' truth. This conviction may indeed explain their readiness to carry through and protect this grand synthesis, if necessary by political means of power and, on the other hand, to use it for political-ideological and legitimatory goals.

It is by no means pure rhetoric in so far as the already cited Foreword in the journal *Unter dem Banner des Marxismus* (*UBM*) speaks of the 'hegemony' of Marxism. In fact, a few sentences later the author very explicitly and freely identifies the most intimate relationship between the establishment and protection of the 'dictatorship of the proletariat' and the opportunity to 'actually take up the ideological commando heights' (*UBM*, Vol. 1, 125/6, 7). He continues by stating that it is precisely this situation that facilitates the emergence of 'that synthesis' in the sciences 'which official bourgeois science is incapable of finding'.

The possibility of grounding the power-political functionalisation of science, of which I originally spoke, is evidently lodged in the basic assumption that social and political progress under the imprint of socialism and the progress of scientific knowledge constitute two sides of the same process. The fact that this possibility of perversion was realised primarily with regard to the social sciences and philosophy cannot simply be explained by the relative weaknesses of this group of sciences from the 'technological' and systematic angle that we have hitherto dealt with (in other words, its weak internal potential for resistance). On the contrary, the power-political use of these sciences may seem much more useful to a dictatorship, at least in the short or medium term, than their uninhibited development, or their actual attempt to remove gradually the mentioned weaknesses.

It is precisely due to the claim that the socialist authority structure is the only one that can be legitimised by science that it is dependent on an ideological system which can be identified as a social science. On the other hand, it is the technological and systematic shortcomings of non-Marxist social science that so convincingly led to (a) its political-practical application, in general, and (b) the connected resolution of problems and systematisation at the cognitive level being propagated as an index of the crucial stages of *scientific* progress. The fact that this constantly asserted claim to scientific backing did not collapse, to the extent that it would have been perceivable even to the most credulous particularly during the worst phase of power-political and ideological instrumentalisation of historical materialism, was of the greatest importance in terms of its political-ideological usefulness. The socialist system of authority had so absolutely tied its legitimacy to the fundamental power of positive empirical-science knowledge[9] that even a policy involving the destruction of all possible development in the social sciences (at least as an unavoidable side-effect) was dependent on the fiction of its highest legitimacy backed by social science.

In the section below I shall deal neither with the eventful history of sociology in the Soviet Union and the other socialist countries in general, nor its almost total suppression during the Stalinist phase, in particular. Numerous analyses of this history are available (cf., for example: Ahlberg, 1968 and 1969; Weinberg, 1974; Kiss 1971; Hahn, 1977) and, indeed, more recently from the socialist countries themselves (cf., for example, Grušin, 1965; Cagin, 1971;

Osipova, 1971; Wiatr, 1971; Osipov and Rutkevich, 1978; Boring and Taubert, 1970). These provide more or less convincing explanations for the repression of sociological research at the end of the 1920s and its revival and development after the Twentieth Soviet Communist Party Congress, although the time periods in which this occurred clearly varied in different countries. It seems plausible that, almost across the board, the dogmatisation of historical materialism had less to do with the 'personality cult' around Stalin (Grušin, 1965, 15) than with the need for an ideological legitimation of the compulsory and violent development of those years that was secure and immune from objection.[10] Similarly, an important point may well be made when the development of 'concrete sociological' research is explained in terms of the necessity for gathering more precise and reliable information about socio-cultural and economic conditions, which had by then become highly differentiated and variable.[11] However, on the whole the analyses in question seem to concentrate over-much on the development of *empirical* sociological research and its economic and political usefulness or disadvantages. These empirical analyses should be regarded as a suitable indicator of the liveliness and fruitfulness of social science and sociological research only in so far as they actually reflect a developed theoretical and methodological problem consciousness. Beyond that even the politically and ideologically decisive controversies refer much less to the existence or non-existence of specific social factors than their adequate and theoretical (causal) interpretation, as well as the importance attached to empirical research in general for the confirmation or refutation of social science theories.

The comparatively open discussion about historical materialism and sociology (of both Marxist and non-Marxist origin) engaged in within the Soviet Union until the end of the 1920s[12] operated primarily on this level of theory and philosophy of science. Similarly, the subsequent dogmatisation of historical materialism operated primarily at this level, which can be easily understood in view of the stated legitimation requirements. Dogmatic historical materialism defends a dictatorial practice of authority and simultaneously explains why empirical analyses of the 'object' of this authority are at least superfluous, if not downright unscientific and counter-revolutionary. Finally, we can talk about a revival in social science and sociological discussion only to the extent that a rational analysis and critique of competing conceptions in theory and the philosophy of science (both of Marxist and non-Marxist origin) has come about. As a matter of fact, this has happened to a remarkable degree, although it varies greatly according to periods and countries.

To conclude these broader observations on the development of sociology and its suppression during the Stalin era, it is worth making a brief critical comment on the 'materialist' way of explaining the Stalinist perversion of historical materialism. However superficial (and, of course, 'un-Marxist') an explanation of Stalinism in terms of the 'personality cult' may be, the 'materialist' attempts at explanation are equally inadequate by focussing *solely* on the economic and class relations in the Soviet Union of the time, and possibly the country's isolation in the international context. To derive a 'law' – that is, an inevitable development towards Stalinism – just from these and similar 'objective' realities does not carry conviction.[13] A multitude of 'intervening' factors should at least be considered here.[14] In particular, an explanation of Stalinism as that of an ideologically coercive system (although one with very physical effects) should take the following background into consideration. Lenin bequeathed to his political-ideological heirs the conviction that in principle there can only be *one* true, all-encompassing conception of historical materialism, which is entirely coherent within itself. But, at the same time, Lenin's death deprived the party of the authority that was to a large extent (though by no means exclusively) capable of protecting and carrying through this one and true interpretation of historical materialism on the basis of its overwhelming and generally recognised intellectual and political competence. Beyond that the party then possessed enough sovereignty to tolerate and even explicitly encourage a remarkable degree of scientific discussion, at least at the inner party level.[15] If, after the loss of such authority, a corresponding conception of historical materialism is held to be inexorable in scientific and political-ideological terms (namely, for the defence of any *true* socialist practice) – and this is in fact the consensus opinion amongst all those who participated in the post-Leninist ideological controversies – then it is not illogical that the ideological struggle literally amounts to a struggle 'of life and death'.[16]

I consider it strong evidence for the accuracy of this assumption (and for the power of that conviction) that, even in the face of death, neither the ideological nor physical victims of the Stalinist purges disputed, but rather emphatically affirmed, the necessity for and legitimacy of a 'monolithic' ideological system.[17] Considerations of this kind also lend themselves to an explanation of the 'personality cult'. The concentration of ideological authority in a small group or (even better) in a single person permits the adhesion to at least the fiction of the cohesive and closed nature of the doctrine. This occurs in such a way that even the serious contradictions and variations in the interpretation of historical materialism do not necessarily lead to greater irritations (see L. Trotzky 1973, 178; also L. Kolakowski, 1967, 7 ff., cited in Kiss, 1971, 120 f.).

2.2 The history of the reception of Weber

The development we have just outlined is closely reflected in the critical treatment Max Weber's work received from Marxist social scientists and philosophers, which I shall now consider. This is not surprising, since Weber's work was and still is seen to be the most influential non-Marxist foundation of sociology, particularly with respect to theory and methodology. In any case, Marxist social scientists and philosophers are far more unanimous in this assessment of Weber than non-Marxists. The way Marxist theorists deal with Weber's work is therefore a very useful indicator of the general readiness for 'free scientific research' and 'scientific critique' (Marx) in the social sciences. It is self-evident that only an acknowledgment of the great scientific importance of any foundation of sociology (and therefore also the Weberian) can create the necessary preconditions for a thorough and productive discussion. This acknowledgment does not, of course, imply that the conceptions under discussion are actually accepted in their entirety or even just in part. After all even an analysis in the form of a critique of ideology of alternative social-science conceptions is absolutely compatible with a conviction of their scientific importance and the basic tenets of 'scientific critique'. The critique of ideology, if carried out by means of rational and empirical argumentation (i.e. in the Marxian sense), is a scientific critique in itself and thus amenable to critical examination on its part and, if necessary, to a critique of ideology in turn.

The ensuing discussion on the Marxist analysis of Weber's epistemology and methodology may provide ample opportunity to elucidate the tenability and implications of the critique of ideology theses directed specifically against Weber and this aspect of his work in particular. Here I primarily purport to discover whether and how far the return of the critique of ideology to the socio-economic or political 'originating context' (i.e. its scientific tenability) of both social science and philosophical conceptions can simultaneously lead to definitive statements about its 'explanatory context'. There seems neither adequate clarity nor agreement on this point among Marxist authors, and indeed, not even when the inadequacy of the dismissive political-ideological treatment given to competing scientific conceptions, as outlined at the outset, is clearly seen and stated.

It is hardly worth mentioning that the method of the 'brief

(political) dismissal' (particularly during the Stalinist era), to which Weber's work was subjected at times, is now considered to be out of the question. Certainly Weber offered particularly easy targets for such a method. Even when he did not explicitly classify himself as a member of the bourgeoisie,[18] it was easy to deduce his 'class' situation from his political opinions and activities.[19] But above all Weber himself emphasised his critique of Marxism in important parts of his scientific work.

Weber was an extraordinarily suitable subject for dismissive political-ideological treatment due to this seemingly quite unequivocal state of affairs, as long as this treatment of all deviations from the 'party line' on social science and philosophical conceptions was seen to be necessary to its power politics. Naturally the possibility of simultaneously interpreting the supposedly unequivocal 'case of Weber' as an example of the whole non-Marxist sociology was considered to be of particular advantage.

The political 'ban' on Weber can be found at least in semiofficial (and even anonymous) form in the second edition (1951) of the *Great Soviet Encyclopedia* (*Bol'šaja Sovjetskaja Enciklopedija = BSE*). As a matter of fact, this seems to be the only fundamental reference to Weber's work in the socialist countries between 1930 and the second half of the 1950s[20] – a reference which simultaneously contains an explanation for this state of affairs. The article presents and dismisses Weber as a 'reactionary German sociologist, historian and economist, Neo-Kantian, the most malicious enemy of Marxism' and as an 'apologist for capitalism' (*BSE*, 2nd edn, Vol. 7, 1951). Only three of Weber's works which were translated into Russian are mentioned (*General Economic History, Agrarverhältnisse im Altertum* and *The City*) and again without further bibliographical details. Similarly any reference to secondary literature is lacking. The only quotation is a statement by Lenin, in which he refers to the analyses of Russian events in 1905 by the 'highly learned' Herr Professor Max Weber and speaks of the 'professorial wisdom of the cowardly bourgeoisie' (*Works*, Vol. 23, 251).

The extent to which the political-ideological anathema has to be ascribed to the special needs for authority by the Stalinist regime is most strikingly illustrated by the *BSE* articles on Weber appearing before and after the Stalinist era (i.e. the first and third editions of the work).[21] At the same time, a comparison between the two articles shows that the level of 'free scientific critique', which had been politically possible up to 1928, had not been reattained as late as 1970.

As a matter of fact the pre-Stalinist Marxist reception of Weber, which definitely deserves a mention, has nowhere been taken up on a full scale, discussed or even carried on by Marxist authors. Even the translations of Weber's work, published before 1928 in the Soviet Union, are not comprehensively (nor bibliographically correctly) listed anywhere.[22] Neusychin's analyses from that pre-Stalinist phase, which undoubtedly represent the most significant and broadest critical treatment of Weber by a Marxist (probably until this day),[23] received and still receive only a hesitant response.[24] Other pre- or non-Stalinist beginnings of a critical examination of Weber's foundation of sociology from a Marxist perspective (from within and outside the Soviet Union) are generally not mentioned, but certainly never discussed at length.[25] The political-ideological grounds for this reserve are obvious with authors who are classified as 'revisionist' (particularly Max Adler, Karl Kautsky, G. Lukács, K. A. Wittfogel and L. Kofler, as well as the representatives of the 'Frankfurt School', including H. Marcuse). This does not, of course, imply that these grounds are scientifically convincing, even if the objection to deviation from 'genuine' historical materialism was derived from the author's inclusion of Weberian categories and arguments, or their slightest affinity to them.[26]

The more recent Marxist literature on Weber has so far even failed to give an account of the reception of Weber by the former leading Soviet theorist of historical materialism, N. Bukharin. This may not simply, however, be due to Bukharin considering Weber to be 'one of the best modern students of religion' (Bukharin, 1926, 178). In terms of its subject matter this appraisal of Weber's sociology of religion by a Marxist who was classified as 'mechanistic' should actually have met with astonishment and interest. It seems evident that for political-ideological reasons even Bukharin's interpretation of historical materialism cannot be discussed with scientific impartiality until this day. This again is probably due less to interpretational problems than to the power-politically inspired liquidation of deviating theories and theorists during the Stalinist epoch, which did not experience a wholesale fundamental review by way of clarification and critical examination (i.e. primarily one that was independent of the vagaries of individual leaders).[27] The more recent critical treatment of Weber's work by Marxist theorists would undoubtedly have benefited if it had followed the threads of the pre- and non-Stalinist Marxist reception and critique of Weber. More than anything, a much more adequate level of objectivity and differentiated problem consciousness would have come about more speedily than was and is possible by the alternative route that was taken.

However, the reception of Weber in Polish sociology constitutes a distinct exception (and – with some reservations and some variation in time — also in Hungarian and Yugoslavian sociology). This cannot be explained solely in terms of the different political and ideological-cultural conditions prevailing in this particular socialist country, but is essentially due to the existence of an independent and important Polish tradition in the construction of sociological theory and research. Moreover, with regard to the reception of Weber in particular it was highly significant that the 'humanistic' theoretical tradition (its leading representative is seen to be F. Znaniecki) has a clear affinity in content to an 'interpretative' and 'action-theory' conception of sociology.[28]

The number of Marxist authors producing analyses of Weber's work (particularly in the socialist countries) has clearly been increasing sharply since the end of the 1950s. It is so vast now that a quantitively comprehensive treatment is impossible even if it were not for linguistic problems. An additional problem is that many of these essays are almost inaccessible since they are mainly produced in the form of dissertations (particularly in the Soviet Union) and therefore command a lower degree of universal accessibility than 'normal' publications. We can presumably conclude from this that the socialist critical treatment of Weber and bourgeois sociology is still largely pursued in a semi-official and, as it were, experimental manner.

3 Epistemological and methodological problems

3.1 Subjectivism or reflection? The fundamental critique of Weber's epistemological position

To begin with the discussion on the Marxist critique of Weber's argumentation concerning issues in the philosophy of science and methodology considers the most general characteristics of Weber's fundamental epistemological position. These comments will be fairly concise and will deal primarily with the ideological aspect of the problem. Both brevity and the critique of ideology orientation typify almost all the utterances of critics on this epistemological problem. Moreover, it is likely that the substance of these considerations is in principle of minor importance for the concrete framework and objectives of sociology. At any rate, Weber's own conceptions concur with this appraisal.

The most general characterisations of Weber's epistemological position, which recur in the critical literature, are: 'subjectivism' (e.g. Kon, 1973, 149 f.; Lukács, 1962, 530 f.; *Wörterbuch*, 467 f.); 'subjective idealism' (e.g. Osipov, 1964, 103), but also – and indeed frequently simultaneously – 'objectivism' (e.g. Paciorkovskij, 1975, 205; *Wörterbuch*, 360), or even 'positivism' (e.g. Bel'cer, 1973, 140, 155); also 'nihilism' (Wittfogel, 1924, 217) and 'agnosticism' (e.g. *Philosophisches Wörterbuch*, 501; Braunreuther, 1964, 62). But the characterisation that summarises all the above is 'Kantianism' or 'Neo-Kantianism' (e.g. Lukács, 1946a, 112; Kuznecov, 1975, 12 and 13; Gajdenko, 1971, 257 and *passim*).

All these characterisations are not merely meant as a critical depreciation (which is by no means self-evident), but rather they seek to show that Weber's fundamental assumptions are diametrically opposed to those of materialist philosophy and that therefore his position should simply be considered untenable. Beyond that, the concepts employed are intended and suited for the purposes of polemic defence rather than precise definition and discussion, i.e. they signal the abandonment of discussion. The critique of Weber's concrete methodological standards and rules, then, becomes comprehensible and debatable only if concretised, particularly in relation to his conceptual constructions of ethical neutrality and the ideal type. Although a concretised (i.e. research-related) discussion of questions concerning epistemology and the philosophy of science, as mentioned, is entirely in line with Weber's thinking, it is nonetheless appropriate to comment on the above general characterisations.

By means of the above characterisations Weber is allocated to the tradition of 'bourgeois' or 'revisionist' philosophy and epistemology on which, in the opinion of not only the Institute for Marxist-Leninism in the Central Committee of the Soviet Communist Party,[1] but also many Marxist theorists, Lenin pronounced the most definitive and scathing verdict in *Materialism and Empirio-Criticism* (all citations below from V. I. Lenin, *Works*, Vol. 14, 1962). In fact, all the arguments recurrently advanced against Weber's philosophical position are formulated by Lenin (and, indeed, with desirable clarity and certainty).

From the perspective of a decidedly party-political stance on which not all of the (special) sciences, but certainly the 'general theory of political economy' and the 'epistemology', are always based (*ibid.*, 342), the philosophical dispute after Lenin is reduced to one simple alternative: idealism or materialism (*ibid.*, 335; cf. 358).[2] According to this view all modifications and intermediate positions (Neo-Kantianism, humanism or even realism, positivism, pragmatism and, of course, Machism) are capable only of disguising this all-important contrast and can thus only serve to weaken the political impact of the materialist position.[3] With respect to those who consider themselves to be Marxist theorists, for example, Bogdanov, Suvorov, Lunarčarskij and so on, Lenin further asserts that 'there is an inseparable connection between reactionary epistemology and reactionary efforts in sociology' (*ibid.*, 335), namely in so far as epistemological 'subjectivism', 'idealism', etc. also and precisely amounted to a denial of the necessity and lawfulness in social reality as well as an antimaterialist overrating of the importance of consciousness and personality factors. In any event, Lenin provides an 'objective, class'-based (*ibid.*, 358) analysis, and hence a critique of ideology, of opposing philosophies and sociologies. According to Lenin, all subjectivistic and idealistic, etc. philosophical tendencies are 'objectively attributable to the class-based interests of the bourgeoisie'. Thus the theoretical directions tending 'towards Kant, neo-Kantianism, the critical philosophy' within social democracy are considered 'petit-bourgeois dross' (Lenin, *Works, op. cit.*, Vol. 34, 386, 379; referred to in the Preface to the first edn of Vol. 14, 19; footnote 12, 367).

The arguments used by Marxist authors against Weber's epistemological or methodological position are based – explicitly or implicitly – on Lenin's demarcations. They see Weber's neo-Kantianism or 'subjective idealism' in:

(a) His complete inability to grasp social reality in its objective 'materiality' and therefore as defining the knowledge arising from it as a product of the knowing subject, rather than its reflection (subjectivism, relativism, idealism).

(b) His intention to offer 'formalistic analyses', typologies and 'empty conclusions based on analogies' instead of 'real causal connections' or 'laws' (agnosticism, formalism) (Lukács, 1946a, 111 and 1962, 530 f.).

(c) His refusal to acknowledge a necessary development of historical-social events, thereby destroying the secure foundation of political practice in social-science knowledge (Lukács, 1946a, 112) and surrendering socio-political practice to 'irrationalism' and 'nihilism' (Lukács, 1962, 533 f.).

Evidently only the vaguest concept of 'Kantianism' is employed here (and, incidentally, in Lenin too). There is no further reference to Kant's specific transcendental philosophical standpoint. The failure to enter into any discussion on the contents of Kant's thinking is so complete that one might be inclined to quote Marx's dictum on the superficial defensive treatment of the dead Hegel (*Capital*, Vol. 1, Afterword to the second German edn, 29).[4] But even the (South-West German) neo-Kantian argumentations, which are much more directly relevant to Weber's conception of science, are not dealt with in any more detailed description and discussion.[5] Furthermore, the crucial distinction between Weber's and, particularly, Rickert's position is no more than suggested, ignoring its full implications.[6] The above bears on the first of the aspects mentioned, that neither Weber's considerations on a sociological 'science of social reality' in general, nor on the role of value relevance in directing knowledge and in constructing objects in particular, are set out in detail and critically analysed.[7] What remains undiscussed, then, is that the Weberian meaning of the 'transcendental presupposition' for all cultural and social science research is neither 'pure' nor arbitrary subjectivity, nor – as in Rickert – a realm of absolutely valid superior values, but rather it represents historical socio-cultural reality (in other words, the real existence of the individual as a 'cultural being').

It is odd that representatives of an empathically 'dialectical' conception of knowledge counter Weber's ideas of a specific subject-object relationship in cultural and social science knowledge with the objectivity of both the social object of knowledge and the reflective character of sociological knowledge.[8] As a matter of fact, Lenin, who once proposed the foundation of a 'society for the materialist friends of the Hegelian dialectic' (*UBM*, Vol. 1, 1925-6, 17), may have prevented any differentiated analysis of the subject-object problematic in the social sciences (as he indeed intended) precisely with his conception of a materialist espistemology. This entailed a concept of knowledge that denoted 'objective reality' as that 'which is given to man by his sensations, and which is copied, photographed and reflected by our sensations' (*Materialism and Empirio-Criticism*, 1962, 130). Such complicated and highly productive mental operations, which form the basis of a developed scientific, and particularly social science, theory (such as that of Marxian political economy), certainly cannot, with any adequacy, be apprehended. Were this concept to imply no more than that, there can be no empirical knowledge without the 'senses' or sensory perception, it would certainly be less controversial and could not be levelled at Weber (nor, incidentally, Kant). According to Lenin's ideas, however, the return to the 'senses' evidently serves to secure nothing less than the 'objective truth' of our empirical knowledge: 'To regard our sensations as images of the external world, to recognise objective truth, to hold the materialist theory of knowledge – these are all one and the same thing' (*ibid.*, 130).

We can raise objections to this conception on the basis that there are no objects whatsoever at the level of mere sensations (but no more than sensory data at the most) and that *a fortiori* the 'objective truth' (i.e. the correspondence to objects) of our knowledge of the real world is not expressed in terms of sensory qualities. There could be nothing more than experience of a very rudimentary and fragmented nature without the active mental incorporation of the manifold sensations. This is by no means a 'subjectivistic' or even 'idealistic' view peculiar to Kant, Weber and others, but a conception which was expressed with some determination even by Karl Marx (particularly in the critique of Feuerbach).[9]

The fundamental principle that active critique and discussion, not passive sensory reflection, constitute the basis of objective knowledge about the real world applies to the whole range of empirical knowledge. This insight was stressed by Marx in relation to the study of the historical world.[10]

It is these preconceptions and interests arising from social experience that also establish the constitutive reference to possible objects of social science knowledge. Social science research can locate its objects only in this manner, and never by appealing to any direct senses.

In respect of the issues we have considered there should so far be a good deal more agreement than disagreement between the Marxist and Weberian positions. On this basis we have presumed that Weber's comments on the 'chaotic' character of reality outside specific value-related perspectives, although sounding 'Kantian' in the narrower sense, should not be seen as metaphysical or ontological statements, but rather serve to emphasise – albeit in a misleading way – the perspectivity of all knowledge and the inexorability of 'selection and construction' by the knowing subject. Accordingly, reality is not chaotic 'in itself' (this is no plausible fundamental assumption for any science based on causal explanation), but only 'for us' – if we permit ourselves to be influenced in a completely passive way without any organising points of view. Only this interpretation permits Weber's concept of 'value relevance' to be combined with the emphatic epistemological interest of 'empirical science'.[11]

The agreement between Marx and Weber also includes the insight that the interest and value orientations determining the 'selection of a given subject matter and the problem of an empirical analysis' (Weber, *MSS*, 22) are in themselves historical in nature in the case of the historical social sciences. They also agree that interests and value orientations change particularly in the course of epochal socio-cultural changes and, indeed, have to change if the social sciences are to undertake an enquiry into the predominant problems of their world. Both theorists share the postulate that this is indeed the task of the social sciences.

In comparison the actual differences between Weber's conception of knowledge and that represented by Marx seem to reside in the following: according to Marx the perspectivity and historicity of social science knowledge do not prevent its knowledge uncovering the 'inherent' essence, i.e. the factors which ultimately and as a whole determine social events. The historical-social grounding of each social science categorial apparatus opens up an understanding of the essential interrelationships, at least if it is concerned with historically 'progressive' social practice. The idea of an *objective* social progress taking place, which Marx adopted from Hegel – standing Hegel on his head – permits him to interpret the (adequate) self-reflection of objective progressive social practice as both knowledge in a historical perspective *and* knowledge that focusses on the essential.[12]

For Weber the idea of historical progress taking place objectively and representatively is no longer tenable.[13] What should be seen as progress of retrogression, leaving aside questions of *technological* improvement, is in his opinion decided by neither an appeal to objective law nor history, but by people themselves who set and are responsible for their 'value standards'. According to Weber, the orientation to something defined in terms of a 'progressive' design of values does not therefore offer a superior understanding of what is *causally* essential. The category 'essential' and even the category of 'progress' should be employed only in the relative sense.

The 'essential' is above all that which corresponds to specific accepted value standards. In this sense a particular conception of the essential expresses itself in a specific 'selection and construction' of sociological objects. The task of empirical research, then, is to discover the 'essential', in the sense of *causally* decisive factors, within the framework of a perspective gained through value relevance. On the basis of this approach reliable statements about causally essential factors in relation to specific research questions are not only possible, but constitute the chief objective of social science research. In contrast, Weber considers unworkable the intention to determine (essential) causal factors deciding the course of social events in general and as a whole 'in the final analysis'. Social events as a whole are not a feasible object for any type of explanation without a more specific determination or limitation. But if we apply a limit we require an orientation to 'value perspectives – for example, if we declare the central social fact to be the emergence and intensification of inequality in social groups' life chances, or if we supply a qualitative definition of what is implied by the 'survival' of a social system.[14] In whatever manner these value perspectives serving the 'selection and construction' of the sociological object are found, we cannot derive them from historical-social reality as such or from an objective and necessary 'trend' approaching such reality.

Weberian conceptions have nothing whatsoever to do with 'subjectivism' in the 'subjective idealism' sense of the term. If this term is to have a reasonably precise meaning, it relates to a position in which not the 'material' of knowledge, but certainly its universal validity and necessity, is considered to be a product of the knowing subject. Despite his explanatory reference to 'modern epistemology which ultimately derives from Kant' (*MSS*, 106), Weber did not advocate Kant's standpoint – albeit one that would at least be worth discussing in the field of empirical social science. Value relevance in the Weberian meaning of the term, even in its elaboration into ideal types, has no comparable epistemological status to, for example, Kantian categories.[15] The categorisations of schemata represented by ideal types are understood as purely ideal (subjective, or even 'utopian') constructions and by no means serve as *a priori* or pure forms of possible experience. Rather they serve to retrace actual categorisations and interconnections, particularly in their deviation from these constructs. It would be more appropriate to talk of a (naive or covert) subjectivism or idealism where ideal constructs or idealisations are no longer perceived or claimed to be such, but are put on a level with reality.

The fundamental problems presented here, which are seen to be equally valid for a materialist conceptual and theoretical understanding not only by Marx himself, but by a number of Marxist theorists too, will be considered further at a later stage (see pages 43–63).

At the start of this section we noted that the classification of Weber's epistemology is generally quickly dealt with. Marxist authors almost across the board point out that bourgeois consciousness is epistemologically reflected in Kantianism in general, and its Weberian expression in particular. Accordingly subjectivism, formalism, agnosticism, nihilism, irrationalism, etc. are no more than the philosophical expression and philosophical rationalisation of the actual decline, and lack of perspective and helplessness, of the bourgeois class in the face of the steadily worsening crises affecting the capitalist mode of production. A thorough bourgeois scientific enquiry into socio-economic conditions and developments remains outstanding, since it would establish that its class domination is doomed to a certain end.[16] Moreover, bourgeois theory dispenses with the knowledge of essential and lawful social interconnections and by means of these epistemological conceptions its position is built up into particularly critical philosophy. Similarly, the principle of ethical neutrality in empirical science research, which is essentially grounded in Kantian philosophy, constitutes a particularly ingenious epistemological device for concealing bourgeois class interests behind the subjectivist-formalist social theories, as it asserts that the distancing from political-moral partisanship accompanied by the distancing of knowledge from the substantial social factors (or society as a whole) is the hallmark of truly objective research.

Weber's methodology represents an 'apologetic product of a high order' (Braunreuther, 1964, 85), precisely because of the combination of subjectivism with the thus understood objectivism.

Since this objective ideological function does not necessarily presume design and consciousness on Weber's behalf, this assessment is not contradicted by the fact that many bouregois (and some Marxist) social scientists are not immediately, or not at all, aware of the apologetic nature of Weberian epistemology and methodology.[17]

The question arises as to how convincing and tenable such general ideology-critical evaluations of the specific Weberian epistemology and methodology are. The last comment regarding the degree of acknowledgment and adoption of the Weberian position amongst non-Marxist social scientists, it seems to me, perhaps points to a fundamental problem. This problem can be expressed in the following questions. Do the critique of ideology theses I referred to concerning scientific and philosophical conceptions relate to actual (causal) historical interconnections, or to ideal or 'elective' affinities? Are they suggesting that these epistemological conceptions in fact owe their emergence, or at least existence, to their asserted ideological advantage to a specific class, or does the critique merely seek to show that these Weberian conceptions, on the basis of their immanent structure, cannot resist, or may even encourage, such ideological application?

It should be generally accepted that the latter case with appropriate proof – assuming it could be plausibly furnished – settles nothing whatsoever regarding the factual grounding or tenability of epistemological argumentation. But in the former case too (the primary concern of the materialist critique of ideology as empirical[18] analysis), a positive answer to the causal question by no means simultaneously supplies or renders superfluous an actual refutation of the epistemological or methodological conceptions.[19] There is no doubt that an unfavourable light is thrown on any type of scientific and philosophical argumentation that can be attributed both functionally and causally to a specific political-ideological context of justification. This state of affairs may lead us to suspect strongly that this argumentation can hardly be well-founded on rational grounds, yet it still does not make a critical examination of its contents unnecessary. This could only arise if we were safe in assuming that the epistemological and methodological grounding or defence of particular scientific methods is consistently and fundamentally ideological in character and could therefore never be refuted by a critique of its contents – unlike the method and findings of empirical (or formal-logical) research.[20] According to this viewpoint then, the sole task of epistemology and methodology would be to legitimise and safeguard the interest and specific class-orientation of scientific research by means of a pseudo-rational philosophical superstructure.

Even the most rudimentary acquaintance with the existing epistemological and methodological endeavours should counteract a general assumption of this kind. The 'merely ideological' character of particular epistemological or methodological assertions, however, would have to be demonstrated by their futility in substance.

As a rule the critique of ideology comments on Weber's general epistemological and methodological position are not based on closer causal and functional analyses. They are limited to establishing more or less plausible 'elective' affinities with bourgeois ideology. Moreover, the argumentation frequently remains *ex nativo*. The real or supposed anti-Marxist character of this epistemology leads to the inference of its affiliation to bourgeois ideology. The result is not merely a questionable obverse conclusion. What remains unexplained beyond that is how far materialist epistemology (or any modification of it) corresponds in content to the interests of the non-bourgeois, particularly proletarian, classes.

As a matter of fact, it is no accident and indisputable that there is indeed a close historical and political link between the labour movement and materialist philosophy. It is also easily understandable that continuity and unanimity even on highly abstract (e.g. epistemological) issues are seen to be an important prerequisite for a successful ideological 'struggle'. After all it is not surprising that the ideological unity of the socialist movement is contrasted precisely with 'neo-Kantian' conceptions in their vaguest meaning: these conceptions have not only proved their appeal to Marxist theorists, but were accompanied by clear deviations in general theory and political practice in those socialist countries in which they appeared.

Under the circumstances – and, indeed, especially under conditions of intensified political conflicts – it is easy to explain why: firstly, an objective examination of the existing epistemological positions has not been carried out. Secondly, it explains why a chance was not given to render problematic (i.e. question) the intimate association of class and political with philosophical orientations, and in consequence to relax, if not actually dispense with, the obligation to a specific epistemological and scientific conception. The contemporary situation should not only allow such dispensation to be effected but is, indeed, long overdue.[21]

With reference to the critical treatment of Weber's epistemological and methodological position, an objective and productive discussion would involve either one of two methods of proceeding, which are not mutually exclusive: on the one hand, the critique of ideology theses reported on thus far should be further developed from mere assertions and more or less plausible associative ties towards exhaustive and differentiated analyses. This presumes that the logical possibilities of such analyses and, indeed, applied to their own position as well, are reflected and presented much more thoroughly than hitherto. On the other hand, an attempt ought to be made to develop a critique of contents on the basis of a detailed analysis of Weberian ideas. Here it would be worth following the good old principle of scientific and philosophical critique formulated by Hegel that one should make the case of the opposition as strong as possible. What has been up to now the most universally used procedure, namely to set the certainty, depth and objectivity of the materialist scientific method in the social sciences in opposition to those considerations of Weber which produce problems, and from that generate an epistemological modesty without any more extensive argument.[22]

The discussion that follows on the specific aspects of Weberian methodology is mainly intended as a contribution towards this critique of contents. Unlike the treatment of Weber's general epistemological considerations, there are some argumentations by Marxist authors, which facilitate and encourage a discussion of contents, on these specific aspects.

3.2 Objectivity and partisanship, ethical neutrality and value relevance

Among the manifold categorial formulae of Weberian thinking the most popular is probably that which identifies such thought with the so-called 'postulate of ethical neutrality'. Like other such characterisations this one is not totally wrong either. If it is apprehended correctly it even leaves room for extraordinarily profound interpretations. In general, however, it is considered in a very 'abstract' (in the Hegelian sense of the term), detached and superficial manner. This applies both to positive as well as negative assessments of Weber and is by no means a specific distinguishing characteristic among a multitude of summary characterisations in Marxist critiques of Weber. Nonetheless, Marxist interpreters of Weber seem, to a particularly large extent, exposed to the temptation of using the postulate of ethical neutrality as a useful shibboleth which renders all further argumentation unnecessary. To justify this they may point out that Weber himself (in the pertinent discussions of the *Verein für Sozialpolitik*) employed the postulate of ethical neutrality, for instance in the critique of

Marxist, or at least quasi-Marxist, positions.[23] Is this not sufficient evidence for the assumption that this postulate constitutes, as it were, the ultimate (alleged) anti-Marxist tendency of Weberian thinking in its entirety?

At the outset I have to repeat what has been said on numerous occasions: however obvious that anti-Marxist tendency of any scientific or philosophical thesis may be, this does not make a thorough examination of its contents unnecessary.[24] Moreover, the postulate of ethical neutrality in Weber's interpretation and application[25] is not even biased against the materialist position. Rather, the scientific weight of his argument stands or falls by the need to justify it as a universally valid principle. Only where it is seen and examined in this way are we really exposed to the intellectual vexation contained within it. Similarly, a critique of the postulate of ethical neutrality is only convincing if it operates at this level of logic. The first precondition of any scientific discussion is an adequate description of the subject matter. The comparatively extensive literature by Marxist (but also non-Marxist) authors on the problem of ethical neutrality is remarkably deficient in this respect. This cannot possibly be because the central Weberian thesis is difficult to identify, 'ambiguous' (Devjatkova, 1969, 9)[26] or complex; rather the extreme opposite is the case. It is conceivable that one might consider the thesis too trivial to give it explicit attention. Were this the case, however, the type and extent of the critique directed against it would be groundless and to no purpose. We are left to suspect that this thesis is not described adequately because it might stand in the way of particular critical objectives. These objectives benefit if one equates some of Weber's statements in the area of the real thesis of ethical neutrality and criticise them instead of this thesis.

Weber's fundamental assertion on the problem of ethical neutrality (which will be called the 'thesis of ethical neutrality' below to distinguish it from the 'postulate of ethical neutrality') runs as follows: 'There is simply no bridge which leads from the really *mere* "empirical" analysis of given reality by means of causal explanation to the establishment or challenge of the "validity" of *any* one value judgement' (*WL*, 61). Parallel formulations are:

> What is really at issue is the intrinsically simple demand that the investigator and teacher should keep unconditionally separate the establishment of empirical facts (including the 'value-oriented' conduct of the empirical individual whom he is investigating) and *his* own practical evaluations, i.e., his evaluations of these facts as satisfactory or unsatisfactory (including among these facts evaluations made by the empirical

persons who are the objects of investigation). These two things are logically different and to deal with them as though they were the same represents a confusion of entirely heterogeneous problems. (*Gutachten*, 113; cf. *MSS*, 11)

And, finally:

> The latter are concerned only with the fact that the validity of a practical imperative as a norm and the truth-value of an empirical proposition are absolutely heterogeneous in character. Any attempt to treat these logically different types of propositions as identical only reduces the particular value of *each* of them. (*Gutachten*, 114; cf. *MSS*, 12).

The simple and actually near-trivial substance of Weber's fundamental thesis on the ethical neutrality of the sciences is that 'propositions' and 'practical imperative' are heterogeneous in character. Logically speaking they are not only fundamentally different, but neither can they be derived from the other.[27] Propositions can no more be derived from value judgements (this should by now really be indisputable[28]) than value judgements can be logically and convincingly derived from empirical tenets. Derivational linkages of this kind exist only within empirical-theoretical systems of statements, on the one hand, and systems of practical norm orientations, on the other. It is true that empirical-theoretical tenets may belong to the ideal foundations of concrete practical conclusions (that is to say, of answers to the question: what ought I do?) but in that case we *always* presume the (highest and ultimate) value premiss which in turn can no longer be derived from empirical facts.

With this distinction science is simultaneously given boundaries *if* it is perceived as an empirical science (including formal logic and mathematics).[29] But in this case (like in Weber's) the concept of 'empirical' can be interpreted in a very broad sense. Thus 'empirical' knowledge is that which addresses the analysis of the 'givenness' of real factors and – in so far as it is possible and required – their causal explanation. In this sense, then, even the 'hermeneutic' analysis of pre-given mental objectifications falls into the sphere of empirical research.[30]

In the main the following critical procedures might be applied to counteract the key idea of the Weberian thesis of ethical neutrality:

(a) One could attempt to show that empirical-scientific analyses may well serve to legitimate value judgements (or at least contribute significantly to them).

(b) One could accept Weber's argument with reference to the

empirical sciences, but show at the same time that there are non-empirical scientific procedures which facilitate the rational grounding of value judgements.

We can talk of a refutation, or at least a clear weakening of the Weberian argumentation only if the first procedure leads to convincing results. In contrast the successful efforts of the second procedure would not touch the core of the Weberian argumentation. But, in so far as they generate rational (though not empirical science) procedures to produce judgements on normative questions, they would undoubtedly be directed against the rigour of Weber's position, and be appropriate to avoid the supposed sole consequence relating to normative grounding, namely purely 'decisionism'.

A third possible (c) critique of Weber's conceptions can be levelled at his demand that scientists (particularly social scientists) should dispense with advocating particular cultural values, so long as they claim to argue in their ('official') capacity or in so far as they give this impression *de facto*.[31] It is essential to emphasise that this Weberian demand is not an inevitable result of the actual thesis of ethical neutrality.[32] Rather, it arises only in connection with Weber's conception, which is worth and in need of discussion, that scientific institutions and their representatives can only fulfil their present duty by strictly concentrating on and limiting themselves to the possibilities of subject-related scientific research, i.e. according to what has been cited above, by the means of logic and empirical research. If scientific institutions and their representatives cannot do justice to this demand, Weber's alternative solution is to at least insist that (a) value judgements in the academic field are always presented as such (i.e. as tenets which cannot ultimately be established through scientific method) (*Gutachten*, 105; *MSS*, 4) and (b) it is ensured that not only theoretical pluralism, but also the pluralism of possible normative positions or entire 'world views' (*Weltanschauungen*) is represented in academic institutions.[33] Weber's opinion on this latter point is that we should not only consider Marxism and socialism, but also the 'most "extreme" tendencies, such as the anarchistic' (*Gutachten*, 109; *MSS*, 7).[34]

In the context of Weber's rejection of all 'professorial value commitments' we often encounter an objection, which similarly is not aimed at the thesis of ethical neutrality itself but very generally at its practicability. It is asserted that the demand to abstain from making any cultural value judgements in the context of scientific argumentation, as derived from the thesis of ethical neutrality, is futile since it is *de facto* constantly violated. This conclusion is occasionally taken further by claiming that the thesis of ethical neutrality itself is meaningless since it has no *practical* significance. The fact that Weber himself often violated his own principles, and not only in his early inaugural lecture on *Der Nationalstaat und die Volkswirtschaftspolitik* (1895), is seen to be ample evidence for the impractical nature of the postulate of ethical neutrality (and therefore the practical meaninglessness of the thesis of ethical neutrality).[35]

In Weber's view, this argumentation, in so far as it refers to the actual non-observance of the postulate of ethical neutrality, has no more to say against the validity and fruitlessness of the postulate, than, for example, in the case of ethical imperatives. Certainly Weber voices great understanding for the fact that:

> The indubitable existence of this spuriously 'ethically neutral' tendentiousness, which (in our discipline) is manifested in the obstinate and deliberate partisanship of powerful interests groups, explains why a significant number of intellectually honest scholars still continue to assert their personal evaluations from their chair. They are too proud to identify themselves with this pseudo-ethical neutrality.

When he maintains 'that, in spite of this, what is right (in my opinion) should be done' (*Gutachten*, 109; cf. *MSS*, 6) (that is to say, that one should refrain from making cultural value-judgements *in cathedra*), this only corresponds to his conception that empirical facts as such cannot determine whether specific evaluations are correct, nor whether they should continue to be represented in practice. In the latter respect it would certainly be of great importance if it were shown that those value orientations *cannot in principle* (or at least only by coincidence) be adhered to under the given real conditions, although, in Weber's view, this had by no means been established at the time. It should have practical importance in so far as it ought to provide the basis for a subsequent determination of the scientific content of 'mixed' systems of statement. However, it is nowhere suggested, and we need not elaborate on the fact, that even if this were the case the actual thesis of ethical neutrality would not be impaired or even refuted in its *logical* meaning.

In what follows I will present and discuss Marxist arguments against Weber's conceptions on ethical neutrality. The last objection (which can occasionally be found in Marxist literature as well) will no longer be explicitly discussed other than by way of reference.[36] This objection will be dealt with in the context of the first more substantial objection, so long as it does not consider the most superficial arguments against value orientations.

Weber's fundamental thesis on the logical heterogeneity of scientific statements (i.e. formal-logical, hermeneutic statements and empirical statements in the narrower sense), on the one hand, and value judgements, on the other, is consistently *not* attacked by Marxist critics. All these Marxist analyses do not, of course, make it clear that this is the key issue of the Weberian argumentation and we are accordingly unclear as to whether the key issue is also rejected. On the other hand, there are authors who express their total agreement with this Weberian thesis. Hofmann, for example, who presents by far the most thorough analysis of Weber's position on the problem from a Marxist perspective,[37] comments by saying that it 'is indisputable' that 'factual judgement and value judgement are essentially different' (1961, 18). Kuczynski (1972, 192) and Kon (1973, 153 ff.), for example, express themselves very similarly, though not with equal clarity, when they insist that cultural value judgements should have no place in the conduct of scientific analyses. In this context Kon refers to the following verdict by Marx on the pertinent 'confusions' (Weber): 'I call "mean" a man . . . who seeks to *accommodate* a viewpoint which is borrowed *from outside* science based on alien and external interests rather than those which inhere in it (no matter how mistaken they may be)' (Marx, 1959, 108; cited in Kon, 1973, 156).[38]

Here it seems that not only the actual thesis of ethical neutrality is accepted, but even the postulate of abstention from 'professorial value commitments' that cannot be conclusively derived from logic. However, the situation is in fact more complex. That is to say, even if the logical heterogeneity of the two forms of judgement is most clearly admitted (as in Hofmann, *op. cit.*, 24 ff.) the opinion is that value orientations are 'derived' from empirical facts. The argument is that all value orientations are based on assumptions about the real conditions under which one ought and has to act. Value orientations conform or correspond in varying degrees to these real conditions. Thus we can say that the objective validity of value standards is dependent on how far they correspond to the true facts about real social conditions. But since the 'real existential conditions' are always group-specific, the 'validity' of value orientations is always 'both objective and conditional' (*ibid.*, 27).

Hofmann therefore summarises his thesis as follows:

> Social evaluations are objective – always, as far as they touch on the relations of people to and in their environment – due to the fact that they *apply* to the *real* relations between social groups. At the outset the objectivity of these norms thus appears in the form of *interests*. (*ibid.*; Hofmann's emphasis)

The claim associated with this argumentation is formulated by Hofmann in the conclusion:

> The *derivation* of value judgements from factual judgements and in the final analysis from the empirical world, from the super-individual experience of real social units – that is to say, the simultaneous grounding of value judgements in the *theory* and *sociology* of knowledge – is offered by the hitherto 'missing link' in the construction of *scientific* value judgements. (*ibid.*, 37; Hofmann's emphasis)

It is indisputable that Hofmann is outlining a 'derivation' (i.e. the possibility of a causal explanation) of value judgements from the *sociology* of knowledge. But the associated epistemological claim, or the claim to logical validity, of an 'empiricist determination of the validity of values' (*ibid.*, 19) is most dubious. This dubiousness is immediately apparent in Hofmann's principle that 'the historically possible actualised is always of social value' (*ibid.*, 32 f.). This principle may well be worth discussing, but it would most probably be mistaken if it was meant empirically (as a causal explanation for the actual existence of a social consensus on values). It can by no means be employed for the positive 'derivation' of what should be done in concrete historical situations. (Fascism was, and probably still is, 'historically possible'; does this imply that it is, and indeed *due to* the fact, 'of social value'?)

Hofmann evidently notices the severe shortcomings of this chain of reasoning and therefore adds to it a further crucial assumption in a subsequent passage. We can find this assumption in all the other Marxist contributions to the problem. In the opinion of these theorists, this assumption is (empirical) scientific in nature: there are universal objective laws in human history. A special version of this assumption continues that these laws are such that they guide the historical-social process in accordance with an 'objective progress' (*ibid.*, 42).[39]

Let us begin with this postulate of 'objective progress'. Weber's fundamental position on this problem has already been outlined above. Accordingly it may very well be possible for the empirical sciences to identify historical developments objectively, i.e. quantitative and qualitative changes in social conditions. Moreover, they may well use the category of 'progress' in the face of such developments, if and in so far as they are concerned with developments within the meaning of technological improvements. That is to say, in this case the evaluative standards of 'worse' or 'better' are themselves in character, since they are bound up with logical or empirical 'measurements'. We can talk about progress in this 'ethically neutral' sense even if the results of any kind of development are neither objectively nor subjectively valuable to *any* individual.

Certainly progress within the meaning of technological improvements is generally seen as valuable and desirable by individuals (e.g. rulers), specific groups (e.g. ruling classes) or even by entire societies (tendentially, indeed, by all people) at the same time. Doubtless this is because the goals these improvements serve are held to be valuable or desirable.[40] In this case the judgement on progress or retrogression is founded upon standards or norms simultaneously defined and challenged by people. Here too the social scientist may use the category of 'progress', but by way of relating historical developments to hypothetically introduced value orientations. That is to say, such value orientations are no longer on their part scientifically demonstrable as empirical or logical realities. According to this interpretation, ethical-political value orientations, for example, are always presumed if – in either everyday or scientific terms – specific empirically establishable changes are interpreted and practically influenced in terms of 'progress', i.e. in the sense of a progression towards something that is of greater value to people. We certainly can talk here about an 'objective' progress, as far as it relates at all to history which really happens, which can be experienced and actively pursued. Progress thus understood is not objective because the evaluative criteria themselves cannot be found as objective facts in empirical reality. Empirical realities no doubt, even if they take on the form of 'trends', can neither be legitimated[41] in themselves for ethical or political goals nor can they as purely empirical facts justify any kind of ethical-political goal orientations.

Materialist theory of history and progress is accordingly confronted with the following alternative: *either*, on the one hand, historical progress is seen purely in terms of a process of unfolding the technological potentialities (of human action).[42] No doubt this can be established by mere empirical-science method, but without any ethical-political dimension. *Or*, on the other hand, in order to be able to speak of progress in the ethical-political sense, an effort must be made expressly to ground ethical-political standards in such a way that these standards cannot be 'derived' from the empirical analysis of realities and trends.

The argumentation presented by Kuczynski seems symptomatic of the existing lack of clarity here. He believes that a stand against the reactionary element in the social sciences should be taken for granted as that in medicine against disease (1972, 199). This attempt to draw parallels between the good and bad in social life with health and disease in physical life is obvious, yet equally unproductive and misleading.[43] Firstly, the decision on the maintenance of physical life is by no means a logical conclusion drawn from empirical science and medical analysis; as we are all well aware by now, independent and very delicate value orientations are necessary here too. Secondly, it is simply impossible to compare the definition of a goal orientation for social life with this simple, ultimate and clear-cut goal orientation for physical life, quite apart from the fact that the argumentation based on pure empirical science is evidently inadequate.

Kuczynski appeals to a 'natural human striving for living in a state of well-being' which 'history accommodates', in his opinion, through the laws of 'progressive development of nature, humankind and society' (*ibid.*, 198). Even if we agreed with everything that Kuczynski implies here (namely that the concept or value of 'the state of well-being' is quite unambiguous, that there is a universal material and possibly exclusive striving for this state of well-being and that historical development provides ever greater chances for its realisation), the question would still not be resolved. The derivation of ethical-political obligations from empirical reality is a 'naturalist fallacy'[44] if this reality refers to a supposed 'natural striving' in the context of specific historical chances of realisation. In addition, Marxist theorists who place such great emphasis on the historicity of practical value orientations must be bemused that the insistence on an 'objective' criterion of 'historical progress' ends with a reference to a supposed fact of human nature. Kuczynski's other demand[45] that one should take the side of a specific class and its interest position in a concrete historical situation surely cannot be scientifically grounded by these means. Quite apart from all the other untenabilities of the anthropological-naturalist argument, it would have to be assumed for this purpose that the struggle of the working class for its *interests* involves ultimate legitimacy *because* it represents the only historically adequate embodiment of that 'natural striving for a state of well-being'.

The appeal to a 'natural striving' of humankind in this context would instead seem to suggest an evasion from the self-imposed task of identifying reactionary and progressive value orientations in the course of a purely empirical-historical analysis. What would be more intellectually and politically convincing than such an evasion is an acknowledgment of the limits of empirical science argumentation in this respect. This would involve a revocation of the idea of an 'objective progress' that can be established by empirical-science method and an attempt to ground the ethical-political and historical superiority of specific interest and goal orientations by other forms of rational argumentation. The reason why this path has not been chosen by Marxist theorists (but is normally even sharply attacked by them), although it would be thoroughly critical of Weber's 'irrationalism' regarding the validity and 'conflict' between ultimate evaluations, will be discussed at a later stage.

The result of the above considerations is that a judgement on substantial, e.g. ethical-political, progress in history always presumes the validity (and acceptance) of particular value standards. These value standards in turn cannot be grounded through an empirical analysis of the historical course of events.

The idea of a lawfully proceeding 'objective progress' is accordingly untenable and useless as a challenge to Weber's conceptions. We could even ask whether the idea of the 'lawfulness' of historical developments as such is sound in this respect.

In fact this idea is frequently used against Weber by Marxist theorists without direct reference to the idea of progress.[46] This seems plausible in so far as the thing to be explained, the evaluative standpoint, is, as it were, 'built into' the explanation – the lawful process of history – in the category of 'progress'; in other words, the argument resembles a tautology.[47] An exemplary and fairly clear formulation of the argument states:

> The crucial refutation of the (Weberian) conception results from the penetration of the absolutely apprehensible objective determinateness and lawfulness of the class struggle, which forms the basis of the conflict between hierarchies of values. This practical, empirically establishable, living relationship is artificially divorced by Weber. (*Wörterbuch*, 207)

To avoid misconception we have to make clear here that Weber himself attached great importance to the opposition of class interests with a view to explaining the 'conflict between hierarchies of values'.[48] But the question nonetheless remains whether Weber's divorce between the problem of causality from that of validity was necessary for 'artificial' or logical-scientific reasons.

To clarify this question we have to assume that the class struggle represents the fundamental dimension of the historical-social process and that its development in accordance with 'objective determinateness and lawfulness' can be unambiguously established by empirical analysis. We are no doubt dealing with highly problematic assumptions here, but they can in principle be discussed within the framework of empirical science argumentation. This applies even to the further hypothesis that the 'conflict between hierarchies of values' can be *exclusively* derived from the lawful course of the class struggle and thus is in turn placed into a context of 'objective determinateness'. But what do all these assumptions amount to? If we take authors who argue in this manner literally it proves that the question concerning correct value orientations is a classical illusory problem, which should by no means be asked in 'situations' produced by objective laws, since it necessarily presupposes that *something else is possible* (or, even better, desirable). If this question regarding values arises in a world consisting of nothing but objectively determined events, then it must be due to an unexplainable aberration of the human mind.

There is something to be said for the fact that the representatives of the 'lawfulness' thesis do not wish to be taken literally in this way. We can find an allusion in conjunction with the assertion cited above. It suggests that 'moreover' Weber's conception also forms the basis of a 'mechanistic conception of the lawfulness of the process of history which does not comprehend that process as laws of human action and class' (*Wörterbuch*, 207). The occasional objection to Weber's 'objectivism' is obviously aimed in a similar direction.[49]

When starting out from the thesis of an 'objective determinateness' of the historical course of events it seems most peculiar that an objection of mechanism is raised *against* Weber whilst also demanding that the 'laws' in question be conceived in terms of human action. Nonetheless, this astonishing *quid pro quo* is not devoid of logic: Weber's thesis of logical heterogeneity is contrasted with the assertion of the universal and objective 'determinateness' of both the historical course of events and human value orientations. Accordingly Weber's thesis is certainly not refuted, but rendered empty of content and the self-imposed restriction to the 'empirically establishable' is maintained. Against the inevitable conclusion drawn from this, namely that the question of the legitimacy of specific value orientations refers to an illusory problem, it is argued that this would presuppose a 'mechanistic' concept of lawfulness. In summary, this two-tier argumentation has to be understood as follows: the historical course of events in general and the emergence of value orientations in particular is determined by 'objective laws'. But this determination does not go as far as to eliminate the possibility and necessity of evaluative standpoints. Objective laws, however, ensure that we can scientifically establish whether specific value orientations or partisanship are congruent with or opposed to the 'lawful' process.

Even this relativised position still contains a concept of historical lawfulness that could well be classified as 'mechanistic' (yet, at the same time, has nothing to do with Weber's conceptions). This concept would be mechanistic because it still assumes that there are 'determinisms' of social life that, when the occasion arises, prevail even against the united will of all historical actors (or against their declared value orientations). But with the explicit critique of a mechanistic conception the heterogeneity of empirical facts and value orientations (of what is and what ought to be, respectively) is simultaneously admitted. It opens up potential for value-related conduct, or a practical approach, to 'laws' of nature as well as social life. At any rate, this fact is neither explicated nor does it lead to a rethinking of the problem concerning the grounding of practical value orientations.

It is most inappropriate to mask the vagueness and inconsistency of this position with the venerable concept of 'dialectic'. In any event, it should be clarified as to how it is possible to arrive at this untenable conception from that of necessity in history employed by Hegel and Marx and the concomitant dispensation with an independent method for the rational grounding of practical (ethical or political) norms. A closer examination, which cannot be carried out here, may reveal that even in Marx we can establish an overestimation of the possibilities remaining with a consistent, empirically based theory of history (founded on Hegel, although admittedly 'standing Hegel on his head'). The substitution of the categories of 'logic' and 'reason' from Marx's early work with the concept of objective historical law, which is consistent with the purposes of the Marxian programme, should be much more crucial to the question that interests us here than Marx himself realised. In particular the Marxian conception that the radical 'critique' of what exists (and the appropriate political practice) represents nothing but the counterpart of his thorough empirical analysis[50] does not seem tenable once the idealistic assumption that history is the practice of reason (or the realisation of practical reason) is actually discarded. This in substance is evidently the most important starting-point for the 'neo-Kantian' reconstruction of Marxism whose general tendency is indeed to limit the scientific claim in order to gain space for independent ethical and political reflection.

It is possible that the latter references harbour an exaggerated expectation regarding the potential of subjecting existing and, to a large extent, habitualised fundamental theoretical convictions to critical scrutiny. In contrast it is undoubtedly reasonable to expect that at least one of the critics of Weber should demonstrate how value standards for socio-political practice, or criteria for decision-making, are derived from empirical statements of law on the historical process.[51] In fact it seems that no serious efforts to demonstrate this have hitherto been made. On the actual 'conflict' we shall have to wait and see whether counter-evidence will be offered (like Weber, *Gutachten*, 118 f.; *MSS*, 16).[52]

Paradoxically it is the tendential consensus between Marxist critics and Weber which has so far prevented another, probably more profitable, line of critique of Weber's conceptions on the problem of value judgement. It concerns the possibility listed above under (c) (p. 31) to establish and develop methods other than those of empirical science for the rational grounding of value standards. That this possibility is not seriously considered and pursued by the Marxist critics of Weber under discussion here is due to the fact that they, even more clearly than Weber himself, equate science and even rationality (or reason) as such with empirical science (including logic and mathematics). Hence, Weber's references to a rational, rather than empirical, procedure of rendering value orientations problematic are not taken up. We are not simply talking about his references to the possibilities of 'value-interpretation' and a 'discussion of value judgements' (cf., for instance, concerning this, *MSS*, 143 ff., 20 ff.; *Gutachten*, 119 ff.; *MSS*, 17 ff. as well as *SSP*, 417 f. and 420 f.), but rather the actual legitimacy of philosophical reflection (*MSS*, 54, 18).[53] The ambiguities and inadequacies of these Weberian references, particularly those concerning the possibility of a rational, argumentative *grounding* of value premisses, would be a very important object of discussion.[54] But the Marxist critics do not see the basis of Weber's 'irrationalism' here or in his thesis of the rational 'irresolvability' of ultimate value conflicts, but in his breaking with empirical-science methods in the grounding of norms.[55] However, in merely *opposing* Weber they do not actually show that empirical-science analyses indeed suffice for the grounding and defence of value judgements. Therefore, the degree of rationality actually held and made plausible by the Marxist authors on questions of evaluation is in fact even smaller than that considered realisable by Weber. It is also in keeping with this fixation on empirical-science rationality that all attempts at developing a method within the broader framework of the Marxist theoretical tradition for the grounding and legitimation of practical (particularly ethical and political) value orientations are very sharply criticised. This applies as a rule both to the older, 'neo-Kantian', approach and the contemporary efforts made by Habermas to clarify the 'capacity for truth' held by practical questions.

The fact that the Marxist stance criticises the shortcomings in rationality of the Weberian position, but does not overcome them and moreover occasionally even surpasses them, is expressed particularly clearly in the discussion of Weber's concept of 'value relevance'.[56] The critique is that the 'value perspectives' themselves, which each determine the 'selection and construction' of the object of social-science research, can no longer be established by scientific method. This incapacity is contrasted with the claim by Marxist social science that it pursues research from the *only* true perspective of historical progress, or rather the interests of the 'vanguard', and hence that it is inevitably capable of grasping the fundamental and 'essential' determinants of the socio-historical course of events. The dubiousness of this claim has already been referred to. *Firstly*, this biased value perspective is based on presuppositions of an empirical nature which – in turn – require an appropriate examination. But, *secondly*, as already shown, it would be no more capable of proving the implied 'progress' itself to be an empirical fact, no matter how convincing the empirical evidence cited, than to make the further logically imperative step of actually siding with 'progress'.

Weber's concept of 'value relevance' appears in a different, by no means 'irrational', light if these objections hold true (and the author of this discussion cannot see a convincing possibility of challenging them). At the outset and above all it should be seen as an indication that social-science research in particular is always carried out on the horizon of historical value perspectives, i.e. those originating in socio-cultural practice. Here resides, as also established above, a fundamental agreement between the Weberian and Marxist positions. Moreover, in Weber's view it is not only possible, but necessary, that the greatest possible clarity should exist or be created about each 'value perspective' guiding research. Similarly, the methods of 'value interpretation' and 'discussion of value judgements' serve this purpose. But the disclosure of value premises could simultaneously lead to, or at least very much encourage, a tendency to avoid idiosyncratic or even group-specific value perspectives and the choice of those which are most universally acceptable in the 'selection and construction' of research objects. Without referring to this specific context Weber in fact demands that researchers orient themselves to the *universal* evaluative ideas of 'cultural values' which move their contemporary worlds. The 'scientific genius' is characterised by the capacity to 'decide' the values which determine the conception of a whole epoch (*MSS*, 82).[57]

The Weberian references and postulates should be seen as rules that not only somehow 'mediate' social-science research with socio-cultural everyday practice, but should serve the greatest possible clarity and universality of the value premises selected by the researcher. Weber's concept and usage of 'value relevance' should not be interpreted as an expression or instrument of a specific 'irrationalism', but as an instruction to the social sciences to attempt the best possible measure of rationality – meaning the generalisability of specific value premises under historical circumstances – in spite of the prevailing value- and interest-related preconditions. This attempt cannot be surpassed by deriving value premises from and siding with that which is empirically given. Here in fact resides a specific source of concealed 'irrationalism' or 'decisionism' – which in this case is frequently expressed in the transfer of ultimate evaluative decisions to political authorities.

It is the logical overtaxing of empirical science (and the systematic dispensing with alternative forms of rational argumentation arising from this) that inevitably produces this result. The fact that empirical assumptions to a large extent also enter into the selection of evaluative ideas for the purpose of 'value relevance' as well as cultural evaluation is, in contrast, very much in accordance with the rationality of this selection. In this context Weber uses the ambiguous concept of 'cultural meaning'. On the one hand, this denotes that which seems particularly 'meaningful' (in the sense of 'valuable' or at least 'interesting') to us (on the most universal level possible) in a given historical situation. On the other hand, as noted, this concept also has a causal meaning, relating to factors which are assumed to have had special original significance for specific historical-social circumstances (again, those of particular concern or interest to us). In the selection, or determination, of such factors in the process of research we obviously need not only value-relevant considerations but also, to a large extent, empirical assumptions (which would, as a rule, be derived in turn from earlier enquiries). The weight of considerations on the empirical-causal cultural meaningfulness of specific factual findings or developments will be greater the more we are concerned with a transfer of 'value relevance' into a concrete research enquiry. But empirical considerations are of great importance even for the rational clarification of the 'value perspectives' or interests themselves which guide research (that is to say, the 'cultural meaning' in the first sense above). This clarification in the form of value interpretation and discussion of value judgements does not have to limit itself to logical (or perhaps hermeneutic-interpretative) analyses so long as it is directed at the generalisability of these value perspectives. Rather, it must seek essentially to clarify that these value perspectives *de facto* possess general validity or could/ought to possess it. For this purpose Marxist analyses would also benefit from their typical guiding value and interest perspectives being supported by empirical considerations and, to re-emphasise this, without needing to raise the claim of an ultimate empirical grounding or 'derivation', even though excessive use is made of this.

At this point we have to refer to one further aspect of Weber's understanding of 'value relevance'. Social science research is based on a multiple ranked sequence of value relations which extends from the most universal determination to a search for true knowledge as such, over the selection from among the various possibilities engaging in science (and ultimately, empirical science),[58] to the selection of specific objects of scientific research within a framework of empirical social science. In principle it is now conceivable that value premisses at all levels are accepted by the researcher as a purely *hypothetical* guiding principle, i.e. the 'as if' mode. For the fundamental value perspectives (including those which ground their interest specifically in social causality) this is, however, neither probable nor worth striving for, since it could express a lack of conviction in the necessity of social-science research. However, in Weber's view, a merely hypothetical inclusion of particular value perspectives is not only adequate here, but has its advantages in respect of the 'selection and construction' of concrete social problems. Under these circumstances the advantage resides in the fact that the fundamentally inevitably restricted range of vision associated with each value perspective is more readily challenged and could, if necessary, also be transcended. Of course such readiness is by no means out of the question if each value premiss was held even at this political level, as personal value orientation. The scientific advantage of this possibility is based on the fact that the relevant research could be carried out with greater motivation and, as a rule, with the background of broader and deeper everyday (including, e.g., political) experience.[59]

At the end of this book I shall return to the issue addressed in these final comments. The traditional Marxist determination of the relation between political orientation and practice in social-science research will be critically discussed with a view to clarifying the potentialities and perspectives of scientific analyses in sociology in a presupposed situation of deep-rooted political divergence. In this context I shall also take up the undoubtedly far-reaching and problematic Weberian demand that political standpoints should be strictly banned from the academic sphere and in turn expose it to a critical examination.

3.3 Ideal types, laws, theories

The entire methodological discussion on Weber's work generally displays a well-defined preference for the theme of the 'ideal type'.

Throughout the Marxist literature on Weber, however, this is the clearly dominant, if not exclusive, point of methodological discussion. With reference to non-Marxist literature it is difficult to explain this preference, which is expressed by an overemphasis of works on the subject. There are Weberian methodological problems that – even in Weber's own view – are more important to the *practice* of social science research in particular. These are especially the relationship between interpretative understanding (*Verstehen*) and causal explanation, quite apart from the question of ethical neutrality and value relevance. In contrast, it is much easier to understand why Marxist theorists take such one-sided interest in the theme of the 'ideal type'. Weber's comments on the ideal-typical character of historical social-science concepts seem to express the anti-materialist tendency of his methodology more forcefully and plainly even than the thesis and postulate of ethical neutrality. In any case, the thesis that ideal types most clearly and conclusively describe Weber's fundamental epistemological assumptions, in the form of concrete methodological definitions and rules, seems very persuasive. In the opinion of Marxist critics the distinctive 'subjectivistic' or 'subjective-idealistic' and, ultimately, 'agnostic' features of the Weberian epistemological conceptions that were discussed above are rendered unambiguously prominent when defining central theoretical categories as 'ideal types'.

The most important and frequently voiced Marxist arguments on the problem of the ideal type will be discussed below. The essential purpose will be to challenge the appropriateness of the fundamental gnoseological interpretations (in the sense of Weber's alleged 'Kantianism') and in contrast to identify Weber's own, philosophically less ambitious, interpretation of ideal types.[60] This method of proceeding will help explain why at least particular Marxist authors are able to establish affinities between the Weberian and Marxian conceptions on the specific aspects of historical social-science constructions of concepts and theories. Finally, I shall deal with an aspect of the 'ideal type' which, although it should arouse positive interest among Marxist theorists, is either not discussed at all or negatively evaluated by them in the course of a wilful misinterpretation. I am referring to the relationship between the ideal-typical conceptual form and the orientational requirements of contemporary social practice.

According to the heavily predominant Marxist interpretation Weber's considerations on the ideal type emanate from the need to rescue the potential of conceptual and theoretical construction in the historical social sciences under the presupposition that (empirical) knowledge cannot be seen as a 'reflection' of reality[61] and, more particularly, that an apprehension of the objective laws of historical social life is impossible. Here, as in general, it is assumed that the replicatory nature of empirical knowledge is proved by the discovery of such laws and hence that a denial or limitation of the potential for establishing such laws amounts to a denial of knowledge as reflection and that this, in turn, is identical with 'agnosticism'.[62]

The main objection to Weber is that the 'Weberian doctrine of ideal types, despite a certain heuristic usefulness' represents 'one of the most ingenious forms of denying the existence of objective laws' (Korf, 1964, 1342).[63] Danilov formulated the same objection in the following manner:

> The category of the ideal type is, in Weber's conception, destined to replace the category of historical law in the realm of historical methodology. By means of the category of the ideal type Weber sought to eliminate the idea of the natural-law character of the historical process from the methodology of the social sciences. (Danilov, 1958, 100)

Weber's comment 'that naturally all specifically Marxist "laws" and developmental constructs – in so far as they are theoretically sound – are ideal types' (and that we are concerned here with 'that ideal-type construction which is the most important one from our point of view') (*MSS*, 103), is accordingly interpreted as an attack on the Marxist theoretical bases of the claim to truth.

It seems to me that this type of argumentation is founded on a grave abridgement (if not distortion) of Weber's considerations. Weber's reservations concerning the epistemological claims *of the* objective lawfulness of the historical social world arise neither from a factually indisputable (or possibly politically-ideologically motivated) 'decision' nor from a prior decision of a universal, epistemological nature.

With reference to the latter possibility in particular, it is a huge mistake to interpret Weber's option for the ideal-typical conceptual form as a direct consequence of the transcendental philosophical conception of knowledge that has been attributed to him. His argumentations on the ideal type are neither the result of transcendental philosophical reflection nor the equivalent of such, as would have been necessary in this case, nor did he attribute the status of *a priori* epistemological forms to the actual ideal types (cf. note 15). Rather Weber's arguments on the grounding and elucidation of his own viewpoints are oriented to the practice of concrete historical and social science research. In fact it would be more justifiable here, as on other points of his methodology, to reproach him on his over-orientation to the requirements and potentialities of research – that is to say, a shortcoming in (ultimate) epistemological grounding – rather than the 'deduction' of methodological rules from abstract epistemological premisses.

Weber explicitly notes that his considerations on the ideal type are intended to explicate a perpetually used method and to make it the object of critical examination. In his opinion 'every historian' needs 'concepts of *this* kind where he uses clear-cut "concepts" at all' (*PE II*, 304). In the cited characterisation of Marxist conceptions Weber establishes nothing more than that these operate throughout within the framework of the universally applied methods in historical research and are exceptional only in so far as they represent particularly successful examples of the endeavour for 'sharper and clearer' conceptual construction in the historical sciences.

The ideal-type character or status of historical concepts thus emanates, in Weber's opinion, from the requirement and necessity to seek 'conceptual clarity' and 'the application of firm and precise concepts' in historical research too (*SWG*, 280). In Weber's view such efforts are a *conditio sine qua non* of *all* empirical science. Moreover he argued that it was utterly impossible to make unambiguous and, therefore, examinable *causal* attributions without them (*SWG*, 288). The question is why, however, the necessity for conceptual clarity and precision in history and the historical social sciences requires the development of ideal-type concepts. Why should it be impossible to satisfy this requirement in this sphere, as it obviously is in the natural sciences, in conjunction with the need for the theoretical comprehension of reality 'as it "in fact" is'? Why is there a need to introduce a separate level of precise conceptual constructions if they are explicitly 'not a description of reality' (*MSS*, 90), but should instead be seen as pure 'conceptual constructs' (*Gedankengebilde*) (*PE II*, 304; *MSS*, 90, 91, 93) or 'mental constructs' (*Gedankenbilder*), as constructions of the 'imagination' (*MSS*, 92, 94) and 'utopia' (*MSS*, 90)?

The crucial explanation of the endeavour for conceptual clarity in the historical social sciences, in Weber's view, is the fact that these sciences – unlike the natural sciences – do not seek to investigate any constant (ahistorical) and therefore relatively easily (conceptually and empirically) isolatable determinants of human behaviour, but rather the effects of genuine historical-social factors. Weber sees these genuine historical-social factors in the 'imputations of meaning' and meaningful organisations that 'constitute' and regulate social life as such at all levels (i.e. also at the level of material social production). It is possible, but in practice improbable (and therefore by no means an *a priori* assumption), that such meaningful organisations exist and operate in social life with the total clarity and consistency of which they are capable in logic. On the other hand, we can (empirically!) assume that there is a tendency towards clarity and consistency of intersubjective 'meaningful relationships' in historical social reality.[64] In Weber's opinion, such a tendency is obviously defined in terms of the necessary 'communicability' of socially established interpretations of meaning.[65]

The necessity to work with ideal-type concepts in historical social science research thus stems from the fact that (a) the requirement for 'conceptual clarity' demands a transparent and consistent construction of *possible* 'meaningful relationships',[66] but that, at the same time (b) it must not be assumed in principle that meaningful relationships, thus constructed, (raised to a meaningfully adequate level of intelligibility) refer to the actual (simple or pure) social references of meaning which determine behaviour.

Weber emphatically insists on the constructive and utopian character of the mental constructs attained by this method, because the temptation to take them as reflections of reality is enormous and particularly widespread in extra-scientific practice. On the other hand, that ideal-type 'mental constructs' are well suited to the analysis of historical-social reality – beyond the fulfilment of the formal prerequisite of conceptual clarity – stems from the fact that it is possible and appropriate to attribute to social practice a *trend* towards 'meaningful adequacy'.[67] Whether and how far this trend actually exists (and certainly in accordance with *each* ideal-type construct) is an empirical question. The employment of ideal types does not preclude its actual existence, let alone to what extent.

Marxist critics of the ideal-type conception as a rule do not consider this background, presented here only in outline. The exceptions will be dealt with further below. Accordingly there is no critical discussion and examination of the specific Weberian assumptions, although their nature is by no means concealed or even metaphysical. In particular Weber's dual interest in both a conceptually clear and empirically profound historical social-science research practice, which underlies his thinking, goes unnoticed. The decisive reason for the inadequacy of the critique in this respect seems to reside in the fact that (a) the contents of Weber's fundamental assumptions about the specific nature of historical-social reality are not taken into consideration and that (b) the ideal-type constructions are interpreted as a ('subjective-idealistic') replacement for empirical theories. Whereas the second point will be explained more closely, I shall return to the first in more detail in later sections (especially in the discussion on Weber's fundamental idea of 'social action').

Weber's well-known observation is that a specific ideal-type construction itself does not amount to a hypothesis, since it is not actually meant to 'copy' reality or its real interrelationships. Rather, in the context of empirical research its purpose is to give direction to the construction of hypotheses (*MSS*, 90), precisely because it demonstrates particular possible interrelationships and trends in a clear and meaningfully plausible way. Marxist critics – but not only Marxists! – seem systematically to overlook the dual nature of the conceptual-theoretical method inaugurated by Weber. There is no other explanation for their belief that they can derive Weber's 'agnosticism', or at least 'idealism', from the 'constructive' and 'utopian' character of the ideal types. They fail to appreciate that ideal types for Weber are *no* substitute for empirical hypotheses or theories but represent a tool, which can be defended on good grounds (although, of course, it can be rendered problematic), towards an adequate empirical description and explanation of real historical-social facts (or particular aspects of such facts). Ideal types, in Weber's conception, should clearly serve the methodologically controlled approximation to the actual determinants of historical-social practice in such a way, of course, that the epistemological interest is in principle focussed on the constitutive distinctness of this specific reality, namely its 'meaningfulness'. In this respect the most appropriate characterisation of the status and function of the ideal types, above all rejecting a transcendental-logical interpretation, in Marxist literature can be found in Neusychin:

> Weber's 'ideal type' is not constructed for the purpose of creating something new. It only serves the orientation of the researcher exploring historical reality; it does not make any prescription. It is a tool for comprehending historical reality that is borrowed from within itself. (Neusychin, 1974, 462)

How does a thus understood application of ideal-type constructs relate to the search for 'laws' in the historical-social world? At the outset these constructions as such – so long as we are talking about tenets of an explanatory nature constructed by means of ideal-type concepts – can, of course, take the *form* of universal hypotheses or statements of law. Because of the specific distinctness of that 'idealisation' which underlies its formation (namely, the construction of 'meaningful adequacy' as 'objective possibility'),[68] however, it is not reasonable to interpret these 'laws' offhand within the meaning of an empirical theory. How far laws are to be attributed to social reality in accordance with – or better, for the purpose of – these idealisations is, as we said, a question of empirical analysis carried out with the guidance of ideal-type constructions. In the context of empirical systems of statements the application of ideal-type concepts and conceptual systems will as a rule be interlinked with explicit findings, to the degree of which (or probability of) the concrete existence of 'meaningfully adequate' social actions or relationships is imputed to the type and purpose formulated in each ideal type.

This is the essential reason for Weber's preferences in making use of the category of *'chance'* in the definition of ideal-type concepts or formulation of ideal-type models of explanation, particularly in *Economy and Society*. Like Weber's overall argumentation, this category is not logically directed against the endeavours for 'nomological' knowledge in the historical social sciences. Neither is it a matter, as Korf suggests, of intentionally reducing the significance of 'establishing laws to a minimum' (Korf, 1964, 1339).[69] Weber is merely seeking to avoid causal attributions, obtained on the basis of ideal-type simplifications and specifications, being automatically confused with descriptions of deterministic laws in the real world.[70] Korf, who very firmly derives Weber's ostensible disinterest in the social-science 'establishment of laws' from the conception of the ideal type, simultaneously throws light on the highly problematic assumptions on which a fundamental critique of Weber's conception would have to be based:

> It is true that the world is undergoing constant change and development, but despite this changeability there are moments of relative peace and stability of things and their relationships and structures within all periods, no matter how much external appearances might change. This peaceful enduring, stable and repetitive quality finds its expression in law. The law is as Lenin, proceeding from Hegel, comments, 'the peaceful reflection of appearances', 'the enduring quality (stability) in the appearance', 'the identical element in the appearance' (*ibid.*, 1333).[71]

'The law formulated by the social sciences reflects real, independent (of the knowing subject), necessary and universal relationships.' (*ibid.*, 1332.)

According to Korf there is no difference between the natural and social sciences in respect of either the scientific status or the application of statements of law in practical research (*ibid.*, 1335). Thus it is clearly stated that the unmediated interpretation of nomological abstractions or idealisations as empirical theories implies that the epistemological interest of the social sciences too has to be guided by and limited to the 'identical' and 'enduring' qualities behind the stream of 'appearances' – this interest being in fact constitutive of the exact natural sciences (a view shared by both Rickert and Weber, as is well known). But in this case the 'identical' and 'enduring', and therefore the 'essential',[72] quality, is the 'material base'. According to Weber there is not even the slightest logical difficulty in conceptually and theoretically reconstructing social conditions and developments from the perspective of 'material production' if one chooses 'meaningful adequacy' as a guiding thread. It is, indeed, this which characterises Marxist 'laws' and 'developmental constructs' according to the cited observation by Weber. It is also possible to appeal to features that apply to 'material production' (or, more specifically, the interplay between 'productive forces and relations of production') under any conditions. But there can be no *a priori* answer to the question as to what such 'idealisations' from a materialist perspective or materialist 'value relevance' contribute to the description and explanation of concrete historical action – even more so when they operate with the most universal (identical and enduring) factors. In any case, the relative causal significance of factors underlying historical change and non-material in character can only be perceived and adequately examined if the materialist constructs – in themselves probably very logical (meaningfully adequate) – are understood and employed as the 'idealisations' of a perspective.

Of course, Weber was of the opinion that an interest in the simply identical and enduring was absolutely uncharacteristic of history and the historical social sciences. On the contrary, as previously mentioned, he believed that these sciences should study what is logically subject to historical change, i.e. social action in as much as it is determined by people conferring meaning and their value orientation on it. This is why he held that the most universal statements of law (e.g. of a psychological type) were indeed possible and admissible, but very unproductive with a view to explaining historical facts.[73] Thus it is not primarily the interest in the historically individual or unique element, as Korf assumes (*ibid.*, 1330 f.),[74] but in history generally that motivates this special form of construction or application of 'clear and unambiguous' concepts.[75] The fact that the everyday experience of history is always 'individualising' (i.e. attached to the respective perspectives of meaning and value) and that the scientific analysis of history ultimately serves this everyday experience, according to Weber, does not imply that the concepts and statements of the historical social sciences have to limit themselves to individual factors in the spatial and temporal sense (i.e. plainly unrepeatable factors). Evidently such a conception would be paradoxical even on logical grounds. The method of ideal-type construction is, like all conceptual construction, a form of 'generalisation'. But it is a generalisation that is not obtained by the subsumption under class concepts of individual phenomena reduced to something 'identical'. Instead it is obtained by assigning concrete historical trends (of varying degrees) to an 'idealised' form, which was initially formed in history 'in an often mediated, broken, more or less logical and coherent fashion, more or less combined with other heterogeneous' (*PE* II, 304), occurring and effective factors. Even the typifications constructed and used in social life may show varying degrees of abstraction. This applies even more to the scientific ideal types. The high degree of generalisation and abstraction that is possible for it (demanded by Weber in large sections of *Economy and Society*) is explained by the fact that in scientific conceptual construction the concrete requirements of orientation to historical-social practice can be 'virtualised' (made concrete) rather than given up or eliminated. Yet this practice still does not operate at a level of abstraction that lies above or beyond all possible historical-social orientation to meaning. Above all, this is expressed by the fact that the practice does not seek to designate *one* dimension of reality to which ultimately all historical-social events can be causally traced back. If Marxist authors mean this when referring to the 'material base' it would seem logically to contradict their observation that materialist theory represents not only a theory of history, but also an 'out and out' historical theory. The Marxist reference must be meant in this way if the statements of law of materialist theory are related to the 'material base' as the identical and enduring element in or behind all historical change.[76] This is even more applicable if the claim to knowledge of social 'laws' in general is derived from such an 'assumption of base' (in the double meaning of the term).[77]

The last comment provides me with the opportunity of introducing some reflections on the more general, although still centred on the problem of the ideal type, Marxist critique of Weber's conceptions regarding the role of social science theory within the framework of an emphatic historical orientation in social science. These considerations should also be useful towards an explanation of the relationship between ideal-type conceptual construction and social practice that concludes this section.

Two interrelated objections to Weber's understanding of social science theory are raised by the Marxist side: firstly, that it is 'ahistorical' and, secondly, 'idealistic'.

The objection of 'ahistoricity' is fairly surprising in view of the above comments. The same authors who raise it undoubtedly seek to set the superior power of generalisation of materialist theory *against* Weber's conceptions. It seems difficult to resolve this fundamental contradiction. But once we leave aside the very logical (quasi-metaphysical) assertions, it is hard to see what the critique of Weber's 'formalistic' categories (particularly in *Economy and Society*) objects to. Herkommer gives the following explanation using the example of Weberian conceptual definitions of class, status, etc.:[78]

> Weberian social science research on the stratification of the population into classes, status groups, strata and other groups does not seem to rise beyond definition while it reduces historical material to a mere example. History is detached in such a manner that the concepts with which the discipline works are no longer understood as historical ones, they are no longer grouped as ideal expressions of historically changing social relations, but are indeed placed above history in poor abstractness.[79] (Herkommer, 1975, 128)

These comments conflict not only with Weber's utterances on the nature and function of conceptual abstraction in the historical sciences, but more seriously with his own application of historical social science categories in research practice, the clarification and elaboration of which he devoted large sections to in *Economy and Society*. The fact that a great number of fundamental categories in the Marxist theoretical tradition have not been clarified until this day does not imply that such clarification is superfluous or even contradictory (since 'unhistorical' in nature). In any case, the temptation to subsume social events and processes under general concepts, or under theorems constructed on the basis of such concepts, seems greater in the Marxist tradition of thought than in the historical social science research based on Weber. This is demonstrated particularly impressively by the way in which Weber's conception of ideal types is contrasted with the epistemological interest in the eternally unchanging, enduring and lawful – however inadequate might be his attempt to determine the possibility of conceptual precision and abstraction on the level of a firmly historically based epistemological interest.

It is indisputable that some Marxist authors also endeavour to establish, conceptually and theoretically, the 'dialectical' relationship between the lawfulness and historicity of the social process. These efforts resume from the relevant, although very brief, references in Karl Marx (particularly in the *Introduction to a Critique of Political Economy* and in the already cited Afterword to the second German edition of *Capital*). Although an adequate presentation and examination of these arguments is not feasible at this stage it is, however, worth referring to an obvious problem. What is sought is the dialectical unity of the conceptually universal and the historically particular, of abstraction and concretisation. Even the terminological choice exposes the philosophical Hegelian roots of this line of enquiry. Beyond that, however, explicit attention is drawn to the superiority of the Hegelian in contrast to the Kantian position on this issue:

> Hegel criticised Kant because the latter 'stopped dead . . . at the assertion that the Notion is and remains utterly separated from reality'. Hegel, in comparison, emphasised the unity of concept and reality, whereby though he raised the concept to the essence of objective reality. (Korf, 1964, 1340)[80]

Against this reference to Hegel we can no less raise the objection that the Hegelian determination of the relationship between 'concept' and historical 'reality', the 'universal' and the 'particular', is completely deprived of its base once we rule out the ontological primacy of the 'concept' as an 'idealistic distortion' (thus Korf, *ibid.*). It is, indeed, *not* possible to retain a necessary unity of concept and historical reality in the Hegelian sense by raising it to a 'realistic' level through the inversion of the causal relationship. To speak of concepts as 'ideal expressions of historically changing relations' (as Korf does) is defensible for Hegel only if and in so far as 'the historically changing social relations' in turn are demonstrable as the realisation of the 'concept'. Concepts can in any case be nothing more than 'ideal expressions' of the 'finite mind' if the absolute subjectivity realised (or discarded) in history is removed. If it is nonetheless asserted that historical-social reality is 'ideally' expressed in the concepts of science, we can at best accept this as a metaphorical way of speaking. This on no account offers a solution to the problem of how the relationship between conceptuality and reality, abstraction and historicity, should be grasped in the historical social sciences. At least in the form in which this observation is presented in Korf's remarks, cited above, it tends to block systematically the view to a solution.

At any rate, this highly problematic formulation simultaneously refers to another issue with regard to which there is paradoxically yet again a certain affinity between Weber's ideal-type conception and the Marxist tradition (particularly if the latter's orientation is emphatically Hegelian). This has prevented, rather than encouraged, intensive critical treatment of Weber's conceptions. Weber relates the necessity of the ideal-type conceptual form to the leading interest of the social sciences in grasping the historical social world in logic as the historical sciences always had practised it: in terms of value-related (i.e. practice-related) 'meaningful relationships'. The construction of ideal-type (objectively possible) meaningful relationships is necessary since there can be no clear and unambiguous concepts in the least suitable for an empirical approximation to *this* reality in the face of the heterogeneity, conflation and diffuseness of meaningful relationships that normally determine social action. As decisively as Weber, on the one hand, emphasises the gap between the ideal-type 'mental constructs' and social reality, so constitutive is, on the other hand, his relation of ideal types to those 'ideas' and meaningful 'syntheses', according to which, in his conception, historical-social contexts of action are constructed, organised and developed.[81] According to Weber, then, there is a relationship between the ideal-type concepts of the historical social sciences and historical reality which is defined in terms of its 'meaningfulness'. *In so far* as this stands it would also be possible to characterise ideal types as 'ideal expressions of historically changing social relations'. But this mode of expression is not commendable because it involves, as mentioned, a hypostasis of social relations to a subject (as opposed to the researcher) who produces concepts or indeed a (historically relativising) reproduction theory of social science knowledge while tending to conceal the idealisation contained in these concepts. The risk of this latter possibility occurring is particularly great because there is a strong tendency in the historical everyday world, not towards *actual* meaningful adequacy, but rather towards a *faith* in the meaningful adequacy given to real social relations or contexts of action, which is firmly embedded in everyday language.

The more general second criticism of Weber mentioned above is an objection to his idealism within his conceptions on theory construction in the historical social sciences. This refers precisely to his focus on the 'meaningfulness' of historical and social reality and his limitation to this dimension – especially in the construction of his ideal types.[82] Marxist authors of a classical or prototypical mould see this theoretical idealism clearly expressed in the essays on *The Protestant Ethic*. To these critics Weber's historical analyses seem significant and acceptable only on the points where Weber shows at least a tentative detachment from his predominant 'idealistic tendency'.[83]

The critique of idealism makes easy work for itself (which is undoubtedly to its own disadvantage) by concentrating to such an extent on the relatively great importance attached by Weber to those factors in specific analyses (yet by no means all) which are allocated to the 'superstructure' in the materialist tradition.[84] The 'material factors' set against this interpretation of idealism are for Weber by no means detached from the field of meaningful historical facts. But the production and class relations, as well as the material elements of social activity in the narrower sense (i.e. productive forces and cultivated nature), are integrated – and indeed meaningfully integrated – constituents, or components, of historical-social contexts of action.[85] In any event, they have a share in the historicity of the human relations under discussion here only in so far as they are *such* constituents. Historicity becomes a problem of the conceptual and theoretical construction related to it only if the 'material base' itself is a product of meaningful social activity by the individual (as Marx in fact asserts in marked contrast to the already cited arguments by Korf).

The view represented here is that Weber's approach to the solution of this problem is *not* linked to an 'idealistic' superstructure perspective, but solely to the definitional presupposition that social action and social relations must be termed historical in so far as they are constructed ('constituted'), maintained and changed through contingent meaningful relationships. Weber's attempted solution can be called 'idealistic' only to the extent that he relates the historicity of human and particularly social existence, and therefore the possibility and perhaps the necessity of history, to the fact that the individual has to lead his life in the form of active engagement with a given reality. This existential form is realisable only in so far as the individual in his actions operates on the horizon of specific interpretations of the self, his own species and the non-human world. This applies even to a (fictitious) Robinson Crusoe type of existence and *a fortiori* to even the most elementary intersubjective life histories. It seems to me that it is this type of idealism that Marx discovered and adopted as the 'realistic' core of Hegelian philosophy (especially in the *Phenomenology of the Mind*). At any rate, I simultaneously believe that the abandonment of any absolute idealistic assumptions in the domain of the historical and social construction of concepts and theories must lead to conceptions that at least approximate Weberian conceptions. It has already been said that neither Marx (though comprehensible from a historical perspective) nor many Marxists until this day seem to have abandoned this Hegelian feature with absolute consistency. This is expressed in a more recent essay on the Marx-Weber discussion in that the 'real historical' process is contrasted with the concept of a 'logically' necessary development (Bader *et al.*, 1976, 385; cf. 324). The crucial distinction between this conception and that of Weber resides precisely in the assumption of a logically *necessary*, as opposed to an objectively *possible*, development based on 'meaningful adequacy'. Even the residue (or *caput mortuum*?) of an absolute idealistic argumentation is explicitly formulated when the authors – at least in the form of a suggestion – bring into play a rationality operating in the process of history itself (cf. 447).

Lukács in *History and Class Consciousness* made a significant contribution (and not only historically) to the clarification of the relationship between the Marxist and Weberian positions on the issue of the historical social science construction of concepts and theories. He is incorporated in the discussion at this stage because he is, on the one hand, directly involved in the problem of 'idealisation' (and, more specifically, with the question of 'Hegelianism') and, on the other, because he shifts our attention to another controversial area, namely the relationship between the ideal-type conceptual form in the social sciences and social practice.

The argumentation by Lukács of interest to us in this context can be briefly outlined as follows: materialist theory of history is capable of seeing through the 'objectivity attributed both to social institutions inimical to man and to their historical evolution' and tracing its 'basis' back 'to the relations between men'. Thus it by no means eliminates the 'laws and objectivity independent of the will of man and in particular the wills and thoughts of individual men'. Rather it interprets this objectivity as a 'self-objectivisation of human society at a particular stage in its development' (1971, 49). Marxist theory can fulfil this (dual) task in that it fundamentally incorporates the perspective of historically acting individuals (i.e. those producing the historical worlds), while it frees itself from the restrictions imposed by the empirical consciousness of social actors. It manages to free itself from the restrictions by relating 'to society *as a whole*', '*as a concrete totality*'. The 'total' perspective permits Marxist theory to perceive the 'state of consciousness' of social actors at the time as one that is *subjectively* true (since explainable 'in the social and historical situation') and objectively as false consciousness (since bypassing 'the essence of the evolution of society') (*ibid.*, 50, emphasis by Lukács). On the other hand, Marxist theory sees through the second dialectic of the actual consciousness that fails to reach the self-appointed (subjective) goals while it unintentionally furthers the '*objective* aims of society' (*ibid.*, 50). Lukács then characterises the method and aims he inaugurated:

> The relation with concrete totality and the dialectical determinants arising from it transcend pure description and yield the category of objective possibility. By relating consciousness to the whole of society it becomes possible to

infer the thoughts and feelings which men would have in a particular situation if they were *able* to assess both it and the interests arising from it in their impact on immediate action and on the whole structure of society. That is to say, it would be possible to infer the thoughts and feelings appropriate to their objective situation. (*ibid.*, 51; emphasis by Lukács)

But as 'situations' vary in accordance with the position in the process of production, i.e. they present themselves as specific class situations, it is necessary to construct a corresponding consciousness of social totality as an 'objective possibility' for each typical life or class situation: 'class consciousness consists in fact of the appropriate and rational reactions "imputed" [*zugerechnet*] to a particular typical position in the process of production' (*ibid.*).

Lukács notes that this method should be related not only to the corresponding approaches in the Marxist tradition of thought (such as the concept of 'economic persona'), but also to 'comparable trends in bourgeois thought' (*ibid.*; footnote). The significance of this source of inspiration is, of course, more likely to be played down than duly acknowledged when he refers to 'Max Weber's ideal types' as an example. Although it may be an exaggeration to rate Weber as Lukács' 'Maître' (Merleau-Ponty, 1955, 44) or 'tutor' (Fetscher, 1973, 501) in *History and Class Consciousness*, the influence is undoubtedly more profound than Lukács himself cares to admit. The reason for this caution may have less to do with considerations of political opportunism than the fact that Lukács was aware of how much Weber stimulated him on this point whilst turning it against Weber's own intentions.

The very crucial difference between Lukács and Weber evidently resides in the following: Lukács, like Weber, lays stress on the non-psychological, but logical, status of theoretical constructs designed within the meaning of 'objective possibility'. By superseding 'man's (psychological) consciousness' (1971, 47), however, the ideal-type construct in Marxist usage does not progress from the 'real motor forces of history'. On the contrary, because of its leading orientation to the social 'totality' (which precisely is not accessible to empirical consciousness) it manages to produce an image of social conditions and processes that has a super-empirical, 'as it were, ontological and normative dignity'.[86] This image is 'ontological' because it determines the 'real motor forces' in social reality as a whole. It is 'normative' because the thus determined 'objective possibility' is simultaneously the objective necessity for social evolution and hence it outlines a clear purpose for social action.

This transition from objective possibility to objective necessity clearly indicates the crucial difference from Weber's conception, but also the great dubiousness of Lukács' argument. That is to say, Lukács operates with a series of highly doubtful assumptions in this 'change of mode'. They are connected with the fact that he naturally – as a materialist theorist – could not make the direct leap from a constructed 'objective possibility' into an absolute necessity, but had instead to seek support in proletarian class consciousness, which – in contrast to the ideological narrow-mindedness of bourgeois class consciousness (*ibid.*, 63 f.) – is capable of forming, or indeed compelled to form, a comprehensive notion of the 'real motor forces' in bourgeois society on the basis of the material situation of this (proletarian) class:

> the same growth of insight into the nature of society, which reflects the protracted death struggle of the bourgeoisie, entails a steady growth in the strength of the proletariat. For the proletariat the truth is a weapon that brings victory; and the more ruthless, the greater the victory. (*ibid.*, 68)

To be sure, for Lukács this does not apply to proletarian class consciousness as it in fact exists in the individual or 'average' consciousness of proletarians. Here again he refers to an 'objective possibility'[87] that cannot be realised of itself due to the bourgeoisie's continuing influence on 'large sections of the proletariat' (*ibid.*, 304). Hence we are not only confronted with the practical political problem of how 'it is actually possible to make the objective possibility of class consciousness into a reality' (*ibid.*, 79). Rather, the legitimate base of a political practice focussed on its realisation faces the gravest danger when he admits to a fundamental difference between the objectively possible and the actually possible class consciousness. This danger can be averted only if a clear, demonstrable tendency exists in historical reality in the direction of that 'objective possibility'. Only under this presupposition can the objective possibility be converted into an objective necessity without too obvious a 'decisionist' leap. Lukács believes to have found the 'missing link' in his argumentation in the Leninist-type Communist Party. According to him, this party, as an '*autonomous*[88] *form*' of proletarian class consciousness' (*ibid.*, 330), presents that objective possibility (namely, the possibility of true understanding of the social totality) as an empirical fact and an indestructible political force – and, of course, specifically for the proletariat as well:

> The Communist Party must exist as an independent organisation so that the proletariat may be able to see its own class consciousness given historical shape. And likewise, so that in

every event of daily life the point of view demanded by the interests of the class as a whole may receive a clear formulation that every worker can understand. And, finally, so that the whole class may become fully aware of its own existence as a class. (*ibid.*, 326)

The Party is nothing but the concretely existing 'conscious collective will' (*ibid.*, 315) of the class on whose side the theoretical and practical 'truth' of the historical epoch resides.

This is an inappropriate point for a detailed critique of this argumentation. A crucial objection against the last step, which crowns and secures the entire chain of reasoning, was formulated by Fetscher. He takes up Lukács' assertion that party consciousness has priority status over the 'direct experiences' of proletarians:

It remains . . . inconceivable how the party, equally consisting of mere individuals, is always and everywhere supposed to be able to formulate in anticipation, i.e. before reflecting on actual experience, the 'objectively possible' class consciousness. The infallibility assumed here is similar to that asserted by dogmatic Leninists, even though less metaphysically grounded. (op. cit., 522)[89]

It seems to me that Fetscher, moreover, sees the reason for the sharp rejection of Lukács' theory of the party by 'Leninist orthodoxy' being due less to the ostensible 'errors' of this theory than 'the fact that the metaphysical nature of the theory of the party in the early Lenin is unmistakably apparent in Lukács' theory' (*ibid.*, 524).

In the present context it is important, above all else, to establish that Lukács' wholly untenable arguments on the status and function of the Communist Party are consistently due to the logical construction of his argumentation, as opposed to having their origins in perhaps accidental grounds, e.g. political opportunism. Krahl noted that in Lukács' theory of the party the Party is declared a 'metaphysical subject of history' while its members are 'the tool of the communist collective consciousness' (1971, 179; cited in Fetscher, 1973, 523). It is precisely this 'Hegelian'[90] expression that is embedded in the premises of the whole of Lukács' train of thought. Lukács emphatically demonstrates the required presuppositions if one wants to free Weber's considerations on historical social science conceptualisation and theorisation from their 'restrictions' and to close the gap, characterised by the concepts of 'ideal type' and 'objective possibility' between historical conceptualisation and historical reality. Lukács adopts the Weberian category of objective possibility because he (justifiably) perceives in this the dual chance of attaining clear and unambiguous conceptual syntheses in historical social science research whilst simultaneously maintaining reference to the historical experience of social actors. Equally justifiably he further recognises that possibilities are contained within the ideal-type conception enabling the transcendance, both in thought and *practical* intention, of each historical reality. Lukács departs from Weberian conceptions, and therefore fundamentally an empirical science argumentation precisely when he converts the construction of 'objective possibilities' into ontological and normative ones.[91]

This *decisive* distinction, so crucial for Lukács, would be untenable even if 'objective possibilities' were determinable with a view to the social 'totality'; that is to say, even if this 'totality' represented above all a possible or necessary reference point for ideal-type constructions. Even statements on those forces which ultimately determine the social whole could at best *only* be confirmed *hypotheses* within the framework of empirical science research.[92] It is indeed more probable that such statements refer specifically to extreme 'ideal-type' constructs. Moreover, if we were to use the concept of 'concrete totality' (likewise borrowed from Hegel), we would have to consider in depth how this category could be given substance within the framework of an empirical materialist analysis, once we had consciously dispensed with not only Hegel's unifying and uniting 'subject' of all social 'concreteness', but also any possibility of a 'synthesis' that logically transcends historical reality.

In concluding this section, one last point that I have repeatedly drawn attention to deserves a little more detailed treatment. It has been suggested that Lukács' reception of Weber, despite its dubiousness, throws light on one aspect of Weber's concept of the ideal type which does not tend to be fully appreciated by either Marxist or non-Marxist interpreters of Weber. The point referred to is that the ideal-type form of reconstructing historical-social realities largely meets the requirements for communication within the framework of concrete social practice. It is not being suggested that 'clear and unambiguous' concepts are generally constructed by these means, even though it would undoubtedly benefit social practice.[93] Rather, the specific advantage of the Weberian ideal-type conceptual form arises from the level and purpose of the conceptual construction characteristic of ideal types. It is both the fundamental reference to historical 'meaningful relationships' and the 'meaningful adequacy' of the reconstructions pertaining to these 'meaningful relationships' that bind ideal types with the requirements of clarification and communication in social practice.

The orientation to practical social goals involves an orientation to the horizon of socially meaningful relationships and this with a view to specific dimensions of meaning and value.

In this context the most important individual aspect is the following: ideal types reconstruct historical social reality in the mode of 'objective *possibility*'. But this is simultaneously the mode in which social practice is contained, so long as it seeks a rational clarification of each historical condition and situation. If social actors were really confronted with statements of law in which the objective 'laws' of the historical and social processes were reflected, there would no longer be action that is mediated by way of a conscious assessment of different possibilities, i.e. conscious and justifiable action. Weber undoubtedly grounds the necessity of the ideal-type conceptual form throughout in epistemological or methodological arguments. But, of course, this does not preclude the specific possibilities of a mediation between social science and practice being contained in this conceptual form (yet these in themselves would not be sufficient justification for the use of ideal types). Besides, this interpretation is in harmony with one basic intention of Weber's methodology, namely to avoid all the misleading, and above all practically dangerous, hypostases of theoretical concepts as well as any confusion between concept and reality in the social sciences.[94] Since ideal-type 'conceptual constructs' reconstruct historical and social reality in the mode of an objective possibility, they may be used as a critical tool in countering the danger of 'reification' (to use Lukács' terminology) to which social science concepts and theorems are exposed in both scientific and – *a fortiori* – everyday usage.

A crucial explanatory feature of the ideal-type conceptual and theoretical form whose importance for the mediation of social science analysis and political social practice ought to be recognised and acknowledged not least by Marxist theorists was expressed in the distancing from social reality 'as it actually is' and in the development of rash nomological modes of explanation (particularly of a deterministic kind). It is undoubtedly consistent to contrast the idea of a scientifically based social practice that corresponds to the conception of the ideal type with the (sociotechnical) 'notion that establishing laws in the social sciences should facilitate the 'control and guidance' of social processes (of course, 'in accordance with progress') (Korf, 1964, 1334). But it is highly questionable whether Marxist theorists, in particular, can adhere to such a (Comtean) positivistic notion as unfailingly as they have done hitherto. Equally questionable, and originating in the same orientation, is the tendency by some Marxist authors to discover the partially correct element of the ideal-type conception in its affinity with the natural science concept of a model (cf., for example, Korf, 1964, 1335 and 1968a, 204 ff.; Korablev, 1968a, 528).[95] Reference to this affinity is not simply wrong, but it does as a rule entail the difference being overlooked. This difference in connection with the last comments should be characterised in the following terms: the models of the exact natural sciences reproduce (physical) reality in a pure sense (i.e. limited to specific constellations of factors – above all those that are quantitatively measurable – which can be isolated at least in experiment), while in comparison ideal types are expected to expose historical-social reality with reference to 'possibilities' or 'chances' (conceived by the guiding thread of meaningful adequacy). As noted, it is this difference that constitutes the specific practical relevance of the ideal-type conceptual and theoretical form.

It is necessary to adhere to this difference even *vis-à-vis* the considerations of the Polish philosopher of science, Nowak, which are by all means worthy of discussion. Nowak (1976; 1971a; 1971b; Kmita and Nowak, 1970, 60 ff.) supplies a reconstruction of the explanatory model used by Marx in political economy that places emphases on the central importance of 'idealisation laws'. 'Idealisation laws' for Nowak's purposes correspond to Weber's ideal types in so far as they have no direct equivalent in the real world. In Nowak's view these laws play an important role not only in the cultural sciences, but (precisely) in the most exact natural sciences too.[96] He considers the shortcoming in Hempel's general explanatory model to be the failure to take account of this. Nowak seeks the difference between Weber and Marx's portrayal of the ideal-type method in Weber, unlike Marx, not describing the transition from those idealisation theorems to empirical hypotheses explicitly as a procedure of progressive 'concretisation'. At any rate, he thinks that Weber's conceptions could 'presumably' be interpreted in this sense (1971b, 146). Nowak contrasts the tendency, equally establishable in Weber, to derive a merely 'instrumentalist' status of idealisations in this group of sciences from an anti-naturalistic conception of social science with the observation that all the idealisations of empirical science, likewise, stand in a logical derivational context with empirical statements (and could therefore also founder on practical knowledge).

However, Nowak misses an important point in his argumentation. According to Weber the ideal types, which are distinctive of the historical social sciences, relate to 'meaningful relationships'. Idealised meaningful relationships, on the other hand, can only in exceptional cases be adequately portrayed in the form of quantitative models. The most important of these exceptions is economic action operating strictly with quantitative units (i.e. 'rational' in a very specific sense) from which Nowak actually selects his examples. Even in this case one could reasonably hold the opinion that the construction of 'idealising laws' is problematic if metric variables are the only ones considered. In any case, it should apply to by far the largest sphere of historical-social reality that the selection of quantitative variables (or 'indices') is indeed justifiable for the purposes of operationalisation and measurement, but that the quantified models arising from this do not generally offer a *theoretically* satisfactory description of social facts. So far as Nowak's proposed procedure of 'concretisation' (i.e. the approach to reality) owes its logical stringency to the concentration on quantified laws, his objections to Weber's inconsistency on this question cannot be tenable.[97]

Finally, in the context of the questions last discussed, it is appropriate to mention Weber's observation that ideal-type constructs would need to change with the social situations of interest due to the 'relationship between concept and reality' (*MSS*, 105), distinctive of research in cultural science research in contrast to the models of natural science.[98] The 'transiency of *all* ideal types', as well as the 'inevitability of *new* ones' (*MSS*, 104) stems from the fact that these constructions are drawn from the perspective of the specific 'value relevance' attached to each historical practice.[99] The historicity of ideal-types – which by no means contradicts the objectivity of research that is led by them – for logical reasons requires distancing from the concrete reality of historical action. But, in so far as this distancing proceeds along the guiding thread of the idea of 'objective possibility', it (as described) simultaneously corresponds to the orientational requirements of historical action in a manner that would be completely out of the question when using 'nomological' models.

3.4 Explanation and interpretative understanding, materiality and meaning

The determination of the relationship between interpretative understanding (*Verstehen*) and causal explanation without doubt belongs to the fundamental problems of the Weberian philosophy of science and methodology. It is striking that the Marxist reception of Weber, which devotes such disproportionate attention to the methodological part of Weber's work, shows so little interest in the central methodological problem of 'interpretative sociology'.[100] It is no great exaggeration to say that this topic has been almost totally neglected in the Marxist literature on Weber. The very brief comments that can occasionally be found could not rank as anything but starting points to a critical discussion.

Considering that the present work set out to discuss the contribution made by Marxist authors to the debate on Weber, it is forced to be similarly restrained on this issue. The comments below chiefly seek to show that it is both necessary and useful to proceed from the existing state of neglect to a more intensive analysis of this problem.

The themes of 'ethical neutrality', or 'value relevance', and 'ideal type' obviously touch on issues that materialist philosophers have long rated as a central problem of their own scientific position (including 'classics' of this tradition of thought). This definitely does not apply to the problem of interpretative understanding. The strictly empirical orientation in general, and its materialist character in particular, seemed to make it impossible, as it were, *a priori* to attribute any factual importance to it within a Marxist context of argumentation. Marxist theorists must have assumed that interpretative understanding could at best be allocated a marginal role in the research process of the social sciences, since even Marx had already disowned the mere 'interpreting' of history and the thesis of the derivational nature of consciousness and its objectifications. This assumption must have gained further ground with the systematic elaboration of the 'materialistic' conception of knowledge in Engels and Lenin.

Various critical considerations have already been presented in the above discussion against the conception of 'materiality' that such argumentation is based on, as well as against the Leninist 'theory of knowledge'. At this stage, therefore, another thesis will be attended to, namely that fundamental epistemological assumptions have only to an insubstantial degree determined the actual development of Marxist theory. The emphasis on the paradigmatic importance of the empirical model of the natural sciences in Marx himself, Engels, Lenin and any other theorists of the materialist tradition, has not led to the emergence of a type of theory that matches the standard of empirical theory in the natural sciences.[101] Evidently, it is quite impossible to transfer the methods of empirical examination, which have been developed and tested in natural science research, to theories of social science origin. Where this is assumed, it seems to serve as evidence that Marxism has 'not always' possessed 'a sufficiently developed theoretical and methodological consciousness of the modes of procedure applied by itself' (Siemek, 1977, 67). But, on the other hand, the procedures of empirical examination (or the confrontation between theory and social reality) that were adequate and under the circumstances distinctive of Marxist theory have not hitherto been elucidated. There are evidently several reasons for this surprising state of affairs.

Firstly, the representatives of the 'orthodox' Marxist-Leninist tendency hold the opinion to this day that historical materialism, as a philosophical theory or world view (*Weltanschauung*), is neither accessible to nor in need of an empirical critique.[102] This immunising assertion, which is by no means compatible with the self-understanding of Marx and Engels, is totally unacceptable and will not be discussed further.

The second, more serious, argument suggests that for Marxist theory political practice is the adequate confrontation with social reality; in other words, that the 'truth' of this theory would be established by the success of self-defined revolutionary action. Thus one of the objections raised against Weber is his 'denial of social practice as an objective criterion of truth' (Fojtik, 1962, 8).

This argument seems to be open to a great number of interpretations.[103] The 'dialectical' interpretation (which in different ways determined, for example, *History and Class Consciousness*, critical theory and the Yugoslav philosophy of practice) consciously abolishes materialist theory as an empirical theory in favour of a dynamic mediation between theory and practice. The theory becomes the medium of 'self-reflection' for social actors. On the other hand, if the argument is understood in terms of political practice being, as it were, the 'test' of the rigorously applied theory (such as Engels' 'the proof of the pudding is the eating'), it indeed follows the logic of empirical method, but needs to deal with the difficult problem of whether such a programme can in fact be implemented. A third interpretation, again primarily advocated by Marxist-Leninist theorists, accepts the political success achieved 'under the banner of Marxism' – particularly the Russian Revolution – as proof for the truth of historical materialism, without further examining the interplay between theory and practice. This interpretation gives rise to the objection that the mere success of any particular political movement (such as fascism) says nothing whatsoever about the truth of the 'theory' that determines it.

Finally, a further reason for the almost universal dispensation with empiricism seems to be that, under the influence of Lenin's epistemological conceptions in particular, the empirical reference to, or empirical confirmation of, materialist theories was regarded as a comparatively trivial problem whose resolution did not in any case require elaborate methodical organisation. Backed by this notion it seems an obvious step to explain the efforts of non-Marxist theorists (including Weber's) towards a critical determination and appraisal of the relevance of social science theory to reality, or their reality content, in terms of the precarious relationship between the bourgeois class and social reality; that is to say, in terms of the 'loss of reality' typical of its class.

These references to the almost universal dispensation with empiricism in the Marxist tradition cannot be pursued any further in the present context. Very diverse opinions as to the actual importance of the above reasons (and perhaps others) are likely to be expressed. The observation that they – in whatever combination – have prevented the question of empirical examination from being acknowledged and discussed as a central problem of materialist theory – particularly in so far as it relates to contemporary conditions – is, however, indisputable.

But this is also the main cause of Marxist critics' failure to appreciate fully the importance of the problem of interpretative understanding in accordance with Weber's considerations. For Weber interpretative understanding denotes a specific way in which social reality *as such* is presented to us both in the everyday world and in scientific practice. This is so because historical-social reality is defined and constituted in terms of 'meaningfulness', in the above explicated broad sense of rationality including the material dimension. Weber's interpretative understanding of the social sciences, as opposed to the understanding of the cultural sciences, does not really stand in diametrical opposition to causal explanation; rather, it is the only method capable of grasping genuine social origins in connection with explanatory endeavours in the social sciences.

In this conception social science theories are accessible to meaningful understanding in so far as they relate to a specific historical-social reality. The construction of 'ideal types' is useful as a device for theoretical explanation in the historical social sciences because it 'counterfactually' presupposes an optimum of meaningful transparency and intelligibility.

The absolutely 'empirical' function of interpretative understanding in the Weberian sense, which establishes or ensures reference to social reality, is most distinctly expressed in empirical research itself. An understanding of socially established and operative meaningful relationships plays a central role when the aim is to determine and 'measure' the driving forces of social life *in actu*. This also explains why the interviewing of social actors on the whole continues to be unrivalled, in spite of the general appreciation of the problems and weaknesses attached to this method of data collection. The objection raised by Marxist social scientists in particular, that this survey method (like all 'interpretative understanding') is at best suited to comprehend the subjective aspect of social events, is already based on a misunderstanding. The 'understandable' is by no means restricted to individual social actors' conscious or designed contents of meaning, but equally encompasses the latent, occasionally highly alienated, 'meaningful relationships' to which individual action is subject in the social context. The logical limit of the capacity to understand social reality resides where this reality is no longer the product of the meaningfully determined and interrelated activity of people.[104] 'Material' realities (such as the forces and relations of production), under which historical action takes place, clearly fall within the scope of reality that can be made accessible by means of interpretative understanding in so far as they are seen as a product of such activity – and there is no doubt, as we noted, that Marx understood it this way. Finally, the category 'alienation' is actually only usable in the context of an interpretative social science, i.e. one that is oriented to meaningfulness of social action. It denotes no more than a form of everyday understanding in which the actual horizon of meaning that determines action, and thus far the 'subjective intention' too, is unconscious to the actors and concealed by other meaningful relations (e.g. of religious origin) and is therefore securely operative in the long term. From the perspective of social science research we cannot only know the condition of 'alienation', but also its genesis (and also ultimately the possibility of its removal) solely by way of interpretative understanding. The reality of alienation, in the Marxian sense, would logically be evaded if the scientific materialist method was in fact defined by its relation to or grounding in immediate perceptible reality 'in the final analysis'.

The problem of alienation in terms of its contents will be once more referred to in the context of the discussion below on Weber's basic outlook and the problem of bureaucracy. At this stage the emphasis is on the methodological aspect that this problem, much less than the 'materiality' of social reality, exceeds the epistemological possibilities of an interpretative social science.

As a matter of fact Marxist-Leninist theorists now regularly refer to material relations as such, rather than the secondary 'reification' of social institutions, in order to demonstrate the inadequacy of an interpretative approach. These theorists consider a special emphasis on the problem of alienation, indeed a development within the Marxist theoretical tradition as well and above all since the publication of the *Early Writings*, to be characteristic of 'idealistic' or 'psychological' deviation.[105] Vincent (1967a, 1848) formulates a generally typical objection to 'interpretative understanding'. 'Social reality is not in fact reproduced in its complexity and involvement, but the way in which it is identified in the ideas and ideological make-up of the consciousness.' This thesis implies that interpretative understanding deals merely with the superficial consciousness of social reality, i.e. the way in which this reality *appears* to social actors. The 'actual' reality of society, its material 'existence' as opposed to mere consciousness, is, accordingly, systematically suppressed. Thus interpretative understanding represents the consequence of Weber's theoretical idealism, whereas the ideal-type conceptual form represents the methodological consequences of Weber's gnoseology. According to this interpretation, restriction to the way in which society *appears* to each actor simultaneously precludes an actual *explanation* of social events. 'He [Max Weber], as the representative of *interpretative* sociology, still owes us the ultimate *explanation* for his thesis. Basically he does not really seek any *explanation*.' (Braunreuther, 1964, 86).[106]

The arguments presented thus far (including those in the preceding section on ideal types) should have shown that these and similar objections are based on a far too limited consideration of Weberian arguments and an inadequate clarification of their own premisses. The assertion that precisely the essence of social reality must not be conceived as historical human creation (in Weber's words, a reality 'on which *human beings* confer meaning and significance'; *MSS*, 81; emphasis by Weber) can hardly be reconciled with the fundamental assumptions of a theoretical tradition originating in Marx. Interpretative understanding, as conceived by Weber, denotes nothing more than that sole form of experience in which this reality is given to us. The depth or superficiality of knowledge in the concrete case is not a problem of this form or experience as such, but depends solely on the care, intensity and (theoretical) imagination with which it is practised. Interpretative understanding thus apprehended is no substitute, but a 'condition of the possibility', for causal explanation in the sphere of research in the cultural sciences. Nowak, who has already been mentioned, justifiably opposes the opinion that is prevalent not only among Marxist critics of Weber that interpretative understanding (*Verstehen*) was intended as a substitute for explanation in Weber's view by making intuitive empirical evidence available through the concept of direct, unassailable 'empathy': '*Verstehen* is a method of explaining and of explaining only' (1971b, 146; cf. also Kmita and Nowak, 1970).[107] Perhaps a better way of saying this would be that *Verstehen* is 'for the purpose of explanation'.

The recent efforts by a large number of Marxist authors to reevaluate the 'hermeneutic' tradition of science seems to demonstrate the growing realisation that the hitherto common Marxist treatment of the problem of understanding was inadequate. Certainly it is no accident that these efforts can be found, as it were, on the periphery of orthodox Marxist self-interpretation. It is also characteristic that the problem of understanding is only discussed within a limited perspective. Marxists of this genre still maintain, more or less resolutely, that the 'material' dimension that determines historical-social reality 'in the final analysis' is not accessible to the interpretative method. Interpretative understanding is thus tendentially accepted, in the narrower 'hermeneutic' sense, in the epistemology of the cultural sciences. According to these conceptions the object of 'hermeneutics' is primarily the actual, 'life world' and consciousness of social classes, especially the 'everyday consciousness' of the working class.[108] Enquiries of this kind originate explicitly in the need to transcend the merely theoretical, or even quasi-metaphysical, statements on class consciousness in order to attain analyses of social actors' real states of consciousness, which are high in empirical content and therefore of political value. As indicated above, it is the interest in the concrete *practical knowledge* of social factors that motivates the partial rehabilitation of interpretative understanding in the context of materialist theory.

However, these authors simultaneously insist throughout that only the 'subjective' side of social reality can be apprehended in this manner, even though they (Marxist-Leninist theorists included) concede a certain importance to the 'subjective method' for the 'knowledge and formulation of objective sociological laws' (Bollhagen, 1966, 91). The problem that remains undiscussed is how those 'objective' social factors could be approached by empirical method and established as facts. The evident presupposition is that the material and, therefore, 'essential' determinants of the social course of events can by no means be made the object of empirical research, but are governed solely by a 'theoretical', or even 'philosophical' determination. Empirical research that operates at the level of the interpretative method is thus not contrasted with a specific materialist empiricism. Such empiricism, if based on direct sensory perception (to use Lenin's term, 'sensations'), could in fact only relate to purely material (i.e. physical) factors which, as such, do not constitute social facts. Of course the view is sometimes expressed that the objectivity of material social relations (as relations of production) can be derived from the fact that those relations 'themselves . . . appear (in the final analysis) as the vehicle and *means* for a mediation within nature' (Colletti, 1972, 39).[109] But this 'naturalistic' (in the literal sense) interpretation of social materiality evidently contradicts all the relevant statements made by Marx and points in the direction of a highly dubious natural metaphysics rather than a specific materialist empiricism.

The prevailing conception has the tendency to limit empirical data in general to an 'appearance' of social reality and to this extent to accept the unalterable nature of interpretative understanding or 'subjective' procedures. However, even this conception is very questionable to the extent that it fails to show non-empirical, but nonetheless rational, methods of grounding or defence for theoretical statements regarding the material 'essence' in the social course of events. The underdeveloped problem consciousness characteristic of the Marxist-Leninist theoretical tradition particularly in relation to the questions under discussion here is most clearly apparent in Sandkühler's 'materialist hermeneutics'. This author makes much of his insight that even materialist research cannot do without a 'hermeneutic' analysis of 'material in the form of language and text' (1973, 403) or of a special 'part-science' respectively (namely, the 'materialist dialectic') that has 'the *text* as the objectification of reflection as its object' (*ibid.*, 400). Sandkühler firmly resists the possible misgivings of less courageous materialists: 'There are good grounds for classifying these sciences as "materialist hermeneutics"' (*ibid.*, 400).[110] It is, of course, very likely that Sandkühler worries unnecessarily on this point. The programme of hermeneutic 'part-science' he outlined is so limited and, besides, so firmly entrenched in the traditional materialist conception of knowledge that hardly anyone could possibly detect an innovation or divergence. Sandkühler sees the specific character of a materialist interpretation of text in perceiving those ideological 'materials in the form of language and text' as 'social-historically determined and historical-logically mediated objectivised reflections of reality' (*ibid.*, 402). A dual restriction is thus expressed and the contribution to the problem of understanding in the historical social sciences is thereby rendered less useful than the above approaches. Firstly, even more clearly than these approaches, Sandkühler restricts his considerations to the type of object that also took a central place in 'hermeneutics of bourgeois cultural sciences', namely to the objectifications of the mind (consciousness) in 'language and text'. All 'meaningful relationships' that do not exist in this specific form (and possibly in no ready symbolically objectivised form), then, are not considered. Accordingly, materialist 'hermeneutics' in particular keeps its distance from the practical formation of contemporay social consciousness.

The second, even more crucial restriction is that, according to Sandkühler, 'materialist hermeneutics' is bound to consider meaning constructs conveyed by 'language and text' as 'reflections' of an objective material reality. Evidently, in his view, this offers the sole possibility of pursuing hermeneutics in a critique of ideology. But this conception is hardly tenable if materialist hermeneutics is distinguished from the hermeneutics of the cultural sciences. According to Sandkühler 'the criterion of its interpretation' is 'practice in its social form' (*ibid.*, 406). The impossibility of conceiving the comprehensible elements of historical-social practice as a 'reflection' of practice would no doubt have become immediately apparent if Sandkühler had been less fixated on the tradition of the cultural sciences and had instead concerned himself with the problem of interpretative understanding in the empirical social sciences.[111] What remains of the 'practice in its social form' if the meaningful relationships that guide it (e.g. economic) are eliminated? To what can we relate these meaningful relationships as 'reflections'? Whatever may logically escape interpretative understanding in the Weberian sense, it is definitely not the *social* essence of human practice. Sartre remarked that 'understanding is nothing but the transparency of practice for its own use'.[112] It seems to me that this is the only conception that corresponds both with the Weberian and Marxist determination of the specific relationship between scientific knowledge and the historical-social object. Endeavours for a Marxist conception of 'interpretative understanding' would have to incorporate this conception.[113]

4 The fundamental theoretical perspective: social action or material relations?

The fundamentally important questions of sociological theory under discussion in this chapter deserve a thorough and independent analysis, even more so than those I have already considered. I can only justify the brevity and preliminary nature of the considerations here by reiterating that this is an explicit discussion of the critical treatment Weber's conceptions received from Marxist authors, and therefore I can merely make some suggestions to pave the way towards systematic treatment.

The impression gained from the critical discussion of the last topic is confirmed here with regard to the extent and intensity with which Marxist theorists deal with the fundamental theoretical issues of Weberian sociology. For whatever reason, Marxist interpreters and critics of Weber seem to approach Weber with greater reserve the more important and fruitful in substance the problem is for scientific work itself. Weber's fundamental theoretical concept of 'social action' is discussed more thoroughly only in works that have distanced themselves to some extent from the conventional and dogmatic interpretation of historical materialism. The following comments will show that concern with Weber's conception need not imply divergence from the fundamental assumptions of Marxist theory, but that indeed an examination of it could prove most useful for a critical self-understanding of the specifications of materialist theory.

An important general reason for the apparent reserve shown by Marxist theorists on questions of sociological theory is undoubtedly that the relationship between the theorems of historical materialism, on the one hand, and genuine sociological theorems, on the other, is unclear and disputed until this day.[1] The question is whether there could be a sociology with (relatively) autonomous *theoretical* legitimacy side by side with historical materialism as a universal theory of the historical-social course of events. Three typical answers to this question can be identified by incorporating Wiatr (1971, 6 ff.):[2]

1. Historical materialism is *the* 'universal sociological theory of Marxism' (Hahn). A number of authors therefore suggest that the label 'sociology' should be reserved for 'bourgeois endeavours'.
2. Historical materialism is characterised as the universal theoretical or 'philosophical' social analysis, whereas the term 'sociology' relates to empirical research and (empirical) generalisations founded upon it.
3. There is a partial overlap between historical materialism and sociology: historical materialism has the most universal laws of social development as its object and thus mediates between materialist philosophy and sociology, whereas the latter deals with 'theories of the medium range', 'theories of social structure', etc. In this conception historical materialism is at least indirectly confronted with the empirical findings of sociology.

There is evidently unanimous agreement amongst Marxists, including the representatives of the various 'revisionist' or 'reconstructionist' tendencies, despite their substantial differences on the most crucial point in this context. Throughout it is undisputed that historical materialism presents a logically self-contained and comprehensive theory of historical-social reality and that there cannot really be an autonomous sociological theory (i.e. one that is not committed to the principles or axioms of historical materialism) beside or within it. Sometimes the assertion goes so far as to say that social science theory as such is identical with historical materialism (cf. the references in Kiss, 1971, particularly 125 ff.; also in Weinberg, 1974, 15 ff.). In other words, it is asserted that a sociology with theoretical pretensions, but without a foundation in historical materialism, can at best be no more than atheoretical empiricism. The view is firmly held, even by those who do not advocate the exclusive theoretical authority of historical materialism, that an acceptable sociological theoretical construction is possible only if based on the fundamental theoretical assumptions of historical materialism. Marxist theorists therefore consider any 'mediation' with the theoretical conceptions of non-Marxist sociologists impossible, due to the fundamental theoretical orientation of sociology.[3] During the course of the very instructive, semi-official discussion on Levada's *Lectures on Sociology* (Levada, 1967)[4] it was established that his reference to the sociological reception of Marxism (such as that by

Durkheim and Weber) was totally unacceptable: such a mediatory endeavour 'objectively serves to unify Marxist and capitalist-oriented sociology' (Kozlovskij and Sychev, 1970–1, 492; comment by K. N. Momdjian).

The same discussion formulates the basic theoretical outlook which, according to a widespread conviction held by Marxist social scientists, does not permit them to see anything but the most determined opposition to materialist theory in the Weberian conception of 'action theory' especially. According to the view expressed there is an inexorable need in Marxist methodology 'to look at society as a social organism, not as a sum of individuals' (*ibid.*, 479; comment by G. E. Glezerman). Levada was criticised for not orienting himself to 'Marx's postulate that the essence of the human being is the totality of social relations' and therefore failing to appreciate the nature of 'social relationships as an objective system underlying the life of society' (*ibid.*). Almost all Marxist theorists put forward this argumentation, with minor modifications, as the fundamental objection to Weber's approach to 'social action'. The apodictic way in which the thesis of the 'totality' and 'objectivity' of society is aimed at a theoretical conception based on the action of social actors simultaneously explains why a more detailed discussion of the Weberian argumentation is seen to be unproductive at the very least, if not dangerous by creating 'confusion',[5] and is therefore not forthcoming.

The following discussion will deal, firstly, with several Marxist critics' presentation and evaluation of Weber's conceptions of social action, and secondly, with the question of whether the asserted logical contradiction between these conceptions and the basic outlook of Marxian theory in fact holds. The concluding comments will also contain brief references to the more recent interesting endeavours towards a clarification of and emphasis on the 'action-theory' dimension of Marxist social theory.

Even those Marxist contributions which are both factual and worthy of serious consideration[6] display ambiguity and a striking lack of clarity in their approach to action. On the one hand, Weber's 'idealistic' and 'individualistic' perspective is contrasted with the materiality and objectivity of social (socio-economic) relations. On the other hand, the same authors generally emphasise that these relations, being social, are a 'natural' product of human activity. A typical, though particularly weak, formulation of this either/or argumentation runs:

> Particular relations of production and class relations are *preconditions* for individual action. The way people act is thus

not determined by their own free will, but objective laws. At the same time, individuals through their action generate, reproduce and change these social relations. To this extent society is simultaneously a *product* of human interaction. (Kretzschmar, 1978, 36)

According to this view, people are governed in their action by 'objective' social conditions that are in turn generated, reproduced and changed through their action. At the outset this formulation does not seem to contradict Weber's conception. Weber, of course, never denied the existence of supra-individual and pre-existing social relations and conditions. His sole assertion was that such relations and conditions, in so far as they really refer to historical-social factors, cannot exist in space or time unless they are constantly 'reproduced' through action: 'Generally speaking sociological concepts such as "state", "guild" (*Genossenschaft*), "feudalism" and categories like these denote categories for particular types of social interaction' (*WL*, 439). 'In the sociological perspective the term "state" denotes *merely* a special course of human action' (*WL*, 440).

The same observation can also be traced in Marx, and certainly consistently whenever he actually comments on this problem. Particularly clear and important statements of the kind cited by Marxist critics of Weber are, for example: 'The relations of individuals under all circumstances *can* only be their mutual behaviour' (*MEW*, Vol. 5, 437). 'What is society, whatever its form may be? The product of men's reciprocal action' (Marx and Engels, 1956, 40). 'Economic categories (private property, commodities, etc.) too, as conceptual abstractions, express nothing but 'social behaviour amongst men'.[7] With these observations Marx not only agrees with Weber that social relations or 'institutions' (including society as a whole) are in reality 'nothing but men's mutual behaviour', but also that 'real'[8] action can be attributed only to men: it is 'the personal, individual behaviour of individuals, their behaviour to one another as individuals, that created the existing relations and daily reproduces them anew' (*MEW*, Vol. 5, 437). The material 'approach' of the analysis in the political economy is through the 'productive individuals in society' or the 'socially determined production of individuals' (*MEW*, German edn, Vol. 13, 615).[9]

How do Marxist critics of Weber defend the thesis of a fundamental difference between the two theoretical 'perspectives', or the 'untenability' of the Weberian conception, given this very evident convergence of Marxian and Weberian statements on the problem? The constantly repeated dual objection raised against the Weberian conception is that it is both 'idealistic' and 'individualistic'.[10]

To follow up the cited statements of Marx, let us at the outset turn to the objection of individualism, which is by no means an objection to Weber voiced by Marxists only.[11] To start with it is necessary to clear up a popular misunderstanding. In Weber's view the individuals to whom 'action' alone can be attributed should by no means be imagined as subjects who consciously (or even unconsciously) pursue their own egoistic ends.[12] No doubt individual action, if engaged in by a majority of individuals, is likely to produce regular outcomes that were not consciously intended nor willed by any of the participants, yet could nonetheless most crucially determine the further course of their action.

> Thus the conflicts of innumerable individual wills and individual actions in the domain of history produce a state of affairs entirely analogous to that prevailing in the realm of unconscious nature. The ends of the actions are intended, but the results which actually follow from these actions are not intended. . . . (Engels, 'Ludwig Feuerbach and the End of Classical German Philosophy', in Marx and Engels, *Basic Writings in Politics and Philosophy* 1969, 271; cited by Kretzschmar, 1978, 35)

This fact, so important for an understanding of 'bourgeois society' in particular, was – as is well-known – stressed by Adam Smith and belongs to the fundamental insights of *every* theory of social action. However, even the 'unintended consequences' of action can be explained only by returning to precisely this action. In so far as they can no longer be explained solely as a chain of 'egoistic' actions of participants under specific 'material' (i.e. physical and temporal) conditions in the narrow sense, the enquiry will have to turn to other dimensions of the participants' action orientation. Apart from the conscious desires and intended goals of individual actors, we would have to draw into the analysis all the intersubjectively (or socially) accepted meaningful relationships of both a cognitive and evaluative nature to which individuals orient themselves in action without being in the least or even adequately conscious of them. Even an action which by no means originates in immediate egoistic needs or action that pursues consciously defined goals can, in Weber's view, be attributed only to individuals, because only individuals can really accomplish the relevance of meaning that constitutes social action. This is by no means contradicted by the observation that those intersubjectively valid, meaningful relationships themselves can be constructed and maintained only by way of an orientation to 'others' conduct'.

Moreover, it is impossible to advance against the Weberian conception that individuals are confronted with social relations or 'institutions' in the 'constitution' of which they have no share, that is to say, not within the latter meaning either. The Weberian thesis does not propound that all social conditions of human action are created by the individuals who are affected by it. Particular institutions may indeed confront particular individuals or groups as an 'alien power' to which they have *no kind* of meaningful relationship. But, at the same time, these social relationships exist only in the meaningful interaction of particular (other) individuals.

Marx notes, in connection with the statement already cited above on the emergence of social relations from the behaviour to 'one another as individuals', that:

> Hence it certainly follows that the development of an individual is determined by the development of all the others with whom he is directly or indirectly associated, and that the different generations of individuals entering into relation with one another are connected with one another, that the physical existence of the generations is determined by that of the predecessors, and that these latter generations inherit the productive forces and forms of intercourse accumulated by their predecessors, their own mutual relations being determined thereby. (*MEW*, Vol. 5, 438)

Marx, then, establishes that neither the totality of conditions of action (which are throughout social) nor each concrete individuality are governed by the designs and arrangement of acting individuals. He nonetheless maintains that all real action is individual action and that social relations can 'under all circumstances only be the behaviour' of individuals.

In terms of the subject matter it is hard to explain why Marxist theorists do not consider this emphatically individualistic fundamental feature of Marxian conceptions while attacking Weber's pertinent theses. It would indeed be worthwhile considering whether the Weberian grounding for the 'individualism' of action could not in principle be applied to the Marxian argumentation. It has been suggested that Weber bases his thesis on the constitutive meaningfulness of social action. But it has been established on numerous occasions that Marx had a very similar conception of the distinguishing characteristics of historical-social practice, both in terms of work and interaction. If we do not wish to assume that Marx related the concept of the individual to the individual organism inclusive of each individual 'make-up', it would seem to follow that we link the 'individualistic' perspective with his concept of historical-social action. Moreover, much could be said for the further thesis that this interpretation alone is compatible with the specific Marxian ideas of political practice.

The latter remarks already touch on the second part of the objection against Weber's conception of action, namely its alleged 'idealism'. It has been shown that the individualistic perspective of this conception of action is directly interconnected with its orientation to meaningfulness, and that applies even if certain misinterpretations on the issue of 'subjectively intended meaning' are rejected. The 'materiality' of socio-economic relations is advanced to counter this fundamental aspect of the Weberian concept of action and, of course, with greater force against a similar interpretation of Marx. It is suggested that the 'reduction' to intelligible action would not – as Weber thought – 'cause the illusion of facticity to be lost, but rather the materiality of real concrete activity, while social relations are rendered subjective' (Koch, 1965, 795). The rhetoric about a fundamental 'materiality' of the conditions of action is marked by an ambiguity that is not always noted by Marxist authors, but of course it is occasionally reinterpreted, in a very underhand fashion, as though it was clear.[13] The two most important problems of reference attached to the category 'materiality' are stated by Hahn. Firstly, social relations are 'material' in the sense 'that they materialise in things and relations, the movement of things, and are embodied in material objects'. Secondly, we refer to the materiality or objectivity of social relations to describe the fact 'that individuals lose power and control over their own relations arising from their individual empirical behaviour and in turn the relations determined by it' (Hahn, 1968, 79).

These two types of materiality should be strictly distinguished in logic and theory, although they appear in the most closely interrelated fashion in social reality (e.g. so that the objectivity of social relations is secured in the second sense by being enmeshed in actual or supposed 'material laws').

Materiality in the first (narrow) sense is of minor interest to us at this point and a brief comment will therefore suffice. A multitude of factors are 'built into' the concrete social context of determination that are not social in character in the sense of the Weberian definition which focusses on intersubjectively constituted and communicated meaning. The impact of these factors accordingly originates in laws that are *not* of a socially contingent nature. We are talking here of factors that belong either to the external or internal *primary* nature or that grounded in natural science, and to that extent also the technology underlying the laws of primary nature (including limits on time). A very important problem of research should aim to clarify to what degree social compulsion is conditioned by the use of natural laws. The fact that human liberation from the direct coercion of nature through technology has to be paid for by particular compulsion at the societal level is neither a paradoxical nor new observation. Indeed Marx held a corresponding thesis for capitalist society in relation to the all-pervasive power of 'modern industry'. He observed that modern industry in its 'machinery system' possesses a 'productive organism that is purely objective, in which the labourer becomes a mere appendage to an already existing material condition of production'[14] (*Capital*, Vol. 1, 364). 'Hence the cooperative character of the labour-process is, in the latter case, a technical necessity dictated by the instrument of labour itself'[15] (*ibid.*, 365).

It all depends on the strict distinction of the thus understood 'materiality' and *its* 'objective lawfulness' from the materiality of social relations in the second sense, denoting objectification, the process of being rendered independent and alienation. Even high degrees of alienation or 'reification' do not alter the fact that the constructs of the 'second nature' are in fact the products of human interaction that could not persist for one moment nor exercise their 'lawful' influence if they were not constantly reproduced in this interaction. If the categories 'essence' and 'appearance' are to be employed in this context at all, we would have to attribute the autonomy or natural quality of social relations to the level of appearance, whereas its 'essence' (or its 'in itself') would have to be seen in terms of its relativity of action, or in the actions constituting these relations, including their 'naturalness'. This by no means asserts that those 'processes of rendering social relations independent from the activity of people' are merely illusory and not 'real'. Koch, who ascribes this conception to action theorists (Koch, 1965, 795), goes on to say a little later with reference to a statement by Marx:

> In capitalism . . . the social character of activity and the social form of the product *appears* because it is governed and appropriated not by the social producers but by capital, "as something alien, material to the individual; not as their behaviour to one other, but as their subjugation to relations that exist independently from them and arise on the impetus of individuals' indifference to one other". (*ibid.*, 796; author's emphasis)

At this point there is no need to analyse the process of being rendered independent and alienation in the social context of action. In any case, such analysis, if it did not dispense with all hypostases of any products of human action (e.g. of capital or relations to capital), would have its purpose transformed into the diametrical opposite. A consistent exposure of the relativity of action of *all* social relations does not permit us to recognise the fictitiousness, but the actual genesis and impact, of 'being rendered independent' and 'alienation'. It is difficult to see how a Marxist analysis can carry out its critical enterprise particularly in the face of the 'reification' characteristic of the capitalist social formation, unless it systematically makes these apparent as specific products of a specific 'interaction'. The insistence on the materiality of *social* relations by simply isolating them from human action is both as anti-critical and anti-enlightening as the thesis of 'individualism' levelled at the Weberian conception of action that the materialist approach has to trace 'individual behaviour' back to 'the behaviour of masses, groups and, particularly, classes, "the individual to the social"'.[16] The tendency of many Marxist authors to attribute a higher form of existence and higher legitimacy to any collectivities than to individuals may have good grounds, but it is at best a political ideology, or even political agitation, by no means scientific in character.

A Marxist analysis can thus impossibly claim its superiority over an 'action theory' by its capacity to *establish* the materiality and 'objective lawfulness' of social relations. Rather, it should enquire into the mechanisms which cause alienation in human action. If it is indeed characteristic of bourgeois society that 'the social relations between men are portrayed, as it were, inversely, namely as social relations between things' (*MEW*, German edn, Vol. 13, 21), Marxist analysis has to show this portrayal to be inverse by exposing its genesis to be *inverse*. We could object against Weber on the grounds that he has not given sufficient detailed attention in his work to the genesis of reified social relations. But, on the other hand of course, Weber's emphatic references to the progressive rationalisation and 'depersonalisation' of social relations in modern societies are directly related to his action theory perspective.[17] The allegation of 'fatalism' in the face of these developments, which is constantly directed at Weber by Marxist critics,[18] is very surprising in so far as only an 'action theory' perspective, if any, is able to identify the starting points of a practical (i.e. *active*) change of ossified relations. An even 'more radical' conception of action to contrast Weber's social action perspective should be the outcome, especially if the decidedly critical and political ambitions of Marxist theorists have any substance. Considering these ambitions it is the height of absurdity to contrast Weberian 'individualism' with a conception of social 'totality' that is not explained in terms of action theory and, in turn, his 'idealism' with the conception of 'objectivity' and 'lawfulness' of the social that is deprived of any foundation in action theory.

In comparison it is entirely consistent if the dogmatisation of a Marxist 'canon' for political and ideological purposes is combined with an emphasis on the objectivity of social relations and processes and a sharp rejection of the action theory perspective. However, this use of historical materialism, the subject of the first chapter of this book, is diametrically opposed to the political function of materialist theory propounded by Marx and Engels. It should therefore definitely not be interpreted as 'divergence' if Marxist theorists have more recently given increasing affirmative attention to conceptions of action theory or even 'interactionism'.[19] On the other hand, this concern seems to be predominantly understood in the sense of an 'integration' of materialist social theory with 'micro-theoretical' conceptions for the purpose of explaining 'small-scale' and/or the directly person-related processes of socialisation, identity formation and so on.

This self-interpretation is not unfounded or even 'wrong', since the existing conceptual-theoretical tools are in fact very much in need of 'integration', not least on the grounds of improving the political possibilities of argumentation. The more fundamental problem that was probably concealed by the reception of so-called 'symbolic interactionism' in particular should, however, lie in the necessity to grasp and develop the action perspective constitutive of the Marxist theoretical tradition in the true sense of the word with new and differentiated conceptual means. In this respect intensified Marxist discussion, particularly of Weber's conception of social action,[20] is probably more important and has greater bearing. This can be explained by the fact that it is the conception of a theorist whose primary substantive interest in the structure and development of extensive socio-economic, cultural and political contexts resembles that of the Marxist 'classics' (and, of course, is essentially inspired by their work). In this respect it is particularly worthwhile to consider that Weber's reflections and theses on the sociological action perspective emerged in the pursuit of his research interest in contents, and to this extent cannot be interpreted as a non-empirical programmatic. (This interpretation would seem to apply to Marx for chronological reasons – in the sense of a contrast between the early and late works – but, as noted, even in that case it is not convincing in terms of substance.)

In the course of the further critical discussion of Weber's conception of social action it will not least be a matter of creating greater clarity on the status of this conception. A number of misunderstandings can essentially be explained in terms of the initial problematic characterisation of the Weberian conception of 'action theory' as it has occasionally occurred in the earlier cited comments. Some clarification of this term is needed even if we cannot dispense with it, although it is a well-known fact that it was not used by Weber himself. It is above all necessary to establish that there is in fact no 'theory of social action' in Weber, if we assume by this that the term 'theory' involves a (hierarchically) organised system of statements of an explanatory nature and that the highest principles (axioms) of this particular theory consist of statements on 'social action as such'.

Firstly, the explanatory statements of a more or less general character contained in Weber's works do not add up to a cohesive general theory. As noted, Weber considered endeavours towards this kind of systematisation of explanatory sociological knowledge at an essentially high level of abstraction by no means impossible, but comparatively unproductive.

Secondly, however, a systematisation of this kind could by no means be based on assumptions of 'social action as such', since such assumptions would have no explanatory power in Weber's view (cf. *MSS*, 68).

Weber's considerations and definitions in his essay on categories and the introduction to *Economy and Society* do not focus on generalised hypotheses of a universal sociological theory. Nor is their purpose *simply* to make a system of comparatively clear elementary concepts available for historical-sociological research. On the contrary, the categories and basic concepts, above all the concept of social action, determine the dimension in which, in Weber's opinion, specifically sociological explanatory endeavours should operate. A sociological perspective defined by social action corresponds with an interest in researching precisely the determinants and 'rules' of human behaviour that themselves originate in the meaningful interrelated action of people and are therefore also capable of exercising an influence or bringing about change through such action.

If we attribute a 'theory of action' to Weber, this does not imply a specific empirical theory, but rather this 'basic outlook' on historical-social reality that serves as the basis and most general perspective of all empirical considerations in sociology. But does this 'approach' not imply – though always qualified – that we are in principle looking for the social determinants of human behaviour at the level of social action? Should the theoretical assumptions possible within this scope not be *integrated* with argumentations in structural, systems or social theory?

Here it is essential to repeat that a conception of social action, such as the Weberian, by no means requires us to dispute the existence of overlapping 'structures' or 'systems' of action. On the contrary, Weber's understanding of social action is *per defi-*

nitionem applied to the formation of such overlapping 'institutions' transcending the here and now of concrete action. Processes of generalisation, structuring and stabilisation of social relations should be directly related to the 'meaningfulness' of social action and explained only in terms of their meaningfulness as *social processes*.[21]

It is therefore no accident that the more recent sociological systems theory of T. Parsons and N. Luhmann is very essentially inspired by Weber's fundamental conception of 'action theory'.[22] At any rate, this reception by systems theory and the 'incorporation' of the action approach simultaneously clearly exposes the risk embedded in a change of perspective from action to structures, or systems. On the one hand, it is possible because of the 'systematic' nature of meaningful social action. Further, for theoretical (abstraction) reasons it seems often unavoidable that one incorporates a systems perspective in the analysis of social facts whilst making extensive use of structural and collective concepts. But, on the other hand, there is always the danger of hypostasis in the sense that structures and systems of action are simply organised in order of priority or superiority; in other words, action is thematised merely as a 'function' of autonomous hierarchies or processes. The relativity of action of *all* social institutions, frequently (though not as a rule) concealed from social actors, is thus logically and systematically masked by the social science construction of concepts and theory (that is to say, not simply for specific analytical purposes). According to Weber's conception, this approach to structural and collective categories contradicts the explanatory task of sociology. Sociology must therefore adhere to the action perspective, in spite of all theoretical-analytical requirements, at least in the form of a firm *'reservatio mentalis'*. Strictly speaking, Marxist theorists ought to be in absolute agreement with this conception. Instead a number of their critiques tend to make extensive and comparatively uncritical use of the conceptions of systems theory. The absurdity seems complete when this tendency is further combined with the claim to a critique of ideology that is emphatically and explicitly directed against Weber's conception.[23]

5 Special problems of the theoretical and empirical work

The aim of this chapter is to present and discuss Marxist contributions on the special theoretical and/or empirical problems of Weberian sociology. To be sure the claims connected with the arguments of this section are considerably smaller than those of the previous chapters. All the problem areas to be dealt with have so many individual aspects of their own right that a more thorough discussion is completely out of the question within the confines of the present work. Moreover Marxist literature is, for obvious reasons, so extensive on the first problem area, which is essentially defined by Weber's essays on the *Protestant Ethic*, that only a separate analysis could pursue the argumentations in detail. In contrast the number and – as a rule – the 'density' of Marxist arguments on the remaining themes decreases sharply, so that it is nevertheless possible to provide the most important information even in this brief description. The intention is to develop some critical considerations on the appropriateness and fruitfulness of the arguments advanced against Weber with regard to all the problem areas covered that serve as useful and essential starting points for further discussions.

5.1 Religion and the material base

It is quite understandable that Weber's paper on the *Protestant Ethic* constitutes by far the most popular object of Marxist critique. What is more difficult to grasp is that acquaintance solely with this, to the exclusion of Weber's other works, has led to conclusions and objections that could easily be shown to be untenable had such other works been read. Also, it is clearly unacceptable when Weber's own arguments in the *Protestant Ethic* are presented in a most slanted and absurd form and are then critically disposed of.[1] A Marxist critique that proceeds in this manner too obviously becomes a victim of its own simplification to be subjected to a thorough discussion. These critics work with the aid of a simple base-superstructure schematic in particular in order to show that Weber had advocated nothing but the obverse of the materialist position. 'Whereas *Marx* explained changing religious ideas in terms of revolutions in material and social conditions, *Max Weber* sought to trace back the development of capitalism to the ascetic character of Protestantism and its rational this-worldly orientation.' . . . 'In contrast to *Marx*, *Max Weber* attempted to invert the close connection between society and religion . . . from an idealist position' (Klügl, 1970, 591). Another author puts it this way: the core of the sociology of religion (and therefore Weberian sociology in general) consists of an 'evidently anti-Marxist' attempt to reach an 'idealistic solution of the relationship between religion and society' (Kuznecov, 1975, 4).[2]

It is difficult to enter into a rational discussion with this kind of crude argumentation. In any case, one would have to clarify at the outset whether the presupposed separation between the material and mental (ideal) spheres can actually be sustained. Marx saw religion as serving the functions of 'moral sanction', 'solemn complement' and 'universal basis of consolation and justification' of an 'inverted world'.[3] Does this not imply that the 'inverted world' could not in fact exist without these accomplishments of religion, and consequently that the 'inverse consciousness of the world' of religion constitutes an *essential* existential prerequisite for a particular material (social) state of being? Indeed, if religion is to accomplish this, does it not need to possess an 'excess' potential for justification that cannot in turn be 'derived' from the given material conditions as such?

In this context Marxist theorists frequently refer to Engels' observation that religious ideas 'react' to material conditions and therefore that Marx had as a matter of fact always admitted the relative autonomy of ideological consciousness. What is crucial in their view is that the 'economic movement' alone could be the determinative and 'necessary' factor in this reciprocal relation 'finally' (Horn, 1958, 112 f.).[4] One may perhaps feel inclined to interpret this assertion as metaphysical and therefore inconsequential for sociological research and let the matter rest there. Depending on what use it made of it, the thesis has in fact considerable bearing on social research under given circumstances. Systematically excluded is above all the possibility that religious or religious-ethical meaningful relationships influence people's economic action, without in any convincing sense being causally derived from the conditions and orientations of any kind

85

of material practice. Weber took it for granted that religious-ethical systems of interpretation are causally or functionally closely interlinked with specific economic relations and class situations and this assumption informs large sections of his analyses in the sociology of religion. However, in his essay on the *Protestant Ethic* he intended to show that the above characterised possibility also gains a high degree of empirical credibility when enquiring into the manifold preconditions of modern occidental capitalism.

The pros and cons of the Weberian argumentation will not be discussed here. These issues can only be discussed and – possibly – settled on the basis of detailed historical analyses. Both the fruitfulness of the Weberian line of enquiry and the difficulty of arriving at definitive and universally valid answers is proven by the volume of the literature on the *Protestant Ethic*[5] alone. In Weber's opinion the purpose of such analyses can by no means be seen in attributing primacy to either the material or ideal aspect, i.e. in attributing the determinative role in the 'final analysis' whatever the case may be. This aim is highly questionable for at least two reasons.

Firstly, an either/or question of this type cannot be settled once and for all at an *a priori* or empirical level. The chain of reasoning presented by some Marxist theorists as to why the material being *must* be seen as the determinative factor 'in the final analysis' is not very convincing. It relates to the – quite indisputable – fact that physical survial and therefore the necessity to 'eat, drink, dress and have somewhere to live' is the first and foremost precondition of all human activity (thus Horn, 1958, 113 and 129 respectively). This very trivial observation is, however, absolutely reconcilable with the assumption that each form of the social reproduction of life is to a high degree moulded by, for example, religious ideas which, in their turn, cannot in any sense be causally explained in terms of the necessity to be able to survive purely as such. In its universality the argument refers at best to an indisputably *necessary*, but insufficient 'in the final analysis' (and by no means always particularly explanatory), condition for the genesis and contents of those interpretations and value systems that are not directly related to material practice. Besides, of course, a broad empirical-historical outlook indicates that people or human groups consciously put their chances for physical survival (to say nothing of the 'good life') at stake for their religious-ethical ideas, but also, for example, their political-ethical (e.g. socialist) ideas.

Secondly, it is highly questionable whether we can work at all meaningfully within the framework of the historical social sciences with the rigorous distinction of material versus ideal factors, as is indeed presumed by the either/or argumentation of the type described above. Here it is useful to refer back to the comments made in the preceding chapters of this book: in so far as the material conditions and relations refer to products of historical-social activity they always and with necessity appear in the context of specific 'ideal' or meaningful orientations. Even the historical-social conflict between the human being and nature is inexorably dependent on such 'ideal' mediations. A variant of the well-known Marxian statement would be that this material reality also exists only as one 'inverted in the human mind', therefore it is *also* ideal. In principle we should be led astray, or into fruitless scholasticism, if we enquire into the possible interrelationship between the previously isolated material and ideal aspects of social practice. If the material (i.e. economic) base of human practice is indeed of an entirely different order to the 'ideological superstructure', it would be hard to explain why this base should universally (and indeed even in socialist societies) be in need of this superstructure and how a 'mediation', indeed the closest involvement, between the two essentially different spheres could be possible. In fact, the 'ideological' interpretations (that is to say, in the narrower sense of religious interpretations) should regularly connect with the 'ideal' bases of a specific mode of production, and vice versa, either by enhancing or destroying it, and not with anything 'purely material' (i.e. physical or concrete).

Considerations of the latter type explain why Weber's first essay on the sociology of religion focusses on the interrelationship between a specific religious 'ethic' and the '*spirit* of capitalism' and why even in the remainder of his writings on the sociology of religion in so far as they concern the problem area addressed here, he always initially thematised the interrelationship between religious-ethical ideas and 'economic *views*', or 'economic *ethics*'.[6] The assertion occasionally still made amongst Marxist critics (e.g. Kuznecov, 1975, 14 ff.), that Weber had attempted to explain modern capitalism as a whole and particularly its material aspect in the narrower sense (in other words, for example, mineral reserves, machines, means and modes of communication etc.) as direct consequences of specific religious-ethical ideas, is therefore based (and this applies to their own position too) on ill-considered reflection.

In contrast, an adequate interpretation is provided above all by Neusychin who also supplies by far the most detailed description of the Weberian argumentation (1974, 422–44).[7] Neusychin observes that Weber had been seeking to clarify the aspect of the sociology of religion in the grounding and justification of those 'norms', or that 'economic ideology', which had guided capitalist management in its development (1974, 445, 446).[8] Certainly Neusychin still distinguishes between this 'ideal' side of the capitalist mode of production and the material preconditions in the narrower sense (original accumulation, availability of free labour, etc.) on which Marx concentrated in his analysis of the historical process, though by no means strictly limiting his attention to this.[9] However, he does not consider it necessary to derive in turn the capitalist economic ideology from *these* material conditions.[10]

Similarly another objection to Weber's sociology of religion in general or *The Protestant Ethic* in particular, which is obviously held to be particularly crucial by other Marxist critics, cannot be found in Neusychin. This objection is that Weber dispenses with an explanation of the *essence* of religion and indeed is forced to in the face of the limited scientific possibility of his argumentation: 'The question concerning the nature and essence of religion . . . is lost' (Kuznecov, 1975, 20; similarly, e.g., Bel'cer, 1973, 145 and Horn, 1958, 131).[11] This is an entirely appropriate observation, but the question is whether, or under what circumstances, this observation can be used critically against Weber.

The 'question concerning the nature and essence of religion' aims at discovering what religion (*all* religion) really is. For Marxist theorists the question concerning the essence of religion is identical with the question concerning its 'truth', so far as religions first and foremost represent systems of ideas or statements about the world (as a whole) and about the final determination of man. In the view of these theorists, but also according to the conceptions of both the radical non-Marxist critique of religion (such as that by Feuerbach and Nietzsche) and specific non-Marxist sociological conceptions (e.g. those of Durkheim, Freud and major parts of systems theory), the general and definitive answer to this question resides in the statement of social and/or psychological origins or functions of those types of statement systems. In contrast Weber did not believe that even the most thorough analyses in empirical science on the social determination and ideological function of religious interpretations of the world could ever lead to a situation in which their importance would be *exhausted* in any particular social or psychological function. Such an assertion can even less be made *a priori*, i.e. without a most thorough examination of the contents of such systems of interpretation and the grounds of validity claimed by them. Weber's reservations about a systematic social science, or psychological 'reduction', or 'deduction' of religious contents of meaning (cf., for example, *PE*, 277 f.), arose from his conception that an empirical form *sui generis* is documented in religions whose own legitimacy cannot in principle be disputed within the potentialities given to empirical science research.[12] Accordingly Weber thought that the analyses in the sociology of religion could only marginally touch on what is 'valuable' to the theologian (cf. *PE I*, 28; *PE II*, 345).

The Weberian conception cannot of course be interpreted as an attempt to provide in a way *ex nativo* 'scientific existential proof for the primacy of religion' with which Bosse reproaches Weber within the framework of a moderate Marxist argumentation (Bosse, 1970, 99). On the other hand, the same author at another point criticises Weber's *dispensation* with an answer to the question concerning truth (*op. cit.*, 138). The self-defined limits of empirical science research that Weber advocated apply on both sides,[13] and Marxist theorists should set out subjecting their continued claims to a more detailed examination and grounding. Firstly, the widespread deduction of the specific social functions of religion to its 'essence' is convincing neither in its structuralist-functionalist nor, which applies to Marx himself, materialist form.[14] Secondly, causal explanations could only be interpreted as explanations of essence if they were able to state the adequate empirical conditions of not only the emergence, but also the meaningful contents, of each religious system of interpretation, including the relevant grounds of validity claimed. One cannot assert that this task is generally recognised in its full complexity, let alone that it has already been largely accomplished.

Weber's enquiries in the sociology of religion show how much (causal) significance he attached in many contexts to economic, political and socio-cultural conditions and 'interests' in the emergence and development of religious ideas, and indeed this penetrated even the explanation of *specific* meaningful contents and their grounding. This, of course, applies to his explanation of the decline in religious interpretations of the world in the course of the growing 'disenchantment' (*Entzauberung*) and 'rationalisation' of the relationships between man and nature and the historical-social world. However, analyses that are oriented in this way, and not only the special theses of *The Protestant Ethic*, are to be counted as the much cited 'Positive Critique of the Materialist Conception of History'.[15] At least this is the case if one links the materialist conception of history to the dual assumption that religious ideas should, 'in the final analysis', always and in every way be explained in terms of economic interests or relations[16] and that this form of explanation at the same time provides a definition of the essence of religion in so far as it specifies its necessary and appropriate conditions.[17]

If this dual assumption is a hallmark only of the 'vulgar materialist' form of Marxism (with which, according to popular opinion, Weber was primarily concerned), then Weber's 'positive' critique, i.e. that based on empirical analysis, cannot be used as evidence of his fundamental anti-Marxism. In this respect it is most remarkable that the two Marxist theorists, Bukharin and Kautsky, who are usually characterised as particularly undialectical and 'mechanistic', seem obviously more able to comply with Weber's differentiated argument than many of their more recent Marxist critics. As Neusychin also observed, this may be due to the fact that Weber's analyses and theses gain greater persuasive power to the extent they are judged from the perspective of empirical science or history, rather than that of a world view.

5.2 Class and status

Weber explicitly emphasised that the explanatory direction he pursued in *The Protestant Ethic* was one-sided (cf., for example, *PE*, 26, 284; *PE II*, 47). However, this is by no means characteristic of his sociology of religion and certainly not of his work as a whole. The cited critique of the particular manifest forms of material 'deduction' or 'reduction' did not stop him from enquiring into the causal importance of economic, or socio-economic, conditions to an extent quite exceptional for a non-Marxist theorist.[18] Class-theoretical assumptions in particular play an enormous role in Weber's entire historical and sociological work – from the essays on agricultural relations in antiquity to the enquiry into the situation of the agricultural workers east of the Elbe, from the analyses of the *Wirtschaftsethik der Weltreligion* to *Economy and Society* – that any special reference is quite unnecessary.[19] It is striking that this very important aspect of the Weberian mode of explanation is hardly noted in the Marxist reception of his work, nor is it discussed in any great detail. We do not go so far as to suggest that the Marxist tradition exercised a 'dominant influence' on Weber in this respect (as did Adler, 1964, III, 35, with reference to Weber's concept of class), but we might well assume its influence to be more complex and indirect (cf. particularly Roth, 1971).[20] At any rate the actual affinity of broad passages in Weber's historical social science analyses with a 'materialist' perspective would seem to urge an argument and critique of these. Here too we can only suspect that the overwhelming, probably politically motivated, desire by many Marxist theorists for clearly defined boundaries may well have reduced their willingness to attend to and discuss this aspect of Weber's work.[21] A more detailed critical treatment of this aspect would certainly have led to *one* result: the popular schematisations, especially the inevitable dichotomy of materialism/idealism applied to determine the class of 'bourgeois ideologues', would have proven to be absolutely useless. Similarly, the specific theses of the type that Weber, in the sociology of religion, had, in the final analysis, replaced an explanation in terms of 'concrete class situations' with an appeal to the 'metaphysical needs of the mind' (Weber) (Bel'cer, 1974, 88),[22] should very rapidly have proven untenable.

Where Marxist authors concern themselves with Weber's conception of class they primarily refer to the conceptual definitions in *Economy and Society* rather than Weber's application of this conceptual set of tools in his empirical, historical essays.[23] There is therefore no discussion of the usefulness of the distinctions proposed by Weber. Rather, the critique by these authors is directed at the very fundamental inadequacies in the theory or philosophy of science (including logic) supposedly apparent in Weber's conceptual definitions.

The first of these objections, presented by Herkommer, has already been mentioned in another context. It is: 'Weberian social science research on the stratification of the population into classes, status groups, strata and other groups does not seem to rise beyond definition while it reduces historical material to a mere example.' The concepts attained in this way would 'no longer be understood as historical ones', but they would take priority, 'in poor abstractness' over 'historically changing social relations' (Herkommer, 1975, 128). To the extent that the fundamental problem of the relationship between conceptual-theoretical, abstraction and historical analysis is addressed here, I refer the reader to the above discussion. This critique by no means affects the status and function of the theoretical concepts of class and structure in Weber's work. Obviously Herkommer interprets the necessarily 'abstract' conceptual clarifications in *Economy and Society*, which nonetheless incorporate a large number of historical aspects, not as the means, but the ends of social science. This is a notion that is utterly incompatible with Weber's own conception and research practice. But if his objection is directed at Weber's endeavours for definition as such, it is to be observed that, firstly, the materialist theoretical tradition by all means possesses and requires a conceptual apparatus of similar, if not higher, abstraction. Secondly, some conceptual clarification and precision is most desirable precisely within the range of materialist class theory. Thirdly, the terminology used in class theory in particular has led quite a number of Marxist authors to attach over much schematic importance to 'historical material' and to use it for the purpose of mere exemplification. This tendency seems to have contributed greatly to the underdeveloped state of concepts in class theory.

This state of affairs, then, should provide some impetus to subject Weber's proposals to closer scrutiny.

A far more crucial objection, which is much more closely related to the distinctiveness of the Marxist concept of class, is that Weber's definition of 'class' and 'class situation' restricts itself to the sphere of distribution while disregarding the sphere of production. It is true in fact that Weber defined class situations in terms of their typical probability for '(1) procuring goods, (2) gaining a position in life and (3) finding inner satisfactions'. The most important distinction – that between the '*property* class' and '*commercial* class' – relates in the first case to 'property differences' as such, while in the second case, it is 'the marketability of goods and services' that 'primarily determines' class situations (*ES*, 302 – Weber's emphases). In a broader sense, according to Weber, it can be said for both classes that the 'class situation . . . is ultimately market situation' (*ES*, 928). This in turn does not imply that the class situation is in every respect and in a like manner *determined* by the market (*RS I*, 1974). Evidently Weber is consistent in his perspective when he terms the class conflict between acquisition classes as the 'price struggle' (*Preiskampf*) (*WL*, 528; cf. *MSS*, 36) or the 'price struggle' *or* 'competitive struggle' respectively (*ES*, 927). However, Weber clearly had no wish for this definition to be taken as being strictly distinct from the sphere of production, as can be seen by his observation that: 'Classes are stratified according to their relations to the production and the acquisition of goods' (*ES*, 937).

Braunreuther labels Weber's form and level of definition as 'economistic' and associates it with the 'idealistic' perspective governing *Economy and Society* as a whole (1964, 102 f.).[24] Nor does he elaborate on the objection beyond establishing that it is the sphere of production that is the 'primary social determinant'. This is not the place to engage in the drawn out and unresolved internal Marxist debate on the relationship between the spheres of production and distribution. But I take the liberty to speculate that the two spheres – particularly within the framework of the capitalist mode of production – are so closely interrelated that the dispute about the primacy of one or the other is purely scholastic in nature.[25] The question alone of interest here is (a) whether Weber's procedure leads to essentially different outcomes (i.e. conceptual definitions) from the approach based on the sphere of production and (b) what could be said in support of this procedure. In this case the restriction to the two chief classes of the capitalist social formation is necessary.

It seems to me that the first part of this question has to be answered essentially in the negative. A glance at the pertinent definitions in Marx and Engels, for example, should suffice as evidence. Throughout the capitalist class is primarily defined in terms of the ownership of capital or the means of production, and the possibility based upon it to buy and exploit labour in the form of 'free wage labour' in the market place (cf., e.g., Marx, *Das Kapital*, Vol. 3, 750; Engels, *MEW*, German edition, Vol. 21, 462). Engels' definition of the 'proletariat' that correlates with this reads: 'By proletariat we understand the class of modern wage labourers who, since they do not own any means of production, are forced to sell their labour power in order to live' (*ibid.*). These definitions thus refer essentially to the ownership of capital/means of production, or 'mere labour power' respectively, and the interlinked possibility/compulsion to buy or sell.

As a matter of fact, Weber's definitions, more decisively than those of Marx and Engels, focus on showing how the different classes or class situations appear in social reality, not least in their latent or overt conflicting nature (i.e. as class *conflict*). Accordingly for him the most important question (though by no means the only one) is how class situations and possibilities of action defined by them, can be or are experienced by the members of classes. This could perhaps also give rise to the interpretation that Weber's definitions are even more definitely linked to the perspective of empirical social science research than the traditional Marxist concepts. If this is an accurate observation it is logically possible that even fundamental assumptions enter into class-*theoretical* analyses on the processes operating in the sphere of production; for example, the assumption that the classes of capitalist society and their conflicts are constantly reproduced through the effect of the 'law of value'.[26] It would be worth considering though how far such assumptions relate to laws that are built into the capitalist processes of production (and exchange), and determine them to a large extent in certain circumstances without in turn being a product of historical-social activity.[27] In this respect Weber's reservations about the sphere of production (in the Marxist sense) may possibly be due to his binding the definitional efforts in *Economy and Society* to the social dimension in the narrower sense.[28] We may criticise this, but not his alleged 'subjectivism' or 'idealism'. But in that case we would have to consider Weber's explicit motives for such distinctions, as outlined in the last chapter in more detail.

In this context the final objection aims at the fact that Weber operates with a fundamental distinction of classes, on the one hand, and status groups, on the other, thereby assigning primarily non-economic characteristics and causes to vertical social status differentiation. Of course Marx too occasionally referred to the relative autonomy of status differentials, but in his view this differentiation arises from economic causes 'in the final analysis' and, besides totally submerges in the class structure in capitalist conditions.[29] That Weber in contrast created a separate category for the 'status group' may similarly be linked to his decided social science orientation. The systematic tendency to attach separate importance to genuine social or socio-cultural factors certainly arises from this orientation. Moreover it is an empirical question whether the status structure, i.e. the structure according to 'lifestyle', 'hereditary or occupational prestige', 'formal education' (*ES*, 305), and possibly also 'monopolistic approbation of economic opportunities' (*RS I*, 274; *ES*, 306), can in all cases be reduced to differentiation by primarily economically determined (i.e. class) factors. This question will not, of course, be discussed in the present context.[30] But the question that is worth asking is what we could hold against a systematic consideration of the possibility that there are heterogeneous sources of social structure. The available empirical evidence seems to support this possibility. The cohesion and closedness of a theory (in this case, the materialist class theory) is not of 'value in itself'. It does not justify sacrificing an eye for a possible and perhaps considerable advance in knowledge, especially if this advance in knowledge has crucial implications for political practice (for example, with regard to political practice in tendentially *class*less societies).

One last note to conclude these brief considerations. Weber's conceptual-theoretical and empirical analyses should be seen as more worthy of discussion the more Marxists distance themselves from any hypostatising or even metaphysical interpretation, particularly in relation to the class situation and class consciousness of the workers (cf. the discussion on Lukács above). There are many signs that something like this is happening.[31] The general reason for this process could reside in the differentiated nature of these definitions and analyses and the degree to which they have substance in reality. Moreover the sobriety with which Weber analysed the categories with a particularly strong political nuance, 'class interest', and 'class action' (cf., e.g., *ES*, 928 and 848 ff.), would seem to have gained some persuasive power by now.

5.3 The city

Weber's essay on the city holds a special position in the history of the Marxist reception of his work in so far as it is the only part that has attracted perhaps greater and earlier attention and appreciation amongst Marxists, rather than non-Marxists. In the Soviet

Union, Neusychin[32] and Stoklickaja-Tereškovič (1925) published extensive review articles soon after the Russian translation (1923, edited by Kareev, a non-Marxist social scientist from Petersburg) had appeared. Moreover briefer, and consistently positive, references can be found in, e.g. Wittfogel (1924), Kautsky (1927, 303 f.) and Kapeljuš (1931, 274 ff.). This reception has not been continued and developed further in more recent times though. However, apart from the references in Anderson (1978, 1979) there are several comments on the 'admirable developments on the city in *Economy and Society*' in a more recent Marxist work (Vincent, 1973, 75; cf. the interpretations on 150 ff.).

It is easy to understand why particularly the essay on the city aroused such strong and positive interest among Marxist researchers and, at the same time, why the decline in this interest has had some very negative effects. *The City* is an historical-sociological analysis that (a) belongs to the range of problems also investigated in *The Protestant Ethic* (the conditions of emergence of 'modern capitalism' as well as the 'modern State' (Roth, in *ES*, ECIII), but at the same time it also (b) systematically tackles those factors and dimensions of reality (economic and political interests, class situations and class conflict) whose elimination in *The Protestant Ethic* to a large extent facilitated the standard schematising critique of Weber.

Thus Stoklickaja-Tereškovič notes that the 'presuppositions of the philosophy of history' held by Weber, who was 'by no means a representative of the materialist conception of history' (1925, 116), had not prevented him from emphasising the crucial role of economic factors throughout the essay (especially in the section on the Plebeian city) and accordingly furnishing his ideal-types with 'contents of a predominantly economic form' (*ibid.*, 117). But even the central thesis of the sociology of religion in the essay on the city (as an element of a complex, multi-factorial, historical-sociological analysis) does not seem unacceptable to any of the Marxist critics. The fact that Weber attributed 'great significance' to the Christian community as 'a confessional association of individual believers, not a ritual association of kinship groups' particularly in the foundation of the association of the medieval city (on the basis of a *conjuratio* of individuals), according to Kapeljuš, merely confirms the Marxist characterisation of Christianity as a 'cult of the abstract human being' (1931, 274).

In the opinion of Neusychin and Stoklickaja-Tereškovič (the latter also originally a historian), the main strength of Weber's essay is rooted in his reluctance to engage in any hasty construction of concepts and theory or the deduction of social historical conditions and processes, whether of idealist, materialist or any other origin. Rather, these authors think that it is the combination of a highly differentiated, multi-dimensional and highly documented (and therefore in fact at times hardly surveyable) historical enquiry, endeavouring conceptual clarification and theoretical abstraction at the level of historical-sociological typologies, that establishes the persuasive power and exemplary significance of the essay. Both authors attach their very detailed and entirely affirmative[33] description of the substance of Weber's analyses to some comprehensive considerations on his method.[34] Regarding their evaluation of Weber's sociological achievement in the narrower sense there are, of course, marked differences between Weber's and the authors' own conception of science.

In Weber's ideal-typical construction of the economic policy of the medieval city Stoklickaja-Tereškovič sees a 'persistent scientific property' and an exemplary use of the 'organising role of sociological enquiry' for historical research (1925, 113). Thus, she holds that 'this marks one of the cardinal methods of making the complexity of historical events manageable', even though large parts of the essay still lack a corresponding sociological thoroughness. 'The ordering function of the ideal-type cannot achieve its full impact and many historical moments from the life of the city remain isolated links which are not integrated into a higher synthesis.' (*Ibid.*, 118.)[35]

In comparison, Neusychin, who even more firmly emphasises the primacy of historical research (and the instrumental function of sociological abstraction), highlights the appropriateness of Weber's way of dealing with conceptual-theoretical abstractions in this essay and favourably contrasts this practice with many sociologists' far-reaching (and above all rash) ambitions for generalisation. In this context he also makes several critical remarks (as again in the essay of 1927)[36] on the introductory 'theoretical' parts of *Economy and Society* (*op. cit.*, 496).[37] He observes that the method actually practised by Weber from the perspective of historical research also constituted an essential prerequisite for an appropriate 'concrete' handling of materialist 'monism', i.e. the materialist theory of history as a dialectical development of productive forces, relations of production and 'superstructure'. Neusychin continues that when Weber referred to the role of economic, military-political, social, legal and even religious processes in the development of the city, he was not offering a 'theory of the reciprocal action of factors', which was unsatisfactory at this stage of research. Rather, Weber had presented a 'history of the reciprocal action of complex phenomena, that reciprocally penetrate each other, combine with one another, oppose each other and conflict with each other' (*ibid.*, 499).

Neusychin does not consider this 'pluralism' eclectic and incapable of explanation, but necessary, making the 'mechanism of that complex reciprocal action' concrete by means of justifiable simplifications and thus preparing the ground for a 'sociological construction'. He believes that Weber's essay on the city was not only a 'valuable historical enquiry', but was of 'enormous value' as a sociological study, precisely because it did not lay down the universal laws of all events, but instead sought to make 'the first step on the path towards a sociological illumination of historical phenomena' (*ibid.*, 500).

Wittfogel gives Weber credit for at least directing the attention of science to the city (or, in any case, to his focus on this research object)[38]. In fact, this author is much more heavily inspired by Weber's work in his own analyses than his numerous explicit references (in agreement and critique) lead us to suspect.[39] Wittfogel sees the particular superiority of Weber's enquiry (particularly in Kautsky's explanations) in the great emphasis placed on the violent military character of the seizure of power introduced by the *conjurationes* (*ibid.*, 75 ff.). Evidently Wittfogel, who at the time supported a very uncompromising theoretical and politically aggressive materialism, sees in this essay an (unintended) approximation to the opinion that the actual process of history has to be explained as the outcome of real, albeit violent (in Wittfogel's view), class struggles. In complete contrast to the opinions held by Neusychin and Stoklickaja-Tereškovič, in principle he certainly considered the 'method' used in the essay on the city entirely unacceptable. While the above Marxist historians are particularly positive in their reception of Weber's guarded approach to theoretical constructions, Wittfogel thinks that Weber had ultimately achieved no more than a 'phenomenal nihilistic chaos' (*ibid.*, 99) because he had refused any guidance by the materialist 'doctrine of the basic law of development that governs all history' (*ibid.*, 28).[40] Wittfogel in turn designed a schema that was to permit the conceptual and theoretical apprehension of the conditions and stages of development of a city bourgeoisie within the context of universal history (*ibid.*, 111). But even from the perspective of Marxist researchers, such as comments by Neusychin and Stoklickaja-Tereškovič seem to suggest, the schema certainly could not represent a scientifically fruitful application of this 'doctrine'.

It is difficult to explain why this early Marxist critical discussion of Weber's essay on the city, which had to start with been greeted with so much interest and far-reaching agreement, has not been resumed and developed until this day.[41] It cannot be on account of the fact that Weber's enquiries have in the meanwhile had a significant impact on, or even played a dominant role in, the research of primarily non-Marxist historical (particularly medievalist) social science on the city. There is no doubt that this essay by Weber is always present in this particular body of literature. The first section of the essay on conceptual explanation has been included in a new collection of contributions made on the subject matter by non-Marxist researchers.[42] However, this does not imply, as one Marxist author believes (Mägdefrau, 1977, 399), that this 'collection of innovative essays', or even the entire non-Marxist research in the field, is characterised by its 'heavy reference to Max Weber's typology on the city'. In fact, this is quite out of the question. The allegation that, for example, Sombart's judgement[43] inspired a remarkable reception of *The City* within the domain of non-Marxist sociology is even less applicable.[44] Accordingly, we cannot even attach an anti-Marxist label to Weber's essay in terms of its 'objective' function (Mägdefrau, *op. cit.*, 381),[45] let alone in the absence of any substantive argumentation in this direction. Rather, all the signs seem to confirm that a resumption of the substantive and methodological discussion contained in *The City* (and this implies, at the same time, the method of historical sociological research in fact practised by Weber in general) would show these categorisations to be utterly useless.

5.4 Problems of culture (science and art)

A broad section of the Marxist critique considers Max Weber as *the* theorist of the cultural superstructure. This firmly entrenched perception of Weber, which is essentially based on misunderstandings and misinterpretations of *The Protestant Ethic*, has led to scant acknowledgment of not only the materialist aspect of his scientific essays, as noted, but also his contribution to the study of so-called superstructural phenomena (at least those in the non-religious sphere). This may be consistent with the assumption that Weber approached this level of social reality in a systematically inverted way, in that he allegedly saw ideal factors to determine the historical-social course of events 'in the last instance'. The present work has repeatedly shown this *a priori* schema of interpretation to be unproductive, and also how it effectively inhibits the process of knowledge. This is strikingly shown when Marxist authors detach themselves from this schema and engage in a substantive discussion of Weber's cultural-sociological analyses. The insight that these analyses (including *The Protestant Ethic* measured by its own limited claims) cannot be seen as an expression of superstructure-idealism by no means suggests in turn that they do not offer some starting points for a differentiated materialist critique. Undoubtedly Weber's enquiries into the genesis of society and the impact of cultural 'meaningful relationships', with all due consideration for material factors, distinguish themselves, and not by sheer accident, from the comparable analyses of a decidedly materialist perspective.

The most important distinguishing characteristic seems to be that Weber assumed an empirical scientist should, in principle, have to concede to these historical worlds of meaning an autonomous 'determination' and legitimacy, i.e. one that cannot be indefinitely reduced to other forms of experience and interpretation. I have already referred above to this fundamental Weberian assumption in relation to his work on the sociology of religion. But Weber logically thought that this also applied to the remaining major cultural worlds of meaning. However, this neither implies that Weber was unable to analyse serious ruptures and contradictions within and between these different cultural worlds of meaning,[46] nor that he had thus deprived himself of the chance to pursue a critique of ideology characteristic of the Marxist tradition. On the contrary, a much earlier hypothesis proposed that the critique of ideology could indeed increase its rigour if it confronted the claimed 'significance' (one that was not seen to be illegitimate at the outset) of historical systems of meaning and value with their real social contexts of emergence and realisation.

The second specific difference of Weber's cultural sociological research is linked to this fundamental perspective. Evidently Weber predominantly worked on the assumption that special importance should be attached to the (internal) meaningful evidence and consistency of the systems of interpretation and value in an enquiry into specific historical-social processes. Thus he did not advocate a quasi-metaphysical notion of ideas as the subjects of history. Nor did he claim a mysterious 'inner dynamic' of meaningful relationships for the purposes of explanation. Rather, the conception underlying the stated leading assumption is that:

(a) all the more complex overlapping and persisting forms of social action are dependent on the organisational and legitimational achievement of developed patterns of interpretation and values; and that

(b) the tendency towards evidence, systematisation and consistency, which represents a universal characteristic of culturally meaningful relationships, is directly interrelated with this social achievement of organisation and legitimation.[47]

All the research-oriented fundamental assumptions of the Weberian sociology of culture originate in the same 'basic outlook' on social action that was discussed earlier. The fundamental assumption of rationality dealt with explains *firstly*, why in 'interpretative sociology' cultural systems of interpretation and value actually constitute the focus of research interest, and *secondly*, why they are thematised essentially according to their immanent rationality and social achievement of rationalisation.

Even the small number of detailed Marxist contributions on Weber's work on cultural sociology do not deal with this fundamental problem. The question of rationality and rationalisation is certainly acknowledged and discussed as a leading question in these enquiries, but its implications and productiveness are underestimated. The fact that Weber, in his analyses on occidental science and art, concentrates on a very specific form of rationality – namely, rationality in a formal and technical sense – is not explained by the special nature of a specific historical development (and perhaps a specific research interest in this development), but by the logical limitations of Weber's perspective.[48]

This limitation should seem far less crucial with respect to the object of science rather than art, for example. As a matter of fact Marxist authors do not criticise Weber's observation that modern science belongs to the sphere of formal and instrumental rationality or that it represents the highest and most effective expression of this form of rationality.[49] This implies that Marxists simultaneously accept that the process of rationalisation encompassing all spheres of social life, *so far as* it is bound up with the emergence and application of modern science, generally possesses this formal and instrumental character.[50]

At this point Marxist theorists are certainly faced with the serious question of whether the absolutely inevitable process of science regulating and governing social practice remains confined to the limits of instrumental rationality in socialist conditions as well, or whether science and the regulating and governing process of science take on an entirely different (i.e. material) character of rationality within socialism. The Weberian conceptions are seen to result in the problem that they do not permit us to make any qualitative distinctions in this respect. However, these conceptions do lead to the assumption, which is completely opposed to that recently held by Weber's successors (e.g. Aron, Habermas and Schluchter), that the largely identical process of science and technology regulating and governing life would entail a progressive structural convergence between socialist and non-socialist social systems (Kvesko, 1974, 13 f.).

Here resides a *logical* difficulty for Marxist theory since it starts out with the dual basic assumption that the sphere of material production has determinative significance on the whole of social life and that scientific or scientific-technological knowledge would, to an increasing extent (and *a fortiori* in socialism), have to become the 'primary force of production'. This basic assumption coupled with the absolutely fundamental and programmatic establishment of materialist theory on scientific rationality make it impossible to put forward convincing arguments against the conclusion drawn by 'convergence theorists'. The fact that the politics of the socialist states orient themselves to a material value system of a political-ideological nature, while being totally independent from perspectives of scientific (economic or technical) rationality on central issues and frequently in diametrical opposition to them, thus working against the tendency towards convergence, can neither be adequately comprehended and explained nor justified on the basis of these theoretical presuppositions. The degree of independence or dominance of the political-ideological sphere seen to be politically necessary and exercised therefore finds no correspondence at the level of scientific discussion on the structure and consequences of the process of rationalisation.[51]

The overall agreement with Weber's formal-rational apprehension of science, as determined by his historical-social science analyses, accordingly generates fundamental problems for Marxist theorists because of its implications on political and scientific policy. The final chapter will discuss the extent to which a political-ideological critique of this concept of science, or its 'realisation' and application by Weber (see also Kozyr-Kowalski, 1964), appears convincing in approaching these problems.

In any case it seems *a priori* plausible that these difficulties could have been overcome by a critique of Weber's formal and instrumental – and thus far the seemingly politically neutral – notion of rationality. This type of critique is, however, a central element of those contributions that critically discuss Weber's analyses on art. Here we are essentially talking about an essay by A. Lunačarskij (the People's Commissary for Education after the October Revolution), which first appeared in 1925, and about a more recent work by P. Gajdenko (1975).[52] Both essays primarily deal with Weber's paper on the sociology of music, but Gajdenko in particular also engages in more general considerations on the sociology of art.

Lunačarskij in his general appraisal classifies the paper on music as one of those 'half-products' supplied by Max Weber throughout his work. But even this 'half-product' was welcomed by the

'Marxist enterprise' and constituted a 'very valuable element' for the socialist construction (1962, 35). Lunačarskij sees the overall cause of Weber's limited potential in Weber's (conscious) dispensation of a 'unified dominant standpoint, a unified method' (*ibid.*, 34). But he traces the specific limitations of the enquiry into music back to the determinative leading idea of 'rationalisation'. In Lunačarskij's opinion this leading idea had crucially narrowed Weber's research perspective, particularly in three respects.

Its first consequences was that Weber had almost totally 'ignored' the 'physical substratum' and the 'physiological aspect' of music (*ibid.*, 37). This dual natural basis of all music could be detected both in 'primitive music', which is a purely 'instinctive thing',[53] and in that evidently all 'rationalisation of music' generally has to 'move within a range of sounds which physiologically please us' (*ibid.*, 37 f.).[54] According to Lunačarskij it is the neglect of the 'natural substratum' that expresses itself in Weber's 'uncritical rationalisation of primitive social thought' in general (*ibid.*, 43).

Lunačarskij's second criticism is intimately linked with this first negative effect of the Weberian perspective on rationality. He believes that Weber systematically neglected the 'emotional aspect' of music whose fundamental importance could, in turn, be clearly deduced from the 'most primitive song of the savage' (*ibid.*, 39 f.). The third relevant shortcoming of Weber's enquiry, according to Lunačarskij, is that Weber – despite a promising start – had not sufficiently clarified 'to what extent the rationalisation of music reflects specific social conditions' (*ibid.*, 41). Lunačarskij thinks that Weber had evidently apprehended the real historical-social conditions as factors that interfered with a process running its course in accordance with rational psychological laws; in other words, that Weber did not interpret the rationality of the process as a genuine social fact.

It is not possible to subject Lunačarskij's critique to detailed examination here. But it is possible and necessary to add some considerations of a more general nature.

To start with the last point, a serious imbalance does exist in Weber's work concerning, on the one hand, the extent and intensity of his treatment of the immanent rationality of musical development and, on the other, the sociological aspect of the process. There is no doubt that one would like to see Weber's brief references to extra-musical causal relationships much more elaborated. However, the fundamental question arising from the introductory considerations of this section is whether processes of rationalisation within specific cultural spheres can lay claim to sociological interest only to the extent that they can be directly and consistently explained as a function of external social factors (for example, the need for economic and political authority).

To begin with a conception of this kind does not adequately consider[55] that, as a rule, cultural (here, artistic) production also has its own social basis, which is more or less differentiated from the total societal context, and that this social subsystem may contain a specific dynamic that is reflected at the level of cultural production as a process of progressive rationalisation. Social differentiation and specialisation of this kind (with this consequence) is evidently a special characteristic of the development of occidental art (particularly since the Middle Ages).

But beyond that Lunačarskij's critique fails to appreciate that a process of rationalisation in any one sphere of culture, if only specific external and internal marginal conditions and general incentives are given, can essentially derive its dynamic and purpose from the fact that the immanent possibilities of a specific cultural creation or invention (for example, specific systems of sound and harmony) are progressively developed and exhausted. Developments in the domain of science in particular can engender the growth of additional crucial impulses and viewpoints in such a process in the sphere of art (but also religion). Weber in fact works with such an assumption in relation to the history of the rationalisation of European arts, especially music and paintings). This is something that is not emphasised by Lunačarskij, but it is indeed rightly stressed by Gajdenko.

The second major point of Lunačarskij's critique argues that Weber's perspective of rationalisation does not permit him to see the 'emotional aspect' of music. As a matter of fact it is true that Weber's paper almost exclusively deals with the problems of musical production (composition and performance) and here again specifically with the 'technical' prerequisites and their development. This does not imply, however, that logically only this intellectual and technical side can be thematised from the perspective of rationalisation and that the affective conditions of production as well as – above all – the reception of works of art should necessarily be excluded from the enquiry. The observation that there could be processes of rationalisation at the emotional level of artistic production and reception may seem absurd at first. However, it is entirely acceptable even within the context of Weber's broader understanding of rationality. It is not only conceivable, but an empirical fact, that the development of a genre or form of art is in a significant respect presented as a process of clarification, differentiation and refinement (sublimation) of the emotional 'meanings' expressed and perceived in artistic creations. But, from Weber's point of view, such a process should be described with the category of 'rationalisation' because this process progressively enhances the 'communicability' of meaningful contents (of an affective type in this context).

This idea cannot be elaborated further at this stage, but I refer the reader to what has been said elsewhere on the interrelationship between rationality and communicability. It was noted then that rationality interpreted in terms of communicability is an indisputable social fact and that it would therefore be inappropriate to proceed from a logical distinction between rationality and sociability, and to then seek or construct possible (more or less accidental) linkages.

At any rate it is established that there are no arguments of this kind in Weber's paper on music nor in his other comments on the sociology of art. On the contrary, Weber concentrated so exclusively on the issue of artistic 'techniques' and their rationalisation that these latter comments are more likely to refer to an actual shortcoming in Weber's work than, for example, to Lunačarskij's critique. To the extent that it relates to Weber's enquiry into music, Lunačarskij's critique is both understandable and appropriate. On this basis it is impossible to draw any general conclusions with respect to research in cultural sociology oriented to the problems of rationality and rationalisation. The references provided should make it clear that to do justice to this discussion one would need much more far-reaching and fundamental analyses, in which the treatment of the problem of rationality within the framework of Marxist theory on superstructure and ideology would have to be included.[56]

Lunačarskij's third point of criticism, namely the elimination of the 'physical', or 'physiological' substratum in Weber's enquiry, is also related to the last considerations. Even if there were a substratum of the type suggested by Lunačarskij – which is still a controversial issue among specialists today – it would as such still not constitute a social fact. Besides, Lunačarskij's notion that 'primitive' and 'primeval' music represents this physical basis 'in its pure state' prior to all cultural superstructuring and that all 'aesthetic rationalisation' not only starts out from this natural basis, but is also determined in its logical possibilities and limits is, to say the very least, most speculative. It cannot be asserted that it is constitutive and essential for a 'materialist' theory of music (and art in general) to appeal to a primary nature in this way. Rather, what Marx observed concerning the 'conflict between man and nature' in general would have to apply to artistic 'work' too: that the 'raw material' here as ever has to be presented as superstructure and mediated through human and, more specifically, social activity. With reference to musical production this means that its historical origin can be located only where the level of the instinctive generation of sounds, or sequences of sounds, is crossed and an (elementary) form of symbolic communication has been reached. This, however, is undoubtedly the case with the 'most primitive song of the savage' to which Lunačarskij refers.

What is particularly questionable though is that Lunačarskij evidently wants to ascribe to that 'physical substratum' a normative quality in the sense that any 'aesthetic rationalisation' is set a definitive limit beyond which music (and art in general) would have to become unnatural. This is obviously the starting point of all efforts to derive a very specific 'realism' as *ideal* art form from a 'materialist' treatment of art and to make it binding for the production of art. According to this conception the detachment of 'aesthetic rationalisation' from the reference to nature necessarily leads to a 'progressist', 'rationalistic', 'technocratic' and 'formalistic' aberration of artistic creation characteristic of the latest developments in bourgeois art (and its aesthetics). In the 'Preamble' to her essay Gajdenko observes that it is precisely these developments in Weber's rationalistic conception of art (more recently adopted and developed by Adorno in particular) that have undergone decisive grounding and justification (Gajdenko, 1975, 115).[57]

In the face of this argumentation it is necessary to establish that the effort to derive normative orientations from an ahistorical and pre-societal nature utterly contradicts the 'founding ideas' of historical materialism. Each abstract dichotomy of ('primitive') nature and society, or rationality ('culture'), and above all each attempt to declare nature the ultimate norm-orienting authority in cultural issues, simply cannot be compatible with the principle of Marxist thinking that concrete nature too has always been mediated by history and society. The endeavours to counter the rationalism, formalism and subjectivism of modern art and aesthetics with the notion of 'natural', and therefore obligatory, art are by no means based on any genuine Marxist presuppositions, but rather on, for example, actual or supposed political requirements.[58] Besides, historical knowledge of such endeavours clearly shows that they, however grounded, did not in any case exactly encourage the development of art.

It does not seem convincing within the framework of a sociological discussion to confront Weber's perspective of rationality with some factors of primary nature. On the same basis it is very questionable whether this perspective is not utterly inadequate for research into the substantive aspect of the 'intellectual ideal contents' of art (Gajdenko, 1975, 122); in other words, it is worth asking whether Weber's perspective should not be labelled 'formalistic' at least in this sense. This question forms Gajdenko's focus in her critical treatment of Weber.

Gajdenko, prior to her critique of the narrowness of Weber's research perspective, notes that it is precisely this research perspective that facilitated Weber's illumination of a very important aspect of the European history of art. Because the leading concept of 'value relevance' was determined by his interest in the problem of rationalisation,[59] Weber had recognised the interplay between art and science in its fundamental significance and had especially appreciated that the visual artists of that epoch 'were the first experimental scientists who resolved the technical problems of their century' (Gajdenko, 1975, 121). Gajdenko thinks (perhaps with some exaggeration) that Weber had in fact been the initiator in drawing attention to this problem.

The shortcomings of Weber's sociology of art, according to Gajdenko, represent the obverse to this constructive perspective: since Weber's interest focussed on the formal-rational and technical aspect of the development of art, and therefore on the interrelationship between science and art, he ignored the wider historical context. The 'intellectual, ideal aspect' of art and its development could become apparent only if the development of science and art was related to the 'essential changes' in 'social, religious and intellectual life' as a whole (*ibid.*, 122).

It is difficult to dispute the observation that Weber's paper on music is characterised by such one-sided treatment. Moreover, one cannot explain this adequately by saying that one is faced with special difficulties when seeking to interpret (i.e. identify and evaluate the embodied historical-social meaningful relationships) the contents of that most abstract form of art, music. Weber's brief references to the visual arts (to which Gajdenko primarily refers) are similarly characterised by a one-sided perspective. But the question is whether we can conclude that Weber's considerations on the sociology of art are logically limited, merely on the basis of his actual neglect of the 'meaningful aspect' (Gajdenko).

Gajdenko asserts that Weberian sociology is thus logically limited and explains this in terms of its linkage with the principle of ethical neutrality. But it is by no means true that the principle of ethical neutrality prevents research into the 'intellectual, ideal contents' of art. It is absolutely feasible to explore this meaningful aspect from the specific perspective of rationality and rationalisation on the foundations of the thesis of ethical neutrality, as the considerations of Lunačarskij's critique have revealed. Neither the formal and technical character of scientific rationality, nor the thesis of ethical neutrality derived from it, imply that extra-scientific meaningful contents and object-specific forms of rationality and rationalisation cannot be thematised on the *side of the object*. The actual limit to social science research, according to Weber, is set where the meaningful contents of art and its distinctive rationality are not merely analysed, but are also subjected to substantive *evaluation*. A particular instance of this is that in the framework of science it is possible to speak of 'progress' in the arts only in as much as the concern is with the processes of progressive formal rationalisation, or developments, on the level of the artistic means or techniques of production. Even the incorporation of more extensive social and cultural processes of change into the analysis of the sociology of art (demanded by Gajdenko) would not fundamentally extend the potential of social science research in this respect. The enquiries of the critique of ideology exploring the 'intellectual, ideal' aspect of art from the perspective of its emergence and function in socio-economic and political conflicts of interest also can only ever lead to *hypothetical* substantive evaluations, and accordingly to *hypothetical* statements on progress in art. Even in this case value orientations ultimately come into play that can no longer be grounded by empirical method alone, as previously discussed (Chapter 3, Section 2).

It is a question of fundamental significance whether it could and ought to be the task of (social) science to give decisive and exhaustive information on the meaning and (relative) value of works of art and their 'ideal contents'. This would involve both considering the meaningful contents attached to art exclusively from the perspective of scientific rationality, however defined, *and* judging it purely by the standard of such rationality. Art would thus represent an incipient form or a fundamentally inferior substitute of science, although useful for specific purposes. It would have to portray, on the level of 'sensory awareness' and via the medium of the 'beautiful illusion', what science comprehends in 'essence' through strict logic. This viewpoint, advocated by Hegel in its classical form, evidently found particular favour among Marxist theorists of art and was adopted by them.[60] However, this conception is dubious not only because of its inherent substitution of the Hegelian concept of science (as absolutist-idealistic philosophy) with the idea of a radical empirical social science, but its expressed claim of dominance, or even monopoly, of scientific rationality that goes far beyond Weber's assumption of rationality that determines his analyses in the sociology of art.

There is no doubt that the above critics of Weber do not themselves advocate this claim of dominance, at least not explicitly. But neither do they make it clear what form a logical alternative to Weber's solution of this fundamental problem in the sociology of art in particular and the sociology of culture in general could take.[61] Weber's solution is characterised by a basic ambivalence. On the one hand, it is based on the assumption that the different cultural systems of interpretation and value can claim a distinctive 'legitimacy' in the face of science. However, on the other hand, his solution is guided by an interest in clarifying the rationality content of these heterogeneous systems of interpretation and value, in general, and their content of formal or technical (i.e. scientific) rationality, in particular. This ambivalence does not harbour any contradiction. Rather, it arises from the need to carry the potential of scientific research into cultural phenomena, and therefore simultaneously to clarify the extent of scientific 'disenchantment', to the furthest possible degree without neglecting the 'distinctive logic of distinctive objects'.

5.5 Rationality, authority, bureaucracy

It is not particularly controversial among interpreters and critics of Weber that the problem of 'rationality and rationalisation' (Weber) dominates the whole of his historical-sociological and conceptual-theoretical work. Not only is this clearly reflected throughout his work,[62] but Weber himself explicitly admitted that this was the main reference point. Weber's far-reaching and highly differentiated scientific research perspective is derived from his initial, entirely concrete, historical and everyday experience of a specific, 'modern occidental', process of rationalisation. This interrelationship between a pronounced extra-scientific concern and a fundamental scientific enquiry, then, constitutes a classical example of what Weber (with Rickert) called 'value relevance', and what is today popularly known as a 'knowledge-directing interest'.

From this perspective, it is both obvious and legitimate for Marxist interpreters of Weber to be particularly concerned with the manifest or even concealed basis of this knowledge-directing interest. Similarly, it is admissible to work on the hypothesis that his interest is, in the 'final analysis', based on class and therefore, essentially, domination. This hypothesis evidently becomes even more plausible if it is possible to attribute an explicit, and above all apparently 'positive', linkage between the conceptions of rationality and domination.

Marxist authors who critically examine Weber's problem of rationality predominantly work on the basis of this hypothesis. Accordingly, the thematic relationship between rationality and domination in Weber's work is approached from two angles.

SPECIAL PROBLEMS OF THE THEORETICAL AND EMPIRICAL WORK

Firstly, they are concerned with this relationship in terms of logic, by looking at those class or domination interests that express themselves in 'rationality'. Secondly, they concentrate on Weber's treatment of the problem of domination, in general, and bureaucracy, in particular, by mounting a critique of ideology within this framework of reference.

Marcuse (1972a) presented the most fundamental, and obviously most influential, critique of Weber's conception of rationality.[63] His central thesis is that Weber's conception of rationality and rationalisation offers an apparently value-neutral framework of reference for social science research and precisely because of this is of great ideological use to particular interests of domination. These ideological contents are concretely expressed in the guiding thread of the rationality question in Weber's analysis of 'modern occidental capitalism'. Since this analysis operates with the apparently value-neutral category of rationality, and beyond that creates the semblance of necessity, if not even 'reason', by means of this category, it 'objectively' serves the defences of domination by a specific class, namely the bourgeoisie. According to Marcuse, it is difficult to see through this interrelationship because the meaning of domination is, as it were, 'built into' Weber's category of rationality. He continues that Weber's rationality is an 'instrumental', or 'technical' and 'formal' reason, but that it could *per definitionem* function exclusively as an instrument of domination and control over both natural and social processes. This leads Marcuse to suspect that the 'concept of technical reason' is inherently ideological.

> Not only the application of technology but technology itself is domination (of nature and men) – methodological, scientific, calculated, calculating control. Specific purposes and interests of domination are not foisted upon technology 'subsequently' and from the outside; they enter the very construction of the technical apparatus. (*ibid.*, 223 f.)

'What a society and its ruling interests intend to do with men and things' is already installed in the technology as an 'historical-social project' (*ibid.*, 224).[64] The ideological-legitimatory function of technical reason is defined by Marcuse in more detail elsewhere: 'Today, domination perpetuates and extends itself not only through technology but *as* technology, and the latter provides the great legitimation of the expanding political power, which absorbs all spheres of culture' (1972b, 130).

The discussion on this type of fundamental critique of Weber's conception of rationality has to clarify two questions in particular. The first one relates to the assertion that Weber had understood and had to understand 'rationality' as technical, instrumental or formal rationality in the final analysis. The second question is closely linked with the first, but is primarily of an empirical nature. This is whether Weber provided an appraisal of the significance of technical and formal rationality for the development of modern capitalist (and socialist) society that was inadequate in logic and possibly even distorted on ideological grounds, and in the process concealed the function of ideology and domination contained in this type of rationality.

Both questions cannot be exhaustively dealt with here. It is, however, necessary and possible to attempt some fundamental clarification.

Marcuse refers to Weber's 'bourgeois reason' (Marcuse, 1972a, 225), but means that of 'the formal rationality of capitalism' (*ibid.*, 224 f.).[65] This is indisputable in so far as Weber, as an empirical scientist, felt 'tied' to the formal rationality of modern science.[66] Moreover modern science can be assigned to the bourgeoisie and capitalism both in historical and socio-economic terms. However, neither of these facts leads to the inevitable conclusion that rationality could be *thematised* merely as 'formal' or 'technical' in the framework of Weberian social science. A look at Weber's conceptual-theoretical as well as material analyses shows that such a limitation is really out of the question. Besides the distinction between formal and material rationality (to which Marcuse also referred), Weber's analyses indicate such a wide diversity of types and dimensions of 'rationalisation' that their systematisation would not only be difficult, but their subsumption under the chief concept of formal rationality utterly out of the question.[67] If we could specify a fundamental meaning of rationality in Weber at all, it would be most suitably characterised as the already cited category of 'communicability'.[68]

Concerning the second question regarding the role of formal rationality in the development of capitalist (and socialist) society, Marcuse's objections (as those of a Marxist) seem surprising at first sight. Weber refers to the significance of specific material (namely, religious-ethical) value orientations to explain the genesis of modern occidental capitalism. In contrast, as we have already noted, Marxist critiques constantly emphasise economic factors as playing the sole determining role 'in the final analysis'. Besides this, and in connection with corresponding statements by Marx, they establish that it is the development of the productive forces that represents the real motive power of history. No one has equalled Marx's rigour in his conception that the laws of movement within capitalist society are a product of economic and technical rationality. Of course Marx also believed that the capitalist mode of production would eventually be transformed into economic and technical irrationality and therefore (still on technical-rational grounds) this would inevitably lead to the abolition of the capitalist relations of production.

But this expectation is neither shared by Weber, nor indeed by Marcuse (who thus far abandons one central Marxist assumption).[69] Rather, both establish that the advanced process of technical rationalisation by no means necessarily entails a radical change in socio-political or authority relations on the grounds of technical rationality, but instead has the obverse effect both in fact and in legitimation, by leading to the stabilisation, if not 'ossification', of existing relations. Further, Marcuse concedes that the *technical* potential for the rationalisation of the capitalist economic and social system even half a century after Weber's corresponding thesis is clearly greater than that of the socialist system.

The opinion shared by Marcuse and many other Marxist authors (see, for example, Bader *et al.*, 1976, 316; Korf, 1971, *passim*; Kuznecov, 1975, 9; Devjatkova, 1968b, 129; Čalikova, 1970, 22; Vincent, 1973, 169 f.) that, faced with this development, Weber's narrow conception of rationalisation merely permitted resignation (or 'fatalism') or else an escape into irrationalism, particularly by showing faith in the liberating power of a charismatic leader, is inappropriate in this context. Although it is difficult to ignore, it is here of only secondary importance that, as noted, Weber by no means conferred an independent claim of rationality merely to scientific-technical and formal-rational positions. This acknowledgment in logic aside, Weber saw in a concrete historical and social situation both the possibility and necessity for contrasting the processes of 'concretisation' and 'depersonalisation' with a *materially* rational and modern idea of value, namely that of human and civil rights.[70] Whether this idea of value could succeed against the power of technological rationality is of course an empirical and above all practical question. It is also a highly discussable problem of how one can realise this idea of charismatic personalities without seriously damaging its content.[71]

In the view of many Marxists the ideological (and consequently fatalistic) nature of linking the conception of rationality with that of domination is shown most strikingly in Weber's analyses on the problem of bureacracy. The fact that precisely this problem meets with extraordinarily great interest among Marxist authors, and that not only Weber's conception of rationality but also his sociology of domination is approached almost exclusively from this angle,[72] has of course its specific and by all means practical political reason. The reason is that critical analyses on the authority relations in the socialist states are, as a rule, primarily directed at the progressive bureaucratisation evidently characterising those states. A critique oriented in this way was expressed at an early stage against corresponding developments in the Soviet Union, and possibly more resolutely by Marxist theorists than by non-Marxists.[73] Marxist critics justifiably appealed to the conception of Marxist classics (particularly that of Marx) that bureaucracy represents a specific expression of (late) bourgeois domination which would have to be eradicated in the course of the socialist revolution and replaced by radical democratic forms of self-administration.[74] In view of this conception and post-revolutionary reality which corresponded so little to it, Weber's assumption that socialist revolution would not lead to the abolition but rather an extension and acceleration of bureaucracy would appear to have been particularly scandalous and in need of critique.

Weber grounded his assumption by saying that 'rational socialism' in particular could by no means dispense with the specific rationality (i.e. especially the transparency, or 'calculability', and efficiency, meaning 'precision', 'continuity' and 'expediency') of a bureaucratically organised 'administration of the masses'. Weber asserted that indeed 'the need for constant, tight, intensive and *calculable* administration' would have to increase in rational socialism, and saw the 'specific rational fundamental feature' of bureaucratic administration as 'power through knowledge' (*WG*, 165). It is this 'specifically rational' aspect of bureaucracy that is evidently of special importance for the development in socialist states. In an earlier section of this book (p. 12) it has already been established that not only the materialist classics, but also the leading Soviet theorists, saw a crucial characteristic of socialist society in its scientific grounding, organisation and direction to an extent that had not previously been experienced nor considered factually as well as ideologically possible in pre-socialist societies.[75] From this point of view it would be absolutely feasible to characterise the specific socialist claim of its legitimate domination, and particularly also in the revolutionary phase, or during the subsequent phase of a dictatorship by the proletariat or 'its' party, with the formula of 'power through knowledge'. At any rate, materialist theorists were convinced that a claim of power thus grounded was in direct agreement with the goal of comprehensive and substantial, i.e. not merely political and 'formal', democratisation of all authority relations, and beyond that an abolition of all domination by people over people. (Evidently this conviction ensures a strong subjective faith in the legitimacy of its own authority among its followers, even if 'formal' democratic procedures are suspended for shorter or longer periods of time.)

Weber's analyses indicate that this type of one-way positive linkage between the radical scientific rationalisation of social contexts of action, on the one hand, and democratisation, on the other, does not exist. There is no doubt that modern mass democracy is dependent on a transparent, calculable, depersonalised (non-partisan) and efficient administration, not only for technical-organisational but perhaps also for ethical-political reasons.[76] But neither this fact as such nor the fact that the 'knowledge' in question is, in principle, both universally valid and universally accessible (i.e. public)[77] could lead us to infer that in such a situation there could be no antagonism. The production and appropriation of the requisite specialist knowledge and (above all) its social and political application necessitates certain organisational rules (specialisms, institutional differentiation, hierarchical structures, etc.) that are diametrically opposed to the principles of radical and comprehensive democratisation.

Weber's fundamental observation in this respect is 'that "democracy" as such, despite and because of its inevitable and unintentional promotion of bureaucratisation, opposes "domination" by bureaucracy and this being the case possibly makes for very perceptible contradictions and inhibitions in bureaucratic organisation' (*WG*, 729). The Marxist critical treatment of Weber's conception of bureaucracy largely leaves this fundamental problem undiscussed.[78] This applies particularly to Marxist-Leninist theorists, although it is precisely these theorists who in general firmly support the idea of the 'scientific guidance and direction' of all social processes. This entails the central point of Weber's argument on the interplay between rationality and domination in socialist bureaucracy also remaining untouched. Obviously Weber's specific 'reference to value', on the horizon of which the antagonisms between sweeping social rationalisation and democracy are demonstrated, is neither noted nor shared by many of these theorists. Thus Kramer, for example, apodictically asserts that 'bureaucratism' is 'essentially alien' to socialism, while simultaneously observing that 'a society which wants to overcome spontaneity, as is the goal of socialism, and is even in a position to be able to do so, naturally needs a highly organised managerial apparatus' (Kramer, 1968, 187). The overcoming of 'spontaneity' is of course an essential characteristic of the process that Weber identified and criticised (for ethical-political reasons) as a process of bureaucratic rationalisation. Kramer thus initially confirms the Weberian thesis that 'rational socialism' *a fortiori* cannot dispense with bureaucracy (in the sense of a 'highly organised managerial apparatus'). In fact this is a conception that is characteristic of all Marxist-Leninist theorists. Neither bureaucracy, in Weber's sense, nor its permeation in all spheres of life are criticised, but only its perverse form of appearance as 'bureaucratism'. Kramer expands on 'bureaucratism' by saying

> that the managerial apparatus becomes autonomous, it begins to assume its own existence and its function is exhausted by purely and simply serving the parasitical section of society, in order to protect and realise its political, economic and ideological goals (Kramer, *ibid.*)

In many respects this conception is problematic and of course particularly in relation to both the traditional Marxist interpretation of bureaucracy and the prevailing conditions in actual contemporary socialist states. Firstly, there is obviously no compelling link between the two elements of 'bureaucratism', i.e. the growing autonomy of the managerial apparatus and its changing function to serve a class other than that of civil servants and functionaries. When, for example, Bukharin and Preobrazhensky find a 'partial *restoration of bureaucratism* within the Soviet order (1966, 183), or when Lenin speaks of 'our genuinely Russian (although Soviet) bureaucratism' (*UBM* 1, 1925, II), these theorists have the 'growing autonomy' of the civil servant apparatus in mind, not its late bourgeois function of ideology and domination. Unless these two factors can make a separate appearance the existence of a socialist bureaucratism would imply that even post-revolutionary societies are still 'antagonistic class societies' (Kramer, *op. cit.*) – something no Marxist-Leninist theorist would care to admit. Finally, the distinction between (good) bureaucracy, meaning a highly organised, comprehensive 'managerial apparatus' staffed by scientifically trained specialists, and (bad) bureaucratism is not in accordance with the radical democratic ideas of self-organisation and self-administration outlined primarily by Marx in his analysis on the Paris Commune and corroborated by leading theorists during the initial years after the Russian Revolution.[79]

Marxist critics see the crucial shortcomings and ideological character of Weber's analysis on bureaucracy in his failure to perceive the 'class base' of bureaucratic domination (thus, e.g. Kvesko, 1974, 16 and Seregin, 1974, 91) and in his thematic treatment of bureaucracy purely as a problem of social rationalisation or organisation (Seregin 1975, 72; Špakova *et al.*, 1973, 79, 83 ff.).[80] But, in fact, the same theorists fail to resume the class-theoretical analysis and critique of bureaucracy inaugurated by

Marx, i.e. that bureaucracy is a specific form of appearance of political domination). On the contrary, the merely alleged class-neutral bourgeois bureaucracy is contrasted with the socialist 'power through knowledge' that embodies a degree of rationality both with a view to its comprehensive and profound basis of knowledge and the organisational efficiency of the planning and managerial apparatus of party and state. The socialist bureaucracy is assumed in logic to surpass the potential of a bureaucracy based on the class interests of a minority. Socialist bureaucracy is obviously even given credit for its material rationality, because it fulfils its function on the basis of scientifically established, and therefore universally binding, substantive goals and norms. Weber (like the bourgeoisie in general), on the other hand, had only been able to demonstrate the bases of legitmacy of bureaucracy in secondary terms, namely in terms of its formal and technical rationality.

But, according to Weber, it is in fact the sheer formal character of bureaucratic rationality which facilitates and necessitates its ethical-political critique (for example, an ethical-political critique oriented to the idea of individual responsibility or to the principles of democracy). Such a critique is obviously ruled out in the case of the scientific planning and managerial apparatus under 'rational socialism', and therefore, by inference, the superior (material) rationality that is embodied, or at least realised, by this apparatus.

This approach, defending the overall tendencies towards bureaucratisation within socialist states, is no longer acceptable to a great many Marxists both within and outside such socialist states. Rather, these tendencies are consistently contrasted with Marx's radical democratic and 'humanist' notions (for example, by 'praxis philosophers', by J. Elleinstein or R. Bahro). At the same time, several Marxist authors fall back on Weber's considerations for an *explanation* of these tendencies (cf., e.g. Tadić, 1973). As a rule though these same authors still hold the opinion that Weber could at best only establish the irrational aspect of bureaucratic rationalisation (Devjatkova 1968, 129) and then resign in the face of it, because of the systematic (and ideological) limitations of his scientific conception. The question is whether existing and even now predominant Marxist theory (and practice) is not determined to such an extent by the idea of scientific rationality that independent, ethical and political considerations are granted even less legitimacy and space than was the case with Weber. The already somewhat dated discussions about the autonomy of ethical principles under the domination of real socialism, and the most recent critical discussions on the issue of 'human rights', not only dealt or are dealing with actual power and interests in maintaining power, but also with a Marxist conception of rationality and legitimacy which

1 accepts ethical and political-ethical considerations only in the context of historical materialism, i.e. including (or so it is claimed) strictly empirically based analyses; and
2 asserts, in the case of doubt, the superior (good) reason of technical rationality and its 'conformity to material laws' (in both the spheres of development of productive forces and socio-political organisation and direction).

5.6 Blank areas: economy, state, law

A review of those fields or dimensions of Weber's work which have been subjected to a more or less thorough discussion in the Marxist critique makes it apparent that above all two large areas have been omitted:

1 Weber's economic sociology in the narrower sense, to which large sections of *Economy and Society* are devoted, goes almost unmentioned. The same applies to Weber's empirical, or methodological research, enquiries into the situation of agricultural and industrial workers.
2 Only small sections of Weber's analyses in the field of political sociology have been covered.

To be sure it is idle speculation at this stage to ask why precisely these, no doubt very important, parts of Weber's work have largely escaped the attention of Marxist research. The crucial reason perhaps is that Marxists assumed that these fields had long formed the centre of interest in the Marxist social sciences, that they were therefore already comprehensively and exhaustively researched and that extra-Marxist endeavours were least in need of consideration. In fact there are hardly any Weberian fields of research whose subject matter more closely approximates the traditional research emphases of the materialist theoretical tradition. But this does not imply that they are therefore uninteresting for the present discussion of Marxism. On the contrary, that the obverse may be true is indicated by several general references.

The significance for materialist theory of the Weberian sociology of economic action and economic orders is that it represents an attempt to apprehend the economic sphere in concept and theory as a sphere of social action of a specific type. From the Marxist perspective a critical treatment of this attempt would in the first place have to clarify to what extent it corresponds with the intention of materialist theory to apprehend and explain 'material' human activity as a historical-social factor. For example, could we employ Weber's conceptual-theoretical analyses to examine the economic process described by Marx in *Capital* from its sociological aspect – or does that 'anatomy of bourgeois society', at least implicitly, contain a sociological perspective of its own? Does the difference reside in that Marx provides an analysis of the 'objective', real structure and laws, whereas Weber limits himself to the subjective or appearance aspect of events – or does this distinction amount to a 'naturalistic' or 'economist' misunderstanding of Marxian theory? Does the decisive characteristic of a materialist theory of economic processes reside in that it considers the constitutive meaning of factors which are not first and foremost 'constituted' through social action (and thus far called 'material') – or does each adherence to a simple extra-social fact contradict the radical social science orientation of the political economy founded by Marx?

These questions are the subject of great controversy in internal Marxist debates, and it is completely out of the question to give adequate attention to them here. The sole aim is to make clear that it is an unresolved problem of the Marxist tradition of thought as to whether material social practice possesses a fundamental dimension that cannot in principle be described by way of genuine social science concepts. Marxist theorists see such a dimension in, for example, concrete nature as such and in concrete productive forces (whose functioning is also subject to natural laws in the narrower sense), or else in that 'second nature' produced by the 'alienation' of human activity. (The differing apprehensions of 'materiality' or 'concreteness' has already been pointed out above.)

It is apparent that detailed clarification of this point is required in order to decide whether a fundamental difference to Weber's sociological perspective is indicated here. This perspective is defined by the assumption 'that all "economic" processes and objects are characterised as such entirely by the *meaning* they have for human action in such roles as ends, means, obstacles, and by-products' (*ES*, 64).[81] In Chapter 4, with references to several Marxian statements on the social importance of 'economic categories', it was surmised that Weber's basic outlook of social action does not constitute a contrast to the knowledge-directing interest of the Marxian political economy. Moreover it was assumed that, despite a logically comparable basic outlook of this kind, it is possible that the directions and levels of conceptual-theoretical abstraction diverge significantly.

This opinion is obviously not shared by Bader *et al.* in the one and only Marxist work devoted to a portrayal of Weber's 'fundamental sociological concepts' of economic action. These authors maintain that Weber, by operating with the background of a 'subjectivist' theory of value could neither adequately apprehend nor explain conceptually the objective (structural) economic realities and determinants particularly of the capitalist mode of production (e.g. value, commodities, money, capital, market etc.) (Bader *et al.*, 1976, 193 ff.).[82] To examine this in more detail should prove a rewarding task in future analyses.[83]

In this context Weber's studies on the situation of agricultural and industrial workers should be of interest in so far as they are marked by their heavy emphasis on 'material' realities and factors in the narrower sense (on the one hand, economic situations, interests and conflicts of interest, and, on the other, material and psychological determinants of working conditions). Even if the different timing and contexts of origination of these works were taken into consideration, it would still be possible to advance and examine the hypothesis that the 'naturalism', or the shortcomings in social science terms, of those works represents merely the obverse of Weber's decidedly sociological perspective on his conceptual-theoretical definitions in *Economy and Society*.

Marxist theorists seem to find Weber's political sociology even less amenable to critical treatment than his economic sociology. The central problem may be that Weber attributed much greater autonomy and independent inner dynamic to political relations and processes than seems possible within the scope of a materialist theory of the political superstructure. According to very widespread opinion it is indeed a constitutive hallmark of materialist theory to apprehend and explain political domination only as an – explicit or implicit – expression and function of powerful economic and class interests. This opinion further suggests that any divorce of the political sphere from the material situations and conflicts of interest is itself an element of that ideology by means of which bourgeois class domination creates the illusion of a 'general will', particularly in advanced and already precarious capitalist conditions.

The theoretical Marxist discussion centring on the materialist theory of the state has been most passionate in recent years and at present constitutes probably the most dominant part-area of internal Marxist argument. The revitalisation of the problem is obviously motivated above all by the dual experience that, on the one hand, the capacity for survival of capitalist bourgeois systems is interrelated with progressive expansion and the intensification of 'state activity' and, on the other hand, the expected 'association of free producers' by no means emerged in the course of the revolutionisation of the relations of production in socialist countries. On the contrary, in comparison with the spheres of production and distribution, the political-ideological and centralist bureaucratic system has proven clearly dominant in these countries.

I cannot even attempt to deal with the extensive and complex internal Marxist debate here. Neither is there opportunity nor cause to develop Weber's political sociology, or at least his theory of the state. Instead a number of comments will be provided on the question as to wherein the distinctiveness, and perhaps also the practical importance, of the Weberian 'approach' resides, particularly with the background of this internal Marxist debate.

The distinctive framework of reference for Weber's political sociology is characterised by the fundamental issue of how legitimate authority is grounded. This is also expressed, and particularly significantly, in his definition of the state as that of a 'compulsory political association' whose 'administrative staff successfully upholds the claim to *monopoly* of the *legitimate* use of physical force in the enforcement of its order' (*ES*, 54; emphases by Weber).[84] It is striking that even on the periphery of the contemporary materialist theory of the state (in Germany, particularly that of Offe and Habermas) the problem of the assumed validity of legitimate state action (in late capitalism) has been receiving increasing attention. This shift in perspective is, on the one hand, motivated by the practical knowledge that the contemporary 'bourgeois' state has specific and 'autochthonic' means at its disposal to secure legitimacy on the basis of its economic and socio-political functions and accomplishments. On the other hand, this change in perspective is certainly connected with the question as to what points of attack, and what character, political action aiming at fundamental change possesses both in the face of these processes and the dissolving confidence in an objective historical law ultimately emanating from material origins. To analyse political authority from the perspective of its basis of legitimacy essentially involves taking into consideration the perspective of the affected social actors bearing or tolerating this authority. This, of course, has to be done with the intention of tracing the beginnings of an irrationality in the consciousness of legitimacy and thus locating a practice able to produce change through enlightenment and the democratic process.

This research perspective seems superior to the conventional materialist explanatory model, both in respect of its power to explain the conditions prevailing in Western societies and its implicit concept of political action. This also applies to those modifications of the model which were explicitly developed to overcome definitions of the state, presented by Lenin in particular but also by Engels, as a mere 'instrument' of bourgeois class domination. Poulantzas, a representative of such endeavours, turns not only against the apprehension of 'economism' by instrumentalist state theorists, but equally against the 'statist' conception that 'apparatuses/institutions (of the state) are the original site and primary field of the constitution of power relations' (1978b, 45; cf. Poulantzas 1976, 74). Poulantzas objects to this conception by asserting that power relations 'until this day' have been carried out primarily by means of class struggles and that the state 'apparatuses and institutions' are a constitutive element of these struggles. Poulantzas discovers 'statism', in the specified sense, not only in 'social democracy and Stalinism' (1978b, 251), but also sees Max Weber as an excellent representative of this position within the realm of political theory (*ibid.*, 45).[85] This assertion will not be discussed here, since it was presented without any explanation and without reference to Weber's writings. However, it is worth pointing out that Poulantzas' own theoretical perspective is so far removed from the real processes of power (particularly from the actual interplay between 'class power' and 'state power') that Miliband called it 'structural super-determinism' (Miliband, 1970, 57) or 'structuralist abstractionism' (Miliband, 1973, 85) and was able to deprive it of any empirical explanatory power (*ibid.*, 88).

Poulantzas in turn objected to Weber's theory of the state for not offering 'any explanation of the foundation of political power' (1978a, 330). Poulantzas obviously sees the ultimate reason for this incapacity in Weber's action theory (Poulantzas terms it 'finalist' – 1969, 70) mode of explanation. He claims that it did not permit a distinction between the fundamental (economic, political, ideological) 'structures' and 'social relations (*gesellschaftliche Verhältnisse*)' and, further, it confused the conception of 'relations of production (*Produktionsverhältnisse*)' with 'social relations of production (*gesellschaftliche Produktionsverhältnisse*)' (1978a, 65). It is true that Weber resolutely opposed such a demand for objectivism and indeed opposed it precisely by means of the action theory perspective from which the central issue of the validity of legitimacy with respect to the analysis of political authority logically arises. But this is the crucial question, especially if contemporary political theory is pursued from the perspective, or in the interest, of political practice. It is appropriate and necessary to examine whether Weber's system of possible types of legitimate political authority is adequate, or whether, for example, the lack of an independent value-rational type of legitimation has to be seen as a serious shortcoming of Weber's conception, as Bader *et al.* (1976, 442 f., 446) asserted within the framework of their comparatively thorough treatment of Weber's political sociology. In this context it is also worth considering the thesis (Offe, 1974) that Weber could apprehend the legitimacy of the modern (bourgeois) state only in terms of its legality or bureaucratic rationality and that he therefore had to neglect the conflict-ridden relationship between this level of legitimation and that defined in terms of performance efficiency, on the one hand, and in terms of 'political consensus', on the other.

At this point it is of no interest whether these objections are actually, or only in this form, tenable.[86] But it is worth noting that this type of critique is not levelled at the fundamental purpose of Weber's political sociology, rather it reinforces it, even, if the case arises, against the critique of Weber's inappropriate self-limitations.[87] This critique is after all determined by the more or less explicit insight that a theory of the state whose key value relevance is defined in terms of citizens' need for orientation and action, is forced to be guided by the question regarding the (actual as well as potential) basis of legitimacy of state power in the concrete historical situation. As shown, it is precisely this insight that underlies Weber's conceptual-theoretical and empirical endeavours.

The problem of the *law* moves into the centre of interest to the same extent that the question regarding the legitimate political authority (incidentally, also, the legitimacy of ownership or 'order of property relations') takes on the crucial 'value relevance' of political sociology. The manifold forms of appearance, or levels of law respectively, essentially define as many possibilities, or levels, of a specifically *rational* mode not only of regulation but also, and above all, justification for the prevailing social conditions of inequality and authority. Looking at it from another angle, this accounts for the fact that Weber's most important analyses on the problem of social rationalisation, in general, and on the European process of rationalisation, in particular, are traceable not only in his essays on the sociology of religion, but also in those sections of his works dealing with the sociology of law. The central significance of the sociology of law for Weber's entire historical social-science work and, of course, for its overlapping and organising key idea has occasionally been acknowledged, and stressed particularly by Winckelmann (e.g. *Erläuterungsband zu Wirtschaft und Gesellschaft*, 5th edn, 107), but has been most inadequately treated in the literature on Weber. Only very recently has it received the attention and treatment it deserves (e.g. a particularly thorough and convincing treatment in Schluchter, 1979, Chapter V). After what has been said, it is entirely within the logic of things that this is happening in the course of a resumption on the issue regarding the 'universal historical', or 'social historical', perspective or purpose of Weberian thought.

More recent attempts by critical theory (Habermas, 1976b; Eder, 1976, 1977, 1981; Eder and Rödel, 1978; Döbert, 1973a, 1977) to 'reconstruct' historical materialism in a theory of development and evolution clearly and explicitly relate to this very controversial interpretation of Weber's work. As a result of this reinterpretation of historical materialism we are encountering a cumulative learning process which allows itself to be designated as a process of social evolution – under the presupposition of a 'level of learning that is instructed by developmental logic' (Habermas, *op. cit.*, 179, 204) – not only on the level of 'applied technical knowledge' and the forces of production that correspond with it, but also and above all on the level of 'moral-practical consciousness' and 'social integration' that corresponds to it. Particular levels of learning of 'moral-practical consciousness' are articulated in extensive 'conceptions of the world', but they develop their impact of 'social integration' in an elaboration of norms and institutions of law (cf. Eder, 1976, 158, 1981 and Habermas 1976, 37, 260 ff.).

At this stage I shall not examine whether this programme in evolutionary theory can in fact be carried out within the scope of a mere 'reconstruction' of historical materialism. However, there is no doubt that the problem of law has been systematically neglected in conventional materialist theories of social evolution, and this is not least due to the restriction of the aforementioned thematic treatment of political, and particularly state, power. Nor is there any doubt that this new determination of the functional interplay between the development of productive forces, domination, religion and law in the evolutionary process represents a specific challenge for a 'Weberian' position. Weber's reservations regarding an overlapping 'developmental logic' of human history emerge more clearly precisely because the approximation of his 'universal historical' perspective of rationalisation is too obvious. Critical theorists admittedly warn against the 'blurring' of logical and historical sequences (Eder, 1977, 507; cf. Habermas, 1976, 33 f.). However, their assumptions about the future stages of 'moral-practical consciousness', or 'social integration', which are bound up with this evolutionary theory, would seem to suggest that the Hegelian and Marxian idea of objective rationality or logic identifiable in the process of history continues to influence this reconstruction of historical materialism, though in a form determined by a developed awareness of the limits to empirical science knowledge.

6 Social science and political commitment

The leading premiss of the Marxist critique of Weber is that one can adequately grasp and fundamentally criticise Weber's conception of science and its practice only if one interprets it ultimately as an ideological expression of specific bourgeois class interests. According to this opinion the contents and direction of impact of the Weberian class position come to light in his private and public political standpoints. Thus it is the confrontation of Weber's methodological, theoretical and substantive argumentations with these resolute and clear standpoints that illuminates the political-ideological function and, simultaneously, the systematic narrow-mindedness and (at best) the limited scientific value of his argumentation.

The thesis that has guided the discussion thus far has repeatedly been that this method of critique is inadequate at least in so far as it does not as a rule eradicate the necessity for a thorough examination of the actual contents of the argumentation under consideration. This anti-critical observation is based on the assumption, which Weber himself firmly held, that scientific and ethical-political principles in the narrower sense are logically heterogeneous. This is the same assumption, then, that for Marxist critics represents the embodiment and expression of the 'growth of reflexity' in the political-ideological tunnel-vision of bourgeois sociology.

It is apparent that future critical discussions on Weber's work would greatly benefit if the mesh of mutually exclusive or conflicting claims to validity could be clarified a little further. Thereby one would have to proceed from the conception represented in the introduction to this book, that the fundamental scientific legitimacy of the procedure used in a critique of ideology is beyond question. Moreover it is at least a possible *modus procedendi* of scientific critique to give priority to the analysis of the critique of ideology over the substantive examination of the conception under investigation. By this means one may gain a more adequate, since context-related, understanding of the central concepts and arguments and thereby be in a position to clarify which parts of the conception under consideration are generally amenable to and worth substantive examination.

With this in mind I shall initially give a brief critical summary of the existing analyses on the class (or political-ideological) determined nature of Weber's scientific works. An examination of the most important arguments presented in this context will offer a clearer and differentiated insight into the fundamental problem. Further, a discussion on the exemplary and problematic 'case' of the scientist and *homo politicus* Max Weber will increase the reflexive degree and experiential content of such general considerations. This particularly applies when this discussion gives special attention to the arguments and experiences from the perspective of the Marxist understanding of science and politics.

The thesis that even Weber's scientific (methodological, theoretical and empirical historical) work is essentially moulded by 'class prejudice' (Cantimori, 1959, 114), or at the very least by very specific political-ideological opinions, has naturally been most resolutely advocated by Marxist critics of Weber. However, with the exception of the essays by Lukács (1962) and Marcuse (1972), which were historically undoubtedly very influential works, the most convincing attempts at grounding this thesis by means of a detailed analysis of Weber's work and political orientations stem from non-Marxist authors.[1] We are talking above all about the works by Mommsen (1974a)[2] and Giddens (1972).[3] The former primarily offers a very thorough and critical portrayal of the development Weber's political conception underwent, whereas the latter (who, like all other similar attempts, uses the material provided by Mommsen in particular) supplies a comparatively painstaking analysis of the link between Weber's political orientations and his fundamental scientific assumptions. Moreover, another work worth mentioning in this context is that of Ferber (1970) who advances the thesis of a general 'political deformation of Weber's basic theoretical conceptions', and a more recent essay by Rehberg (1979) on social action as a 'bourgeois action model'.

In the following discussions I shall refer equally both to Marxist and non-Marxist works. This procedure is not hampered by the fact that, as a rule, non-Marxist essays operate with less deterministic assumptions, particularly with regard to the link between class interests and political position.[4] For the problem that interests us here it is not of *crucial* importance to decide initially whether political value orientations in turn can or must ultimately always be explained as an expression of class interests.[5] We can more usefully discuss how necessary or productive this more extensive analysis is, once the conclusions of the following, more limited, considerations are presented. These considerations, however, already take adequate account of the Marxist critics' arguments since, in their opinion, it is class interests in their politically reflected and articulated form that exercise a direct influence on Weber's scientific work too.

At this point the arguments of the critique of ideology will not be discussed in any detail if they have already been referred to and discussed in previous chapters. In general this applies particularly to the arguments levelled at Weber's epistemological and methodological position, and in particular to the concept of the ideal type and the thesis of ethical neutrality. Additionally this also applies to the critique directed at the 'idealistic' framework of reference employed in Weber's historical analyses, particularly those concerning the conditions of development and continuity of capitalism. The arguments I referred to portray the ideological character of Weber's assumptions in the following terms. When dealing with Weber's epistemological and methodological assumptions, Marxists see the fundamental determinative feature as his denial of the possibility of a secure knowledge that encompasses the objective laws of the historical-social course of events. Even the thesis of ethical neutrality is considered only as a logical conclusion drawn from his limiting the possibilities of social science knowledge. The objective political-ideological 'meaning' of this type of epistemological argument is that the bourgeoisie, which is doomed to decline, deceives itself and others about the necessity of this historical process and particularly about the ethical-political superiority of competing class interests.

According to this interpretation the same purpose is expressed in Weber's material analyses in so far as they, at best marginally, touch on the vital (material) dynamic laws of capitalist society and limit themselves to an investigation into derivative phenomena. It is claimed that such 'theoretical idealism' not only systematically prevents the knowledge of the main determinants of the social process, but that even the self-interpretations and self-defence of capitalism would be confirmed rather than laid bare in their ideological function.

In the literature on Weber I have referred to there are, side by side with this type of sweeping and superficial argumentation, some more specified and better documented theses on the links between Weber's political position and the specific characteristics of his scientific work.

The references to the reflection of Weber's own political value orientations in his analyses in the domain of political sociology are certainly especially convincing. There is no doubt that the 'selection and construction' of the dominant objects of enquiry is here determined by Weber's political value relations as well as his practical political values. The perspective of a 'consistent as well as realistic nationalist and imperialist' (Mommsen, 1974a, 443), on the one hand, and the decided option for bourgeois freedom and democracy, on the other, form the tense political framework of reference of his purely scientific analyses too, i.e. those focussing on the description, explanation and prediction of empirical social development. Clear examples of the determinative importance of his nationalist or imperialist perspective can be found, for example, in the report on the situation of agricultural workers east of the Elbe and – at least to an important degree[6] – in those considerations dealing with the possibilities of political leadership in modern, highly bureaucratised mass democracies; whereas the liberal-democratic framework of reference is expressed particularly in his concern with the problem of progressive bureaucratisation (but also, for example, in his analyses on revolutionary events in Russia).

This kind of interrelationship between the leading goal orientations of an author, on the one hand, and the 'selection and construction' of the central objects of his social science anlyses, on the other, are by no means uncommon or problematic, but are – from Weber's perspective too – taken for granted and necessary. Thus this critical discussion will not fundamentally question the legitimacy of this causal relationship, but it will investigate whether and to what extent the political value orientations of Weber the researcher have impaired his capacity for understanding and therefore the explanatory power of his assertions. That politically determined causes have impaired Weber's scientific capacity for understanding can definitely be established. This applies although Weber the scientist undoubtedly made a conscious and determined effort to disclose the facts 'inconvenient' for his own political opinions.[7] Weber's unsuccessfulness in the practical political domain seems to have been due not least to his strongly felt need to keep his mind free from all political considerations and all *sacrificia intellectus* in his scientific analysis.[8] This need also dictated his reluctance to represent political goals clearly running counter to the position he reached with each of his scientific insights. In this context Weber's comment in the letter to the Chairman of the German Democratic Party (*Deutsche Demokratische Partei*) accompanying his resignation is telling: 'The politician should and *must* be prepared to make compromises. But I am an *intellectual* by profession. ... The intellectual may not make compromises nor conceal "absurdity".' (Cited in Mommsen, *op. cit.*, 334).[9]

Weber in fact adhered to these maxims to a considerable degree in his scientific work,[10] but this by no means rules out that politically determined restrictions can be established in such works. Both Weber's underestimation of the durability of changes introduced with the Russian Revolution of 1917 (thus Aron in Stammer (ed.), 1971, 99) and his blindness to the dangers of perversion of a 'plebiscitary leader-democracy' (Mommsen, *op. cit.*, 435), for example, would have to be explained in terms of this political factor. Even his idea that the cultural level and prestige of a nation is essentially a function of a nation's international (economic and political) power standing seems to have been determined more by his political fixation on the idea of national power and greatness than by scientific insight (which, 'in itself', was undoubtedly at his command).[11]

There would not be much force in a contrast between these, and perhaps other, politically determined limits to Weber's scientific power of judgement with the idea of pure influence-free and therefore 'objective' scientific research. In view of Weber's constant emphasis on the constitutive role of ethical-political perspectives for social science work, one can reasonably only ask the question whether the price, which always has to be paid for such an obligation, was too high in Weber's case. Even if this question cannot be answered on the basis of a precise cost-benefit analysis it is nonetheless possible to establish that a systematic and all-pervasive 'tunnel-vision' of Weber the scientist is out of the question. A comparative evaluation of the great classical social scientists should prove that Weber does not occupy a particularly bad position in this respect. For that matter one could find politically determined misjudgements with no lesser bearing than those of Weber particularly in the materialist theoretical tradition, even among those authors who are most astute, knowledgeable and highly concerned with intellectual honesty. Some central assumptions of Marx, Engels and even Lenin regarding the conditions, course and short- and medium-term results of the socialist revolution, in general, and the emergence, function and post-revolutionary fate of the bureaucracy, in particular, which have hardly been confirmed by developments to date, have obviously been much more strongly determined by political goal and value orientations than by the findings of purely scientific analyses.

It is inconceivable that knowledge-inhibiting influences of this type and origin can once and for all and in principle be removed.

However, it is equally unnecessary to accept them as concrete entities, for example, by pointing out their ideological nature and function. Rather, the progress in social science knowledge is due not least to the fact that conflict between such perspective-bound positions helps to make the narrow vision inherent in any perspective apparent as such and to eradicate it in the course of further scientific research. This fundamentally inconclusive process, however, presumes that political positions or 'standpoints' are not used to suppress new empirical insights, not even if these insights stem from researchers with different political orientations. This can only appear as an unfair or unrealistic prerequisite if it is assumed that political orientations possess or have to possess the character of highly affective or quasi-instinctive obligations or identifications. But this conception by no means corresponds with the classical Marxist notion of the nature of political commitment. To the extent that Weber's utterances point in this direction they should be criticised by appealing to corresponding inconsistencies in his thought and conduct as well as the actual requirements of democratic practice.

The concluding remarks of this section will return to this problem. Prior to that, however, the discussion on the possible influence of political-ideological factors on Weber's work will be continued, but on this occasion on another, deeper level. The question is no longer whether Weber's 'selection and construction' of concrete research objects is governed by conditions and limitations of this kind, but whether such political influence can be demonstrated in the conceptual-theoretical bases of Weber's sociology.[12] Such evidence would surely carry different qualitative weight to that of the interrelationships considered so far. It might imply that the epistemological possibilities of his sociology are logically limited or 'deformed' in a specific way. But this would above all have negative consequences for the possibility and productiveness of the above postulated conflict between Weber's conceptions and those conceptions which originate from a different political context of experience and value.

Weber's basic category of 'social action' in particular and the theoretical 'individualism' linked with it have been made the object of such a fundamental approach at interpretation. Additionally and partly in connection with it similar attempts at interpretation have been provoked by the central position occupied by the categories 'conflict' and 'selection'.

Marxist critics combine Weber's 'individualistic' perspective (and *a fortiori* the terminology of conflict and selection) with the chaos and brutality of social communication in competitive capitalist society. They therefore interpret the basic category of social action as an attempt to transform the 'plight' of actual social relations into the 'virtue' of rational conceptual construction and thus, of course, to provide existing relations with the immediate semblance of inevitability and universal validity.[13] This interpretation was countered above (Chapter 4) with a reminder of not only Weber's logical scientific grounding for the action perspective, but also referred to the goal orientation of political enlightenment that explicitly co-determined the choice of this perspective. Of *this* political background non-Marxist critics are no doubt aware, but they similarly interpret it as an indication of the systematic limits to Weber's perspective.

Mommsen is still rather careful when relating Weber's fundamental 'individualism' to the 'European humanist tradition and its esteem for the individual' (*op. cit.*, 68) and interprets only Weber's notion of charismatic political leadership as an expression of 'aristocratic individualism' (without attributing it to class) (*ibid.*, 448, 451). Rehberg, on the other hand, locates an 'action model' in the basic concept of social action itself, by means of which 'the individualism of the high bourgeoisie' or 'bourgeois aristocraticism' articulates its specific needs and possibilities of action (1979, 216 and 217 respectively). Rehberg believes that in this concept of action is expressed the self-understanding of strata which are 'prepared for action' and do not see themselves as yet fundamentally separated from 'actions of adopting methods and actions of establishing and changing the order of society' (*ibid.*, 216). But such action, in the full meaning of the term, is grasped through the category of *domination*.

> The privileged possibility of action in social structures whose order readopts and in repetition enhances all the characteristics of definition of the concept of action: leadership calculation, pre-established rules of conduct, analysing and restricting possibilities of action being executed – that precisely is 'domination' (loc. cit., 215).

Accordingly 'routinisation' and 'conflict' are the central characteristics of such action being executed by domination, and conflict therefore underlies all socialisation from this 'high bourgeois' sociological perspective (*ibid.*, 212 or 222 respectively).[14]

Ferber's thesis of the 'political deformation of Weber's fundamental theoretical concepts' is comparable to Rehberg's interpretation, even though Ferber distances his 'sociology of knowledge' analysis from all attempts to derive the deformation from Weber's 'party-political or class-linked position'. Ferber detects in Weber's definition of social action precisely those characteristics which correspond to a notion of political action centring on 'the creative freedom of the leader' (Ferber, 1970, 90) and the idea of force: namely, 'timelessness' corresponding to the 'interventionist' character of political action; the 'attachment to persons' showing the margin of freedom given to political leaders; and 'subjectivity', pointing to the enhanced need of such leaders for a consciously meaningful orientation to action (*ibid.*, 90 f. or 97 respectively).

This is not the place to describe and discuss the interpretations outlined in more detail. Even the question whether those authors base their interpretations on an adequate assessment of Weber's conceptions will not be investigated more closely. However, it is necessary to point out that Ferber derives his crucial objection to the 'usefulness of social action as a basic concept of sociology' (the objection to 'blindness to structure' (*ibid.*, 98) from his confusion of 'subjectively meaningful' with 'conscious' action (*ibid.*, 95). This misinterpretation is very common even among Marxist critics of Weber and has already been sufficiently dealt with earlier on in this book. What is also striking is that all the advocates of such interpretations not only dispense with a detailed portrayal of Weber's conceptual definitions and derivations, but they fail to make a single mention of Weber's logical scientific grounding (also considered in an earlier section) of his 'individualistic' approach to action. This latter omission is particularly grave because the implications of sociology of knowledge or critique of ideology analyses of this kind can ultimately only be settled if they are combined with logical scientific considerations. It is absolutely legitimate to tackle the, in Mommsen's words, 'strategy of suppressing Max Weber's sociological work in the face of possible political critique' (Mommsen, *op. cit.*, 446).[15] It is equally permissible to attempt to demonstrate that not only particular thematic preferences, but also the fundamental conceptual-theoretical orientations of Weber the sociologist, are interrelated with time- and class-linked political conceptions which are no longer acceptable today. At any rate the question is what in principle can and cannot be demonstrated this way. To resolve this question one needs to assume that such interpretations gained a much higher degree of plausibility than those of the first approaches to the problem at issue.[16] Is it possible *solely* on the basis of such evidence in contemporary sociology to settle the question whether 'social action' is still a 'useful' basic sociological concept today (Ferber, *op. cit.*, 98), or what the possibilities and limits of application of 'Weber's abstract and methodological concepts' (Rehberg, *op. cit.*, 223) are? The authors cited seem to hold this opinion: in their view the changed 'social positions' of the strata producing and using sociological knowledge (Rehberg), or the changed political relations and orientations (Ferber), fundamentally challenge the usefulness of the categorial apparatus of Weber's sociology.

Conclusions of this kind would appear to be rash, if not also questionable in logic. It may well be possible that the usefulness of social science concepts arising from the intellectual incorporation of a concrete and committed historical practice is linked to the continuity of existential conditions. But the question is not whether basic sociological categories, like Max Weber's, are appropriate both to 'conceptualise' and transcend a specific historical-social and political situation. Marx formulated the possibility of conceiving such an interrelationship in that he established that specific elementary social processes or facts (for Marx, especially, 'work, pure and simple' or 'abstract work') made their appearance as such and were conceptually conceivable only under highly developed conditions. Even if one does not wish to get involved in this specific Marxian conception (for example, because of its implications for universal history or the philosophy of history) one should not see an irreconcilable contradiction in, on the one hand, the limitation to time and place of the 'invention' of specific basic social science concepts, and, on the other, the claimed universal significance and applicability of these concepts. Presumably this applies to almost all basic concepts of the different theoretical perspectives (for example: *'Gesellschaft'* and *'Gemeinschaft'*, 'mechanical and organic solidarity', 'class', 'material relations', 'alienation', 'role' and so on), that they were developed in the context of a specific, and also essentially determined by practical interest, explanation of specific socio-political relations and processes. Their developmental and organising power is nonetheless not limited to the specific 'object' (e.g. capitalist society) nor the specific interest perspective (e.g. the elimination of alienation), nor even the specific historical subject/object constellation. There seem to be two interrelated reasons for this. On the one hand, the social conditions producing the need for a radical social science enlightenment were in fact progressively reduced to elementary mechanisms of social interaction stripping away all specific cultural superstructures and mediations. But, on the other hand, this actual background of experience corresponds to the profession-specific interest of the founding fathers of sociology in comprehending social reality as such. The specific practical political orientations, which further determined their scientific efforts, did not limit this striving for radical knowledge, but on the contrary actively promoted it. On the other hand, the practical political determination of the perspective must have involved each categorial apparatus being similarly characterised by a specific perspective and representing various fundamental possibilities of intellectually categorising the social world – with their respective typical strengths and weaknesses. In this respect the most important distinction seems to be that between an 'individualistic' and a 'holistic', or 'collectivistic', perspective – as it is employed in all history of sociological dogma for the purposes of systematisation. Even the further-reaching differentiation within these two basic perspectives should to a large part be understandable and explainable with this background in mind.

But the crucial point here is that there is no arbitrary number of such possibilities of categorisation. After referring to the 'humanistic' framework of reference of Weber's individualism, Mommsen notes that the selection of an utterly different, for example, collectivist, 'basic conception' would 'formally speaking' have been just as conceivable (*op. cit.*, 65). This remark is misleading to the extent that it gives the impression that fundamental theoretical options are purely a function of ethical-political value premises, or corresponding historical contexts of action. But as a matter of fact there are internal scientific criteria which set definite 'formal' limits to the arbitrariness of the decision and probably even permit the construction of a system of possibilities which can be justified on good grounds. These criteria are not only brought into play with hindsight and for the purpose of rationalisation, rather they are explicitly declared, examined and considered in all important attempts at laying a foundation.

In the light of the above reflections on the sociology of knowledge and critique of ideology theses relating to Weber's basic conceptual-theoretical perspective, the following preliminary result emerges: the evidence that sociological categories can be assigned to a specific historical-political context of discovery and usage does not cancel out the possibility of making use of these categories, as 'basic concepts', even outside this context. It can be shown that historical-political 'contingency' and the universal importance of such concepts *need not be* mutually exclusive. This decision cannot be made in the concrete situation without first examining the immanent scientific (logical scientific) arguments of proof which were presented, or had to be considered by today's standards, by the representatives of the relevant basic perspective. Such considerations on Weber's 'action theory' perspective have already been dealt with in an earlier section of this book (Chapter 4). They revealed that there are good immanent scientific grounds for sociology to continue to base its considerations on Weber's basic approach. At the same time, of course, one must bear in mind the precise scientific-logical status of this basic perspective. We are not dealing with an empirically substantive theory here, but with the structural preconditions for its development. Similarly neither does it rule out that the sociological construction of concept and theory operates on a level of abstraction that is utterly remote from the perspective of real social action.

However, according to these considerations there are not only good scientific-logical, but perhaps also some good political, grounds for not discarding the action perspective as historically outdated. The above critical arguments against the Weberian approach are thus not problematic purely in terms of their epistemological conclusions, but they are perhaps also far too one-sided regarding the political-ideological classification of this approach. Within the context of earlier considerations the thesis has already been formulated that the action perspective seems indeed to correspond well to a decidedly democratic ethical-political framework of reference. It is therefore all the more surprising that critics like Mommsen, Ferber and, less explicitly, Rehberg (but, of course, all Marxist critics) detect a pronounced anti-democratic 'bias' in Weber's basic concept of social action. This appraisal is due to the fact that the critics, by proceeding from Weber's personal political action ideal, only thematise social action in its unique and, as it were, 'pathetic' form – that is to say, in a form in which action is in fact, or allegedly, realised by the much called-upon 'great individuals'. In this context they are led by the assumption that the constitutive characteristics of the allegedly universal Weberian concept of action can be gathered, or derived, from this very specific possibility of action. But, in fact, it does not seem to be this 'imperious' action, which sets and carries through its own goals, that provides the value-laden framework of reference for Weberian conceptual construction. This framework of reference, on the contrary, is defined by the much more elementary *possibililty* of human action to develop a conscious (or self-assertive) and therefore productive and critical relation to the meaningful relationships that determine it. The concept of meaningful social action is conceived in terms of the possibility (rather than necessity) of consciousness and a conscious approach to the historically determinative bases of social conduct.[17] Obviously this also contains political 'value relevance'. But this value relevance can be linked much more easily to the need for comprehending democratic courses of action in general than to the wish to assign exemplary, or even ideal, importance to the dominant power-related action by extraordinary individuals.

In Weber's definition of social action both intersubjective orientations and regulations of action are conceived in terms of their meaningfulness or 'communicability', and therefore in terms of their possible 'rationality'. By 'rationality' Weber understands both the subjective *capacity* for consciousness and conscious control as well as the intersubjective 'communicability' and, at a higher level, the capacity for consensus on the determinative grounds of action (cf. concerning this, Weiss, 1981a). The systematic clarification of the chances of realisation of rationality thus apprehended – which should not, of course, be confused with substantive 'rationality' – is a specific prerequisite for all 'democratically' oriented politics. The same applies to the 'individualism' of Weberian sociology, which is in this sense intimately connected with the problem of rationality. This 'individualism', as noted, precludes neither the employment of the structural or systemic concepts as theoretical abstractions, nor has it anything to do with the 'counter-factual' assumption that the chances for individuals' self-determined conduct (and therefore the chances to realise 'democracy') have to improve continuously in the historical process. Rather, its practical political meaning resides in adhering, in the face of all the necessity for an abstract construction of concept and theory and all the 'depersonalising' tendencies of the social process, to the insight that the reality of society consists of the meaningful interrelationship of individual actors. A conception of political practice building on 'enlightenment' and rational conviction has to take account of this reality in a much more fundamental and decisive manner than all the competing notions of political influence and control. As noted earlier, here too an important reason for the original individualism of Marxian social science seems to reside.

The observation by the cited critics that Weber personally tended towards a pathetic, power-oriented and 'interventionist' understanding of political action obviously can easily be illustrated. It is also true that such action can adequately be described with Weber's own sociological concepts. The obverse conclusion of a political 'deformation' of Weber's categorial apparatus, however, is neither logically convincing nor factually plausible.[18] As a matter of fact it seems to be less the basic sociological concepts in the narrower sense, but rather the more fundamental, as it were, 'ideological' (*weltanschaulichen*) categories of 'conflict' (*Kampf*)[19] and 'selection', on the one hand, and the concepts of 'charisma' and 'force' (*Gewalt*) from his political sociology, on the other, that can be related to Weber's own perception and evaluation of specific requirements of political action. If we want to locate more than the (conscious) considerations of specific, politically important, possibilities of action in Weber's basic sociological concept of social action, and attribute to him a specific political *tendency*, then according to the above, it is a tendency that more likely contradicts, rather than corresponds with, Weber's personal ideal of action. Aron's thesis[20] that Weber had 'betrayed himself' with his political conceptions (namely, betrayed his fundamental scientific beliefs) could on this basis be corroborated rather than contradicted.

But at the same time it is worth observing that this interpretation does not seem reconcilable with Weber's own ideas of a strict divorce between the 'political' and 'economic' spheres. The fact that a particular political idea of order is not only considered a possibility in the basic sociological conceptualisation, but 'built into it' as a tendency, does not seem to correspond with Weber's ideas any more than the view that political standpoints could 'betray' scientific conceptions.

These latter comments already indicate that in the defence of Weber's scientific conceptions against specific political objections, or the critique of ideology, one would perhaps have to discard some of Weber's fundamental meta-scientific assumptions on the relationship between political and scientific opinions. In the following and concluding reflections an attempt will be made to draw some fundamental conclusions from the debate on the proposed programme and reality of this relationship in Max Weber. In this instance I will have to appeal more strongly to the explicit arguments presented by Marxist authors which are throughout universal and logical in nature.

The desirable lucidity and concentration of the following considerations is best served if the outcomes of the above discussions are once again summarised by thesis:

1 The thesis of ethical neutrality presented by Weber (and others) in the form referred to above (Chapter 3, Section 2) has to be seen for the time being as irrefutable. There are no logically convincing derivative relationships between empirical statements, on the one hand, and 'ought' tenets (e.g. ethical-political) on either side.
2 Very important interconnections and causal relationships between the logically separate spheres nonetheless exist on both sides:
2.1 Not only immanent scientific, but also ethical-political value orientations, or (at least) hypothetical value relevances, possess constitutive importance for the 'selection and construction' of concrete research objects, or the *constant* perspectivistic approximation to historical-social problems. Ethical-political 'value perspectives' or interests that move the researcher will always be expressed in social science enquiries, although more or less latent or mediated. This basically applies even to the most general conceptual-theoretical tools of which the researcher makes use. Of

135

course, causal relationships are as a rule very indirect. Immanent scientific aspects obviously also gain increasing importance with an increasing level of abstraction. A clear correlation, as can frequently be demonstrated on the level of relative historical categories, is therefore generally no longer assertable on the level of the highly generalised conceptual-theoretical orientation.

2.2 Ethical-political value orientations are faced with a multitude of methods of scientific critique. These methods cannot, of course, directly relate to the claim of the validity of value perspectives. However, logical and hermeneutic enquiries into the bases of validity, latent dimensions of meaning and meaningful consistency and so on, on the one hand, and empirical enquiries in the narrower sense into the actual conditions of origination, validity and realisation of value orientations (including the undesirable side-effects of such realisation), on the other, represent the tools of 'critical examination' which may greatly influence the acceptance, refutation or modification of ethical-political value orientations. This influence is, of course, linked to presuppositions concerning the nature of ethical-political 'positions' and will be thematised further below.

3 These observations in principle portray nothing but a review of Weber's conceptions. If looked at more closely, however, both 2.1 and 2.2 contain implications that render very problematic a further conception of Weber's, i.e. that ethical-political and scientific standpoints need to be strictly divorced both in material and institutional terms. As noted above, this demand is by no means an inevitable consequence of the thesis of ethical neutrality. Beyond that this stands in clear contrast to Weber's view on the necessary reciprocal interplay between cognitive and value-oriented (in this case, ethical-political) elements in the process of social science knowledge.

In Chapter 3, Section 2 I attempted to show that the Marxist critique has not developed a plausible alternative to the thesis of ethical neutrality in the narrower sense. The real difference between the critique and Weber's position will therefore have to relate to the observations contained in thesis 2 above and the contradiction specified under 3.

With reference to the reciprocal relationship between scientific and ethical-political orientations the superiority of the Marxist conception is seen in its dissolving the 'on the one hand this – on the other hand that' of Weberian argumentation in a dialectical unity. According to this the capacity for truth held by scientific knowledge would be a function of the 'correct' political and class position just as the correctness of this position could be demonstrated by scientific proof. But the second part of this 'dialectical' argument evidently presumes the invalidity of the thesis of ethical neutrality and is therefore untenable. However, with this being the case, the first part becomes simultaneously dubious, since there is no longer any possibility of establishing the correctness of any political position within the scope of empirical science other than through the productiveness of the research perspective it has opened up. But this latter implies that such establishment is *post festum* and can only be hypothetical. Faced with this difficulty Marxist thinking is exposed to a danger which has already been clearly demonstrated in the earlier discussion on Lukács' *History and Class Consciousness*. The impossibility of empirically demonstrating the sole rational political perspective guaranteeing true knowledge (or classifying it as such) induces Marxists to construe this perspective as the 'objective possibility' of a fictitious subject and then to assign this fictitious subject a representative in the real political world, namely the party. This solution is not only afflicted with serious logical flaws and unfounded presuppositions, but neither has it stood the test of political practice. The assumption that the party or its leadership is capable and entitled to determine not only the political goals, but at one and the same time the divine road to true knowledge, has been discredited so clearly and absolutely by historical experience that there are good reasons to support its abandonment.

Evidently Marxist theorists underestimate especially the possibility of a politically oriented scientific practice and scientific critique that remains *after the dispensation with* such assumptions. Presumably the critical treatment of Weber's work encourages this kind of scepticism because Weber in principle referred to this possibility, but practised it himself only in part (which in turn is connected with *his* underestimation of the possible rationality of political value orientations). The attempts, illustrated and discussed above, to subject Weber's sociology to a politically oriented critique may well demonstrate the necessity and fruitfulness of such methods, even if they do not fulfil the claims linked with them in the concrete case.

In contrast to the Weberian conceptions dealt with so far, Weber's assertion that ethical-political value orientations have no legitimate place within the material and institutional limits of science seems logically untenable. This Weberian assertion, or demand, underlies a series of further assumptions beyond the thesis of ethical neutrality, which by no means share the persuasive power carried by this particular thesis. This applies particularly to the dual assumption that contemporary universities should exclusively serve the promotion and mediation of rational knowledge *and* that the only contemporary form of rationality is represented by modern science, or to be more precise (provided that it concerns knowledge relating to the real world), by modern empirical science. Since evaluations cannot in fact be verified on the basis of this science they belong to *the* domain of the human construction of meaning, in which there are no methods of rational persuasion but, logically speaking, just the eternal 'conflict' between personal 'ultimate positions towards life' (Weber, *FMW*, 143).

Weber's argumentation is thus neither convincing nor tenable even if one not only accepts the thesis of ethical neutrality, but also Weber's demand that the primary and governing goal of academic institutions must be to 'produce' and impart intersubjectively valid, or examinable, knowledge. If, as Weber assumes, all social science research in particular is determinatively based not only on hypothetical value relevance but, as a general rule, also on practical value orientations, and if far-reaching consequences ensue from social science research for the justifiability and enforceability of political goals or interests – as Weber also suggests, although not as plainly – then there is every reason to believe that even within scientific discourse all biased value perspectives should be disclosed and discussed. This does not have to entail the intermingling of normative and empirical questions in a logically inadmissible fashion, nor the repression of facticity and 'intellectual honesty' of scientific discourse about 'conflict', emotionality, demagogy and manipulative modes of argumentation.

The first danger stressed, above all, by Weber would be much greater, and indeed much more difficult to discern, if the value positions and their ranking and function within each research process were not disclosed and explained. But the second danger, the loss of rationality threatening internal scientific communication, is not dependent on a thematisation of normative-political conceptions as such, but on the way in which these conceptions are advocated. In this respect one can expect that in a material and institutional context, which is governed by specific requirements of rationality, the treatment of evaluative questions has to follow the rational criteria of facticity, clarity and truthfulness – at any rate to a degree impossible outside this context, such as in the field of the political 'power struggle'. In order to confirm that such a tendency is given with the scientific context of communication, one would also have to substitute Weber's postulate 'Politics is out of place in the lecture-room' with the explicit demand that even the thematisation and discussion of political standpoints be bound by the above type of rational criteria (which, of course, needs further specification). There are in general two reasons why Weber does not consider this possibility, or at least not systematically. The first, rather accidental, reason is that Weber saw the academic relationship between lecturer and student as characterised by a strong asymmetry and he feared that this asymmetry, which was unavoidable within the framework of purely scientific enquiries, would lead to the development of a leader-follower relationship on the political level, which was by no means justifiable in terms of the nature and authority of the professoriat (Weber, *FMW*, 146 and 149). Not only the change in academic authority relations, but also the now widespread insight that scientific and political authority are heterogeneous in nature and by no means have to coincide should have largely abated this fear since then.

Weber's second and crucial reason is that ultimately there is in principle nothing but an 'irreconcilable conflict' between the different 'value spheres' (*ibid.*, 147 f.) on questions of ethical-political constructions of meaning or value orientations, and therefore efforts towards rational communication in the field are 'meaningless' to begin with. This argument is based on his identifying 'science' with rationality (or better, non-science with irrationality) which is hardly convincing today. Besides, it is by no means reconcilable with the definition and application of the category of rationality within the framework of the whole Weberian sociology.

No doubt Weber conceded several crucially important indications to the possibilities of a rational *substantive* discussion on ethical-political standpoints. He assigns to these methods (discussion and analysis of principles), belonging to the scientific context and allocated to the faculty of philosophy, the unenviable task to help the individual to 'give himself an account of the ultimate meaning of his own conduct' (*ibid.*, 152). But on account of his basic perspective Weber held back from systematically clarifying the implications of these considerations.[21] This may be largely due to Weber's conception, corresponding to that basic perspective, that political action does not have to be based on the persuasive power of rational argumentation, but rather on the 'weapons' used as 'swords against the enemies' (*ibid.*, 145; cf. also Giddens, *op. cit.*, 46).[22]

A productive way of overcoming Weber's conceptions could start with his understanding of politics, which in turn was by no means derived solely from scientific insight – with due consideration for relevant political experiences – but very essentially from normative orientations. A firm orientation to an enlightening and democratic idea of politics, which not only affects the goals but also the methods of political action, must lead to a very detailed examination of the possibilities and limits to a rational treatment of political-normative questions.[23] One result could be, for example, that even when we are dealing with, irreconcilable (in logical or actual fact), and thus far 'ultimate' value orientations, there is absolutely no need to speak of equal positions in every respect. Even in this case the quality, relative importance and distribution of 'good reasons' can greatly vary. Moreover the fact that two value positions are actually irreconcilable does not even rule out the possibility that both arguments have to show they also carry intellectual persuasive power. (This is frequently the case even within empirical science.) If we nonetheless talk of an absence of rationality in this context, we evidently understand by rationality an absolute and substantial rationality, which permits in each case only *one* possibility – generally or at least for the specific historical situation – to characterise the only valid possibility. It may be that Weber too could only conceive of practical rationality in this way and therefore had to arrive at his thesis of irrationality once his faith in such rational authority was shaken.

Marxist critics have been particularly firm in their rejection of Weber's postulate of a material and institutional divorce between 'science' and 'politics'. However, they have not shown the same determination to develop an intellectually persuasive alternative to this, in fact dubious, postulate. Even if Weber's thesis of ethical neutrality was accepted, this did not as a rule lead them to examine the existing formulae of political science and the politically partisan science nor to a search for more solid proofs of their own position. Above all they adhered and still adhere to the idea of a law determining the entire course of history, which is to be interpreted as both the 'logic' of history and – in practical respects – historical 'reason'. They ignore the fact that the Hegelian idea of a 'logic' operating in real history and therefore binding upon each rational practice cannot be 'carried over' into a decidedly empirical approach to history. Rather, this idea is for better or for worse linked to absolute idealism. Had the inevitable conclusions been drawn from an understanding of this situation, it would have been impossible in the first place to assert of any real historical practice (or its goal orientation) that it was true *per se* or rational in the ethical-political sense. That this conclusion was not drawn as a rule is obviously connected with Marxist critics' fear that they would thus lose every possibility of a rational grounding of their own political goal orientations. But this fear in fact *confirms* the truth of Weber's conception described above, namely that there can be no rationality outside the limits of modern science and, more particularly, that it had become impossible to proceed rationally in the grounding and defence of ethical-political goals and norms.

The resulting aporia leads some Marxist authors to make political partisanship an issue of spontaneous and unconditional 'solidarity' with goals, persons and groups, or with a 'standpoint' capable of reflection and explanation.[24] The fetishisation and mystification of these 'standpoints' can thus assume degrees that may in fact only be traced in the sphere of conscious anti-enlightenment 'decisionism'. The full implications of a thus understood political standpoint for a 'partisan' social science in this sense are documented by historical experience and need not be elaborated any further in this book.

A promising path to overcome Weber's 'irrationalism' from a Marxist perspective can only be seen as corresponding to the 'distinctive logic of distinctive objects' (Marx) in the domain of ethical-political goal orientations. According to the opinion expressed here this involves two things.

Firstly, it is necessary to discard the convertible claim that the truth and inevitability of socialism as an idea of political order can be demonstrated solely by way of (empirical) science. Instead it should be shown which (value-)rational considerations of an ethical-political nature support this idea of order. The persuasive power of this argumentation would certainly increase if it was accompanied by a meta-ethical reflection on the 'conditions for the possibility' of a rational treatment of normative-ethical questions. For this purpose I cannot see why Marxist theorists should not examine, more seriously than hitherto, the pertinent endeavours by, in particular, Habermas.

Secondly, with reference to the obverse, causal relationship, it should be clarified in a more systematic and rational fashion than is common what is meant by the socialist partisanship of the social sciences or how it is generally possible to determine the influence of political positions on scientific orientations from the perspective of this political option. In this respect it would be particularly worth considering whether there is in fact a convincing logical relationship between the/a political option for the socialist idea of order, on the one hand, and the adoption of historical materialism as a social science concept, on the other. After all the thesis that these can easily be divorced has been advocated not only by Weber[25] but – just as long ago – by several Marxist philosophers and social scientists.

Notes

1 Introduction: the origins, purposes and outline of the discussion

1 I am referring to the following papers (all in Russian):
   (a) 'Max Weber's Sociological Enquiries into The City' in *PZM*, 1923, No. 6, 219–50.
   (b) 'A New Attempt at Constructing a Systematic History of the Economy' (relating to Max Weber, *General Economic History*), in *Archiv Marksa i Engel'sa* (Marx-Engels-Archive), 1924, 425–35.
   (c) 'Max Weber's "Empirical Sociology" and the Logic of the Historical Sciences', in *PZM*, 1927, Nos 9 and 12, 113–49 and 112–37.
   The papers (a) and (c) are reprinted in A. Neusychin, *Problems of European Feudalism. Selected Works*, Moscow, 1974 (in Russian). Concerning the biography and work of Neusychin (1895–1969) cf. A. I. Danilov, 'A. I. Neusychin – Historian, Medievalist, Intellectual and Teacher', (in Russian) in *Srednie Veka* (The Middle Ages) 32/1969, 5–12 (with bibliography); L. T. Milskaja, 'Problems etc.', 7–32; 'In Memory', in *Zeitschrift für Geschichtswissenschaft*, 1970, No. 3, 419; 'Neusychin, Aleksandr Iosefoviče, in *BSE*, 3rd edn, Moscow, 1970, ff., 4 vols, Col. 1566.
2 Among the critics of Weber this is also noted by Fojtik (1962, 12). He nonetheless speaks of a contemporary 'Weberianism' (*Veberianstvo*; 4, 12 ff.), as does, for example, Kvesko (1974, 4). This 'Weberianism' to which Fojtik allocates theorists such as Mannheim, Mills, Aron and Jaspers is – vaguely enough – characterised by the following: (a) the assertion of the impossibility of knowing the substantial laws of social life; (b) general epistemological and ethical 'relativism and subjectivism' (18 f.).
3 Weber's relationship with Marx and Marxism has already been dealt with very thoroughly in several works. Cf., in particular, Roth, 1968, 1971, 1977; Mommsen, 1974; Giddens, 1973a; Mayer, 1974; Zander, 1978. On Weber's view of socialism and its scope for development,

see also the critical discussion in Lenhardt, 1980 as well as Cacciari, 1979 and Bedeschi, 1979.
4 Jaeggi provides a similar delimitation of 'orthodoxy' in the non-polemical sense of the term (Jaeggi and Honneth (eds), 1977, 145).
5 Even a very limited familiarity with the extensive Polish literature on Weber proves that it cannot be adequately considered under any circumstances within the framework of the present work. Nonetheless I very much regret that the essays by S. Kozyr-Kowalski, L. Nowak, J. Kmita and J. Szczepanski in particular are either only partially or not at all available to me.
6 Of course there is also a drawback with regard to this that cannot be ignored: the dissertations I referred to were as a rule only available in summaries ('self-survey') supplied by the candidates for the oral defence of their thesis. One would have presumed that these 'self-surveys' are systematically distorted, particularly on questions of political-ideological interest. The extent of this distortion can only be roughly estimated.

2 The political and ideological 'ban'

1 Cf. in this context Engels's complaint about 'how few of the young literary men who fasten themselves onto the Party give themselves the trouble to study economics, the history of economics, the history of trade, of industry, of agriculture, of the formations of society' (Letter to C. Schmidt of 5 August 1890, in Karl Marx and Friedrich Engels, *Selected Correspondence*, 1956b, 497). Here also belongs Marx's comment cited by Engels (*ibid.*, 496) about certain French 'Marxists': 'All I know is that I am not a Marxist.' Finally I draw attention to Marx's speech about 'free scientific inquiry', as well as his comment: 'Every opinion based on scientific criticism I welcome' (Preface to the 1st German edn of *Capital: A Critique of Political Economy*, 1977a, Vol. I, 21, Lawrence & Wishart).
2 Cf., for example, the comments about the dialectical character of the method employed in *Capital*, in the Afterword to the 2nd German edn: this includes 'in its comprehension and affirmative recognition of the existing state of things, at the same time also, the recognition of the negation of that state, of its inevitable breaking-up'; it is 'in its essence critical and revolutionary' (Karl Marx, *Capital*, *ibid.*, 29).
3 We shall not therefore abide by the principle of interpretation constructed by Marcuse (1971, 16) in his analysis of Soviet Marxism (indeed Marcuse failed to abide by it consistently himself). This principle states that in the case of Soviet Marxism we *can by no means* question the scientific tenability of theorems, but solely their 'political intention', or political appropriateness. Although this sounds decidedly materialist, it is not compatible with the propogated claim of even the Stalinist interpretation of historical materialism. It is of doubtful advantage that by means of this method of interpretation (immanent critique) we can assign some truth (in terms of practical reasoning) to scientifically untenable ideologisms,

yet which are useful in power politics, or even that we can distinguish between 'false' and 'true' consciousness (*ibid.*, 74 ff.).

4 The most prominent victims of this method were probably the Einsteinian theory of relativity, on the one hand, and the doctrine of hereditary transmission (genetics), on the other. Cf. concerning different controversies of this kind in the domain of the natural sciences: G. A. Wetter, *Philosophie und Naturwissenschaft in der Sowjetunion*, Hamburg, 1958 and Graham, 1974; concerning specifically the 'Lyssenko case' see Z. A. Medvedev, 1974 and – a critique from the Marxist viewpoint – Lecourt 1976 (with a foreword by L. Althusser, in which he comments that historical materialism should not continue to repress its own history). Cf. also the examples from the natural sciences and technology cited by S. and B. Webb (1936, Vol. 2, 1000 ff.) which were based on a critical *Pravda* article by A. I. Stetsky ('Simplification and the Simplifiers', *Pravda*, 5 June 1932).

5 What Wittfogel remarked once (1922, 70) on the pluralist position of the bourgeoisie towards the different sciences could more justifiably be applied to the attitude of the Communist Party (KPdSU) during that period: 'It wants – almost entirely – the exact natural sciences. Biology – sociology with reservations – but by no means in the modern, merely positivist, form; in the old form (because any allusion to the field is already risky) only the very unavoidable existential minimum.'

6 Cf., for example, the comments on the two initial All-Union Conferences on Planning Scientific Research (1931 and 1933), in Webb and Webb, 1936, Vol. 2, 957.

7 German edition, Vol. I, 1925–26, 6. Here the necessity for a 'scientific monism' is based on the needs of the 'growing socialist economy', not those of science or epistemology.

8 V. I. Lenin, *Karl Marx and His Teachings*, 1973, 24 and 7 (Moscow: Progress Publishers). Cf. the following assertion from 'Materialism and Empirio-Criticism': 'By following the *path* of Marxian theory we shall draw closer and closer to objective truth (without ever exhausting it); but by following *any other path* we shall arrive at nothing but confusion and lies' (*Works*, Vol. 14, 143). Finally, see the speech about 'Marxist philosophy, which is cast from a single piece of steel', from which one cannot 'eliminate one basic premise, one essential part, without falling a prey to bourgeois-reactionary falsehood' (*ibid.*, 326).

As a more recent essay in which non-Marxist sociology is confronted with the alternative of final disintegration or unification in the sense of Marxist orthodoxy, cf. Krysmanski and Marwedel (eds) 1975 (particularly Part I).

9 Cf. material and references from the early post-revolutionary years in Webb and Webb, 1936, Vol. 2, 948 ff. Even the first 'programme thesis' of the Sejatel 'social democratic' opposition group in the Soviet Union seems to belong to this tradition. It runs: 'Scientific-democratic management of society, scientific reorganisation of the authority mechanism' (reprinted in Lewytzkyj, 1972, 147).

10 Hofmann (1970, 229) also sees the beginning of the 'intellectual contraction of "Marxist-Leninism' in the Soviet Union and beyond that already in the resolutions of the Tenth Party Congress (1921) against splinter-group formation within the Soviet Communist Party (KPdSU). Hofmann explains these resolutions in turn by emergency measures and 'party dictatorship' (instead of the Soviet system) required by the economic misery together with the raised expectations amongst particularly the proletarian population following the revolution. The exacerbated economic difficulties coupled with the rigour and economic-technological ambitions of the rulers, in Hofmann's view, accordingly led to the 'manipulative-pragmatic character of all approaches in theoretical thinking' towards the end of the 1920s, and to the doctrine of the 'alleged "monolithic" character of communism' (*ibid.*, 245) derived from Stalin's doctrine of the 'monolithic character of the Party'.

11 'The rational self-enlightenment of the system by means of the social sciences became necessary under the changed economic and political circumstances.' (Kiss, 1971, 113.)

12 Non-Marxist sociology, which in the early years after the revolution was centred at Petersburg University, rapidly lost its chances of development from 1922–3 onwards (Sorokin, 1926, 463 f.; Weinberg 1974, 2 ff.). For the current assessment of the Petersburg episode from a Soviet point of view, cf. Čagin, 1971, Chapters I and III and Klušin, 1964. Weber's *The City* and *General Economic History* were also published in Russian by Petersburg scientists in 1923.

13 'It would be paying lip service to a fatal historical determinism if we sought to evaluate the excessive development of power under Stalinism as the inevitable result of circumstances.' (Hofmann, 1968, 39.)

14 Schulze (1977) in this sense refers, for example, to the conflict-prone relationship between the two camps within the ruling intelligentsia: the 'agent of legitimation' and the 'agent of production'.

15 Concerning this, see, for example, Lenin's programmatic remarks in Volume I of *Unter dem Banner des Marxismus* (*PZM* 1/1922, No. 3; German edn: 1/1925–6, 9–20).

16 In the middle and at the end of the 1920s Roj Medvedev (1973, 43) justifiably writes about the 'struggle between tendencies': 'The quarrel within the party was bitter from the first day, and each side tried to make the other appear in the worst possible light. Frequently opponents' statements were distorted beyond recognition and repeated, while misunderstandings were magnified beyond all measure. Both sides subscribed to the grossest slanders.'

17 See, for example, the 'Last words of the accused Bukharin' on his confession 'that the naked logic of the struggle has not pushed us, the counter-revolutionary conspirators, into this foul illegality . . . this naked logic of the struggle was accompanied by a distortion of ideas, a distortion of psychology, a distortion of ourselves, a distortion of humanity' (in Bukharin and Deborin, 1974, 277).

At this point we should also refer to Lukács's *Selbstkritik* (1934) in which he confesses to a 'determined ideological intransigence and uncompromising integrity towards all divergence from Marxist-Leninism'.

18 See, particularly, 'Was heisst Christlich-Sozial? Zu F. Naumanns Gesammelten Aufsätzen', *Christliche Welt* 8/1894, Cols. 476 and 477. Further, Weber's remark in *Gesammlte Politische Schriften*, 26, as well as Marianne Weber, *Max Weber. Ein Lebensbild*, Tübingen, 1926, 521 and 523. The reference to 'a certain economic involvement with the ruling class' (thus Korf, 1971, 32 f. – with respect to Weber's income being derived from interest payments on capital) in Weber's case should have no more explanatory power for the class-determined tunnel vision than in the case of Marx and Engels who are well known to have been much more involved in material affairs.

19 At the same time a more detailed analysis, as it was presented by Mommsen in his book *Max Weber und die deutsche Politik 1890–1920* (2nd edn, Tübingen, 1974) in particular, does not only produce greater clarity on many points, but also some inconsistencies, which are not to be neglected. Here we should not only remind ourselves of Weber's at least temporary political rapprochement to social democracy (though not in his *Weltanschauung*) (cf. Mommsen, *op. cit.*, 179 and footnote, and Baumgarten, 1964, 607 f.), but also of the great reputation Weber enjoyed as political analyst in the post-war years, which came from far beyond the bourgeois camp. Cf. Bab, 1920 for evidence of the hopes put in Weber as a political leader as well.

20 References to Weber's work during this period can also be found in Kapeljuš, 1931 and Maschkin, 1953.

21 *BSE*, 1st edn, Moscow, 1928, Vol. 9, Cols. 129–31 (author A. Neusychin) and *BSE*, 3rd edn, 1970 ff., Vol. 17, Cols. 1031–2 (author R. P. Devjatkova). Cf. also *Great Soviet Encyclopedia* (translation of 3rd edn), New York/London, 1974, Vol. 4, 680–1.

22 Cf. the details in the bibliography. At *first* glance it is surprising that the essays by Weber, edited by non-Marxists between 1923–5 (*General Economic History*; *Agrarverhältnisse*; *The City*) are mentioned with less embarrassment than those printed in the Marxist journal *Ateist*. The translation of Chapter 1 of the *Protestant Ethic*, translated and introduced by M. I. Levina and published in 1972, leads a bibliographical shadow-existence until this day. According to personal information a complete translation by Levina in manuscript form has been submitted in the meanwhile. Besides Levina (2 f.) refers to a part-translation of the *Protestant Ethic* in Neusychin's posthumous writings whose author is unknown.

At this point we should note that the Russian translations of Weber's essays of the years 1923–5 obviously relate to the first translations of Weber's works in general. The English version of *Wirtschaftsgeschichte* (General Economic History), which Winckelmann believes to be the earliest translation, was published in 1927 (preface to the 3rd German edn, 1958, XIII).

23 This is also Kon's assessment (1964, 150), who himself emphatically

referred to Neusychin's essays (however, without more detailed consideration) and who incidentally also contributed to rendering the Marxist reception and critique of Weber factual.

24 Cf. also the references in the bibliography. The first reference to Neusychin's essays probably stems from Markarjan (1957, 28 and 29). The fact that neither Neusychin himself (who died in 1969) nor Danilov (a colleague or student of Neusychin's, a conclusion reached from his 1969 obituary and the editorship of his book of 1958) nor any other appreciation of Neusychin's work, referred to these early essays on Weber, seems to be due to tactical political considerations. Politically motivated restraint probably also explains why the two most important essays by Weber are indeed reprinted in the omnibus edition of 1974, but without any commentary, and more particularly without a reference as to why the continuation and conclusion of the second essay was no longer published.

In this context reference should also be made to the essay by M. N. Pokrovskij, 'New Tendencies in Russian Historical Literature' (in Russian, first published in 1928, reprinted in 1933) in which the author sharply attacks the reception of Weber by the medievalist D. M. Petruševskij (308 ff.). The fact that Neusychin's name or essays on Weber are not acknowledged could well be interpreted as the next higher level of politically motivated disapproval (on Pokrovskij, cf. R. Medvedev 1973, 552, 554; on Petruševskij, see the references in *BSE*, 3rd edn, Vol. 32, 623).

25 Osipova (1971, 179) makes reference to the critical preoccupation in the 1920s, operating at a 'highly ideological, theoretical and scientific level', with the sociological works of Durkheim, Simmel, Tarde and Weber.

26 For the purposes of political-ideological defence such 'family likeness' to Weber was attributed to, for example, Marcuse (in Korf, 1971) and Lukács (in Fojtik, 1962, 14).

27 Cf., for example, the most meagre critique in Čagin, 1971, Chapters V and VI. There is no reference to the period between 1929 and 1936 in Čagin's essay of 1967. Čagin (1971, 158) identifies the *positive* aspect of the ideological struggle from 1927–8 'for the purity of the Leninist doctrine' with the following quotation from Sčěglov (1967, 117): 'Numerous new cadres of philosophers developed in the course of these discussions.'

28 Concerning the special case and history of Polish sociology cf., for example, J. Matthes, 1962 and Markiewicz, 1971 (in Wiatr (ed.) 1971, 97–135). On the humanistic conception of sociology in particular (and its relation to Weber) cf. above all the essays by Mokrzycki and Z. Bokszański (1968).

3 Epistemological and methodological problems

1 Cf. the preface to *Materialism and Empirio-Criticism*.
2 Lenin in turn (in 'Ten Questions to a Lecturer', *Works*, Vol. 14, 15–16) refers to the pertinent method employed by Engels.

3 According to Lenin, this also applies to Kant's original philosophy. Whereas the 'Machists' criticised those 'from the right' on the basis of their remnant of 'materialism', a Marxist critique 'from the left' in contrast had to disclose its 'idealism and . . . agnosticism' (*ibid.*, 194 ff.; here 204).
4 There is a very vulgar materialist argument in Wittfogel (1922, 31) for the thesis that a closer examination of Kant has become obsolete on account of Machism: 'bringing Kant into play against Mach involves advancing the small business and manufacturing business of the eighteenth century against Stinnes and Krupp'.
5 Beginnings can be found, for example, in Danilov, 1958; Heise, 1962; Devjatkova, 1969.
6 Weber's position on Rickert is evidently seen and evaluated in various ways. Whereas Neusychin (1974, 414) establishes Weber's progressive distancing from Rickert (and, indeed, towards an approximation to Marx), Gajdenko, for example, criticises the fact that Weber had abbreviated Rickert's conceptions in a positivistic manner (1971, 257). Comparatively detailed explanations on the relationship between Rickert and Weber can be found in Kon (1973, 132 ff.). Korf (1968a, 42 ff.), Kramer (1968, 130f.) and Devjatkova (1971, 188f.) also refer to the differences between Weber and Rickert on the question of value relevance.
7 This is discussed in more detail in Weiss, 1975, particularly 33 ff.
8 Cf., for example, Hofmann, 1968, 74 f. for a critical evaluation of Lenin on this issue from a Marxist perspective.
9 Fojtik (1962, 7 f.) speaks – at least – only of an overrating of the active part of knowing in Weber.
10 On this and what follows, see Kocka, 1973 (here, 62 f.). It seems to me that Kocka underrates Weber's 'sociological science of social reality' orientation in favour of 'Kantian' expressions.
11 Concerning this interpretation cf. also Henrich, 1952 and Kocka, *op. cit.*, 60 f.
12 Regarding this, see also the appropriate critical remarks in Kocka, *op. cit.*, 65 f., 68, 69 ff.
13 Cf., for example, Weber's explanations in 'The Meaning of "Ethical Neutrality" in Sociology and Economics' (*MSS*, particularly 27 ff.).
14 Or, ultimately, that we are enquiring into the 'general cultural significance of the socio-economic structure of the human community and its historical forms of organisation' (Weber, *MSS*, 67).
15 Devjatkova (1969, 8) thinks that ideal types in a gnoseological respect refer to an 'idealistic interpretation of the model and the process of its construction'. Fojtik (1962) does not only speak of the 'subjective idealistic theory of "ideal types"', but in this context even explicitly employs the concept of '*a priori* forms' (8). Similar interpretations can be found in, for example, Korf (1964, 1340; 1968a, 98, 112, *passim*), whereas Kon (1973, 48) and Kramer, 1968, 140 ff.) use more differentiated arguments.
16 Thus, for example, *Das Philosophische Wörterbuch* (Vol. 2, 782): Neo-Kantianism had attempted to prevent the same level of precise

research in the 'field of the social sciences' as in the natural sciences 'for reasons of maintaining class domination and concealing exploitative relations as well as giving religion higher status'. Cf. also Bergner and Mocek, 1976, 58 ('It is contrary to the ideological function of bourgeois social theories to reflect reality as it actually is.'), and Korf (1968a, 6).

17 For bourgeois social scientists Braunreuther (op. cit., 86) explains this in terms of "many a wilfulness on part of the author" (Weber).

18 It is well known that this is a term favoured by Marx and Engels in the *German Ideology*.

19 A very good example of the philosophical 'insufficiency' of critique of ideology analyses (on Kant and Weber) is the essay by W. Lefèvre (1971). Kant's theory (or should we say 'invention'?) of transcendental subjectivity is 'explained' by Lefèvre in the following manner. In bourgeois society 'concrete individuals in their conduct are either indifferent or even antagonistic to each other. It does not seem possible to base rational conduct to reality on their empirical subjectivity, on their interests, passions and intrigues' (*ibid.*, 12; a comparable argumentation on Weber's postulate of ethical neutrality can be found on 100 f.). Lefèvre does not waste a thought on the empirical fact that Kant's philosophy never became the 'ruling idea' in bourgeois society (or even the basis of the typical capitalist 'rational conduct to reality'). This seems to show that his thesis deals at best with an associative nexus.

20 Cf. the comment by Lenin cited above on page 22. Lenin (in *Materialism and Empirio-Criticism*) certainly saw a substantive critical analysis of 'subjectivistic' epistemological theories as a prerequisite for their political-ideological classification.

21 H. J. Sandkühler's 'Self-Criticism' in the introduction to the 2nd edn of the reader *Marxismus und Ethik* (ed. by H. J. Sandkühler and Rafael de la Vega, Frankfurt 1974) is disillusioning evidence for the continuing and evidently deeply rooted obstacles to a more open discussion of precisely the 'neo-Kantian' conception of Marxism. In the 1st edn, after admitting the need for a critique of the conventional Marxist orthodoxy on ethical questions, Sandkühler now states 'emphatically': 'Revisions – including the neo-Kantian – are offered to scientific socialism from outside while disguising bourgeois standpoints on class under Marxist cloaks' (II). Sandkühler in this sense grounds his own revision primarily with the necessities of the political struggle. With his distinction between 'within' and 'outside' he effortlessly transfers the political friend-enemy schema to the level of scientific and philosophical discussions.

22 The only attempt at a comparative discussion of the relative strengths and weaknesses of Marxian and Weberian epistemology that I am aware of is the essay by J. Kocka (see above).

23 The liberal economic 'fraudulent use' of the seemingly interest-free values of 'productivity' and the 'national interest' (*Volkswohlstand*), which in fact reflected entrepreneurial interests, provoked Weber's critique in the so-called 'second' methodological dispute among the

Verein für Sozialpolitik (1909) (cf. 'Diskussionsreden auf den Tagungen des Vereins für Sozialpolitik', in *SSP*, 417 ff.; see also in Baumgarten, 1964, 394 ff.). Considering that it is Weber's position on the 'divorce between values and science' which is attacked by the left today, Bryant (1976, 244) notes that Weber and his colleagues in their time were the 'radical "left" who accused the establishment'. If 'radical' and 'left' are here understood in the Anglo-Saxon, rather than Marxist, sense of the term, this historical relativisation is certainly appropriate. As a matter of fact, some Marxist authors (Braunreuther, 1964, 78; Kon, 1973, 160 f.; with reference to Marcuse) also establish the political-ideological ambivalence of Weber's thesis or postulate of ethical neutrality. That Weber's position has not only been particularly sharply attacked from the side of 'monopoly capital' (as Braunreuther thinks), but the decidedly politically reactionary side does not, of course, lead to the usefulness of the political-ideological, opportunistic considerations in philosophical and scientific questions being fundamentally examined for once. Concerning the political sociological context of the dispute on value judgement cf. Ferber, 1965 and Hofmann, 1961, 47 ff.; as well as Franz Boese, *Geschichte des Vereins für Sozialpolitik 1871–1932* (Schriften des Vereins für Sozialpolitik, Vol. 188, Berlin, 1939).

24 It is thus totally unacceptable when Moskvičev (1974, 79 f.) thinks he can conclude from the content of particular Weberian sociological assumptions, which were critical of Marxism (especially with reference to the concept of the ideal type), 'that alone tells us that his "ideal types" are bound to carry an ideological bias'.

25 Lukács (1946c, 594) notes the conservative critique of Weber's thesis of ethical neutrality (here by Freyer), but does not take the opportunity to challenge the assertion of a specific anti-Marxist tendency in the entire Weberian methodology.

26 In fact the author provides a generally adequate description of the central Weberian thesis elsewhere (Devjatkova, 1971, 193 ff.).

27 The assertion (Lewis, 1975, 59) that ethical neutrality in the Weberian sense involves accepting the validity of the actual operative value orientations (e.g. in the capitalist economic order) is diametrically opposed to the unambiguous Weberian observations. Not being able to refute evaluations solely by scientific method certainly does not imply that one has to accept them.

28 Thus, even in this respect, Kuczynski (1972, 192) expresses his total agreement with Weber – and refers to the pertinent utterances by Marx, Engels and Lenin.

29 According to Weber, scientific method (in the narrower sense) is defined by the use of and restriction to the 'method of logic, on the one hand, and empiricism, on the other' (*Gutachten*, 124).

30 Weber occasionally refers to the analysis 'of the internal structure of cultural values' as the third task of the sciences apart from 'empirical observation' (empirical analysis in the narrower causal sense) and the 'establishment of mathematical and logical facts' (Weber, *FMW*, 146; cf. also *MSS*, 53 ff.).

31 Here Weber speaks (*MSS, ibid.* and *passim*) of 'professorial value commitments' or – more polemically – of 'professorial prophecy' (*MSS*, 4); cf. also the well-known remarks ('Politics is out of place in the lecture-room') in 'Science as a Vocation' (Weber, *FMW*, 129 ff., particularly 145 ff.).

32 Thus Weber himself (*MSS, op. cit.*, 9 ff.). This demand is of an equally scientific-ethical or scientific-political nature; that is to say, it is based on practical evaluations and not – unlike the thesis of ethical neutrality – on logical analysis.

33 Roth (1971, 239 and 246) points to Weber's attempts to promote the academic opportunities of young colleagues with a socialist orientation (Sombart and Michels).

34 Weber in fact expects – which seems to contradict his opinions I hitherto reviewed – a specific scientific advantage from participation by 'extreme' political positions because an 'Archimedean . . . point outside the conventions and presuppositions which are so self-evident to us' would be asserted through them. 'Fundamental doubt is the father of knowledge.' (*MSS*, 7.) In actual fact there is no contradiction here to the opinion Weber generally held. For the fruitfulness of ethical-political orientations implied here, it is absolutely adequate (if not downright necessary) that these function in the form of hypothetical value relevances, not 'practical' evaluations (*MSS*, 11, 22, 39).

35 Weber's later critique of the unsophisticated nature of these arguments and his comment that he could 'no longer identify' himself 'on many important points' (*Gutachten, op. cit.*, 127) should indeed not be neglected, but the arguments have no impact on the accuracy of this general observation.

36 Ossowska (1968) advocates a 'modified' version of the postulate of ethical neutrality in view of the difficulties in applying it.

37 Because of this we are looking at Hofmann's argumentation in more detail, although he does not belong to the set of authors who form the primary focus of discussion in this work since he distances himself from Marxist endeavours towards orthodoxy.

38 Some still clearer comments by Marx on the necessity of absolute 'scientific impartiality' and 'consistent adherence to the purely theoretical standpoint' (Marx) are cited by Steinvorth (1978, 294).

39 Accordingly Hofmann justifiably emphasises that once the 'certainty of progress has been lost, science' could 'assume nothing but the attitude of a declared and practised absolute ethical neutrality'.

40 This argumentation would be entirely identical in structure even in the fairly common case that the means become an end in themselves.

41 Even the maxim 'that which succeeds in historical practice' is 'legitimate and valuable', of course, contains an enormous value judgement and in case of doubt is of Social Darwinist origin. Kuczynski's assertion here (1972, 193) that 'the objective historical process favours the case of the working class', that 'partisanship for the working class, or the oppressed in general' is politically and ethically essential, is as unreflected in logic as the previous maxims.

Should we help the 'oppressed in general' to gain their rights, because they will be the historical victors at any rate?
42 In fact Klaus and Schulze (1967, 140) in this sense designate – no doubt resuming from Lenin – the 'development of the productive forces' as the 'highest criterion of social progress'. Lewis (1975, 130 ff.) argues very similarly. The authors obviously do not take into account how close this conception is to the otherwise sharply criticised 'technological determinism' (Mtschedlow and Rutkevitsch 1975, 261) nor how weak it is in demonstrating the progressiveness of the socialist countries.
43 It is a well-known fact that Durkheim sought to demonstrate the link between true sociological theory and correct social practice in a similar fashion (in *The Rules of Sociological Method*).
44 In a comparable context Weber speaks of 'naturalism' (*WL*, 425).
45 See note 41 above.
46 Thus, for example, Lukács (1976), Kuczynski (1972, 192), Kon (1973, 157), Assmann and Stollberg (1977, 356), *Wörterbuch* (207), *Philosophisches Wörterbuch* (1157).
47 At this stage I should mention that Weber already saw himself confronted with two identical versions of the objection to the thesis of ethical neutrality. He notes (*MSS*, 51) that the first appeals to 'an unambiguous evolutionary principle', the second to 'immutably invariant natural laws'.
48 See, for example, the repeated references to this context in *Gutachten*, *op. cit.*, 111, 131, 133. The assertion by Assmann and Stollberg (1977, 356) that even the use of the concept of 'class struggle' would have to be rejected by Weber as a 'mere value judgement' is conclusive proof of the authors' unfamiliarity with Weber, something that could be redressed by even the most superficial reading of his historical analyses.
49 Thus, for example, in this context: Braunreuther, 1958, 59, 121 and 1964, 79.
50 Marx cites the following description of his critical method by a Russian reviewer (Afterword to the 2nd German edn of *Capital*, Vol. 1, 27):

> If in the history of civilisation the conscious element plays a part so subordinate, then it is self-evident that a critical inquiry whose subject matter is civilisation, can, less than anything else, have for its basis any form of, or any result of, consciousness. That is to say, that not the idea, but the material phenomenon alone can serve as its starting-point. Such an inquiry will confine itself to the confrontation and the comparison of a fact, not with ideas, but with another fact.

Marx sees this portrayal as being 'striking and generous' and notes that the reviewer had (unintentionally) described nothing but 'the dialectical method' (*ibid.*, 28).
51 There is no equivalent reference either in the articles on 'value

judgement', or the 'dispute on value judgements', in the *Philosophisches Wörterbuch* (1155–7).
52 The philosopher Loeser's (Humboldt University) attempt to measure the social-ethical value of action by means of strict empirical method and mathematical models can only show how this method could definitely not be employed (Loeser, 1972). The crucial question why 'social stability' should be approached as the highest moral goal remains completely open in this foundation of a 'truly scientific theory of morality'.
53 Cf. the reference to Kant's practical philosophy (*Gutachten, op. cit.*, 117; *MSS*, 16) with the suitable comment on the misconception that these did not contain 'substantive indications'.
54 For example, what is also worth discussing is the question whether Weber's reference to the distinction between 'cultural ideals' and *ethical* norms (*MSS, op. cit.*, 15, 57) suggests that the latter have another, *better*, chance of being rationally established in his view.
55 Lukács (1962, 534, 537) sees in Weber a 'refined', as it were, enlightened irrationalism at work which rescues the scientific nature of sociology with 'ethical neutrality' by shifting 'all the irrationality' onto 'value judgements', 'standpoints' or '*Weltanschauungen*'.
56 Even in Marxist literature this concept has by no means been given the intensive attention and discussion it deserves. Beginnings can be found, e.g. in Devjatkova, 1969 and 1971.
57 Korf (1964, 1333) thus provides an adequate portrayal of Weber's conception when she describes it in the following way:

> Every researcher is guided entirely by subjective ideas of value at the start of the study of social phenomena. The researcher's individual epistemological interests permit him/her to select from the infinite stream of appearance only that section which is of personal value . . .

Cf. similar arguments in Korf, 1968a, 44 ff. Weber saw the interest guiding his own work on the process of 'rationalisation', in general, as well as in the existential conditions and consequences of 'modern occidental capitalism' (and socialism), on the progressive 'depersonalisation' and the trend of 'basic laws', etc., in particular, undoubtedly to be determined primarily by universally operating value perspectives. On the category 'depersonalisation' cf. *RS* I, 547; *RS* III, 544; *SSP*, 405, 414, 444; further: 'Was heisst Christlich-Sozial' in *Christliche Welt*, 1894, 475. Concerning 'the idea of basic laws to which we are nevertheless indebted for not much less than everything' cf. *PE*, 245 as well as *PS*, 59 ff.
58 Kozyr-Kowalski (1964) deals with the normative bases of scientific epistemological efforts which reach far into methodological and methodical decisions. His opinion that the problem of the rational defence of norms could be resolved in this case, if science were seen as a 'form of socio-historical practice' (Abstract 164), does not seem tenable at any rate since no social practice, either in philosophical or logical terms, can be self-legitimatory.

59 Cf. concerning this the already cited comment by Weber about the usefulness of the most extreme value premisses (in this case: anarchist) for social science (in this case: juristic) research.
60 In comparison a more detailed and systematic description of the Weberian conception has to be dispensed with. Here again I can only refer to my arguments elsewhere (1975, 65 ff.).
61 Korf (1964, 1330), in particular, emphasises this aspect.
62 Thus, concerning the ideal type, for example, Braunreuther, 1964, 62.
63 To the historian Pokrovskij Weber's conception of the ideal type represents 'the final attempt by a bourgeois historian-idealist to rescue the idealistic conception of the historical process'. But this 'rescue' is considered to 'resemble a simple capitulation in the face of historical materialism' (1933, 314).
64 Henrich (1952, 101) formulates the even more fundamental background assumption 'that meaningful consistency is the distinctive human possibility'.
65 Compare Weiss (1981a) on Weber's category of 'communicability'.
66 This *is* the specific way in which we obtain a 'distinct' and unambiguous image of social relationships even in everyday life.
67 Concerning 'meaningful adequacy' as the crucial criterion for the construction of types, see *WG*, 9 f. Here a reference to Weber's characterisation of the ideal type as a 'purely ideal limiting concept' (*MSS*, 93) is necessary.
68 On the category of 'objective possibility' cf., for example, *MSS*, 92 and 93. I shall return to this category at a later stage.
69 Concerning Weber's appraisal of the law of generalisation in the historical sciences (and, of course, before the development of his specifically sociological 'generalisations') cf., for example, *MSS*, 79.
70 Fojtik (1962, 9; *passim*) *criticises* the 'non-deterministic' nature of Weber's concept of theory.
71 The Lenin citations are taken from *Aus dem philosophischen Nachlass* (undated), 70 and 69 respectively.
72 Thus Korf with a further Lenin citation (Korf, *op. cit.*, 1333).
73 Weber stated this particularly clearly against psychologically oriented critics (Fischer, Rachfahl) of *The Protestant Ethic* (cf., for example, *PE* II 33, 49 ff.; *MSS*, 74, 88).
74 'The ideal type in fact is the logical device for discerning the individual, unique and irretrievable.' This observation is relativised a little later by Korf herself (*op. cit.*, 1332, 1335).
75 That Weber had distanced himself from the 'unlimited idiographism of neo-Kantianism' is noted not only by Neusychin (1974, 461), but also by, for example, Devjatkova (1969, 4), Kon (1973, 147) and Bel'cer (1973, 142).
76 Kuczynski, for example, attributes such statements of law to historical materialism (1952, 95). Accordingly Marx had formulated this fundamental law with the thesis that 'it is not the consciousness of individuals that determines their existence, but rather their social existence that determines their consciousness'. The Marxian prin-

ciple is also seen as such, for example, by Bader *et al.* (1976, 99) in the context of a generally much more problem-conscious discussion.

77 Korablev (1969, 15) provides an even 'more metaphysical' version of this fundamental assumption when he observes 'that the unity and lawfulness of our experience, and therefore of understanding [this relates to *Weber's* concept of interpretative understanding; author's comment] is based on the unity of existence which consists in its materiality'. In Korablev's view Weber had relapsed into the 'subjective-idealistic nominalism' of the conception of the ideal type because he had failed to appreciate this 'indisputable fact'.

78 The pertinent critique in Bel'cer (1974, 93) refers to the same group of categories.

79 Another author (T. Neumann) in the same publication thinks that there are 'masses' of examples in Weber's and Simmel's works for 'using general definitions as general conditions of historical reality' (*op. cit.*, 71). According to this, Weber would have apprehended his ideal-type 'definitions' in conceptually metaphysical terms as real social conditions. I refer here only to Weber's comment in his essay on objectivity (although an earlier publication, but in substance he always adhered to it) in which he formulates his critique of the belief 'that the "true" content and the essence of historical reality is portrayed in . . . theoretical constructs' (*MSS*, 94).

80 The Hegel quotation is taken from *Science of Logic*, Vol. 2, 226, London, 1929.

81 Weber occasionally defines 'ideas' in this sense as 'thought-patterns which actually exist in the minds of human beings' (*MSS*, 103). On this and the entire context of argumentation, see Weiss, 1975, 71 ff.

82 Concerning this common objection of idealism cf. Devjatkova, 1968, 1357; Braunreuther, 1958–9, 119; Danilov, 1958; Cassano, 1971.

83 Thus, for example, Devjatkova, 1969, 8; Osipov, 1964, 104; Bel'cer, 1974, 89. In contrast Levina (1972, 15) observes that the 'critical thinking through' of the 'theoretical problems' posed by the *Protestant Ethic* represents an 'important and worthwhile task' for Marxist sociology.

84 Assmann and Stollberg (1977, 359), in a vastly oversimplified fashion, thus contrast Weber's 'philosophical idealistic superstructure-base doctrine' with the 'Marxian teaching of base and superstructure'. The authors explain the fact that Weber had 'not directly' advocated such an either-or schema by saying that he was 'too wise' to do that and therefore went about it in a 'very ingenious' way. A similar 'explanation' can be found earlier in Braunreuther (1964, 87). (Weber ingeniously leaves it to the reader to draw the idealistic conclusions.)

85 Weber made it very plain, particularly in his essay on objectivity, that he saw a 'materialist' perspective not only as a possible, but indeed as a very essential, dimension of the 'programme of knowledge' he advocated (cf. especially *MSS*, 64 ff.). Besides this it is of course demonstrated in all of his historical analyses. Obversely we should remind ourselves at this juncture that for Marx the whole elementary

and pre-social human activity logically distinguishes itself from animal activity by its basis on a preceding meaningful 'imagination' (*Capital*, Vol. I, 174).

86 Thus Fetscher (1973, 509) in his very stimulating comparison between Weber's and Lukács' conceptions. Cf. on the relationship between Weber and Lukács, Weyembergh, 1973 and Coniavitis, 1977.

87 "*The objective theory of class consciousness is the theory of its objective possibility*" (1971, 79).

88 That is to say, separated from the really existing proletarian class by organisational measures as well.

89 Cf. in this context Weber's sharp critique of the 'pseudo-scientific operation' found in the assertion of a 'talented author that the individual may be in error concerning his interests, but that the class is infallible about its interests' (*ES*, Vol. 3, 930). In Roth's opinion Weber's comment is levelled directly at the young Lukács (*ES*, Vol. 1, LXXXI).

90 The historicity of the 'transcendental' party volonté générale brings the reference to Hegel much closer than that by Krahl to Kant. In fact Fetscher (*op. cit.*) also speaks of a 'transformation of Max Weber's categories in the tradition of the Hegelian dialectical ontology'.

91 Lukács' self-criticism on *History and Class Consciousness* may well be interpreted in this direction: that he had worked with an 'over-extension of the concept of practice', which made the abrupt change of the 'imputed' consciousness in revolutionary praxis appear like 'a miracle' (*History and Class Consciousness*, 1971, Preface to the new edn (1967), xix; cited in Fetscher, *op. cit.*, 224 f.). The question, of course, is whether it is possible to adhere unreservedly to the Leninist conception of the party, as Lukács does, without such exaggeration.

92 Kon (1964, 145) sees in the emphasis on the hypothetical nature of scientific statements a contradiction to the endeavour of knowing the 'objective relations between things'. Korf (1968a, 95) advocates an equivalent conception. Kon unjustifiably identifies the ideal-type – i.e. in fact focussing on merely 'objectively possible' relations – status of specific conceptual-theoretical constructs with the hypothetical nature of all empirical science explanations, including deterministic laws.

93 And, indeed, particularly in the case when the ideal-type nature of the thus gained clarity is noted.

94 Here I only refer to Weber's allusion to the anti-enlightening function of 'collective conceptions' in which he perceived 'a cloak for confusion of thought and action. It is, indeed, very often an instrument of specious and fraudulent procedures. It is, in brief, always a means of obstructing the proper formulation of the problem' (*MSS*, 110).

95 Špakova *et al.* (1973, 83) especially point out that Weber's ideal-type conception of bureaucracy is accepted by Marxist authors (Devjat-

kova and Štoff, 1970; Gvišiani, (1974, 1970) in so far as it fulfils 'some of the gnoseological functions of a model'. The fundamental acknowledgment that Weber's conception of the ideal type (because of the mediation between historical and theoretical perspectives that occurred within it) received in Neusychin and Stoklickaja-Tereškovič (cf. Chapter 5, Section 4), and yet again in Markarjan (1957, 29) can no longer be found in more recent Marxist literature. Naumova (1968, 59 f.) constitutes the only exception in his very positive comments on Weber's mediation between history and sociology and on the corresponding function of Weber's typology of action. It is regrettable that Neusychin was no longer able to present the announced (1974, 470) closer analysis of the ideal-type method. Evidently the historian Neusychin took a sceptical stance to the abstract ('purely sociological') sections of *Economy and Society*, particularly in 'Basic Concepts', even though he detected Weber's 'historical sensitivity' even in this work (*op. cit.*, 415). However, Weber's approach to ideal-type constructions in research practice (such as in the *Protestant Ethic* and *The City*), according to Neusychin's opinion, signals the end of the 'eternal dispute between sociology and history', between 'abstraction and concretion'. Neusychin thinks that one could say that Weber 'in his methodological practice had overcome not historical materialism, but the logic of Rickert's cultural sciences' (*op. cit.*, 471; cf. 461 f.).

96 According to Nowak, a classical example is Newton's law of inertia with his assumption of objects not affected by any forces (Kmita and Nowak, 1970, 67). Besides Max Adler (1964, 145 f.) voiced a similar opinion at an earlier stage.

97 At this point I should refer to Kempski's essay 'Zur Logik der Ordnungs-Begriffe, besonders in den Sozialwissenschaften' (in H. Albert (ed.), *Theorie und Realität*, 2nd edn, Tübingen 1972, 115 ff.), which contains the starting-points for a further clarification of the questions outlined here (cf. Weiss, 1975, 79 f.).

98 Weber (*WL*, 6; *MSS*, 89) notes that the (by no means exclusive) specific use of ideal types distinguishes the 'cultural sciences' from the 'exact natural sciences'.

99 Kmita and Nowak classify Weber's 'ideal type' concepts as 'anti naturalistic instrumentalism' (1970, 67). The pejorative meaning connected with their concept of 'instrumentalism' seems questionable at least from the perspective of the considerations outlined here.

100 On the other hand, the essay by Ionin (1974) on the problem of understanding, which is dedicated to Cooley, Mead, Thomas and Schütz, contains no reference to Weber. Ionin refers (*ibid.*, 2) to some other Soviet publications on the subject which I was unable to take into consideration.

101 This observation applies even to those authors who, in their own and/or others' interpretation, advocate an emphatically 'mechanistic' form of materialist theory.

102 Kretzschmar (1978, 35) formulates this widespread opinion with a carelessness characteristic of her entire work.

103 Sandkühler's (1973, 249 ff.: 'Die Praxis als Kriterium der Wahrheit') discussion, for example, gives us a good idea of this ambiguity and opacity, which was not least furthered by Lenin.
104 It is another question whether one therefore (like Weber) identifies the limits of 'the social' with the limits of intelligibility or 'communicability'.
105 Cf. concerning this (particularly as a critique of Fromm), for example, Andreas Gedö, *Der entfremdete Marx. Zur existenzialistisch- 'humanistischen' Marxismus-Deutung*, Frankfurt, 1971.
106 Weber's comment cited by Braunreuther as evidence is absolutely useless for this purpose as could be expected. It relates to the (actual) impossibility of a *full 'causal explanation* of an *individual* fact', by no means to the general impossibility or worthlessness of causal explanation in the social sciences.
107 In P. Winch's opinion, which is explicitly directed at Weber's establishment of causal explanation in the social sciences, it is totally inappropriate to see a 'radical elaboration' of the Weberian ideas (Bader *et al.*, 1976, 102).
108 The works of, for example, H. Lefèbvre, Agnes Heller, K. Kosik, T. Leithäuser *et al.*, belong to this category.
109 Similarly, e.g. Koch (1965, 791) on the fundamental problem 'of materiality or the material unity of society as a part (a partial unity, a part-system) of the cohesive material world surrounding us'.
110 As Sandkühler emphasises elsewhere (1972, 977) 'the attempt to found the materialist alternative on the bourgeois hermeneutics in the philosophy of history' cannot after all appeal to the 'citations of classics'.
111 Although Sandkühler is generally not exactly sparing of references, Weber's considerations, for example, do not appear in his essay.
112 W. R. Beyer, 'Artikel Hermeneutik', in *Philosophisches Wörterbuch*, 475, cites this in agreement (taken from: Sartre, *Critique de la raison dialectique*, Paris, 1960).
113 Starting points are offered in, for example, the already cited essays by Kmita and Nowak (1970), Bader *et al.* (1976, 83 ff.) and Siemek (1977).

4 The fundamental theoretical perspective: social action or material relations?

1 On the history of the critical discussion (in the socialist countries) cf. especially Wiatr, 1971, Kiss, 1971 (especially 106 ff.) and Hahn 1977. Kvesko (1974, 12), for example, draws attention to the undecidedness of the controversy in Soviet discussion.
2 Kon supplies a comparable, although slightly divergent, three-point characterisation (1961, 46).
3 Some of the divergence from this heavily predominant conception will be dealt with later.
4 Concerning the background and course of the critical discussion, cf., for example, Hahn, 1977, 39 ff.

5 Thus on Levada (*op. cit.*, 491).
6 Klügl (1970, 591), for example, gives a very odd description of the alleged Weberian conceptions. A large section of Kretzschmar's (1978) arguments are clearly beyond the limits of what is worthy of scientific discussion.
7 *The Holy Family* (cited by Tuchscheerer, 1973, 224). Cf. the observation that '*economic categories* are only *abstract expressions* of these actual relations', in a letter to Annenkov (Marx and Engels, *Selected Correspondence*, *op. cit.*, 45).
8 Marx, in *German Ideology* (*MEW*, Vol. 5), also emphasises that the only 'prerequisites' for his own analysis, 'which are establishable by pure scientific method', are 'actual individuals, their action and their material conditions of life'.
9 Hahn (1968, 71 *passim*) compiled this and a number of further proofs, though he completely ignores the affinity to an 'individualistic' action approach in the Weberian sense.
10 Thus, for example, Koch (1965, 793 f.), Bakurkin (1975, 22 f.) and Paciorkovskij (1975, 204). Besides Paciorkovskij provides relatively speaking the most adequate description of the Weberian conception of action.
11 Kiss (1971, 48 f.), for example, endorses this.
12 This misinterpretation can also be found in the essay by Bader *et al.* (1976, e.g., 25, 226, 345, 492), which otherwise contributes much to a differentiated approach to the problem. It seems not least due to the misunderstanding of the Weberian conception on this point that these authors ultimately also adhere to the contrast between 'individualistic' and 'social-theoretical' perspectives.
13 Cf. the cited (note 77, Chapter 3) retransposition of social reality into the material unity of nature.
14 In contrast Marx notes: 'In manufacture, the organisation of the social labour process is purely subjective; it is a combination of detail labourers' (*Capital*, Vol. 1, Chapter XV: 'Machinery and Modern Industry', 364).
15 In the already cited letter to Annenkov Marx insisted that 'the way in which machinery is utilised is totally distinct from the machinery itself' (Marx and Engels, *Selected Correspondence*, *op. cit.*, 44).
16 Thus Bakurkin (1975, 22) with reference to Lenin's critique of 'subjectivistic' sociology.
17 Cf., apart from the better-known statements, the following:

> Today's capitalist economic organisation is a monstrous cosmos into which the individual is born and that is given to him, at least as an individual, as a factually irrecovable capsule, in which he has to live. It forces the norms of its economic action upon the individual in so far as he is integrated into market relationships. (*RS* I, 37).

18 Cf., concerning this, especially Korf, 1971. Bader *et al.* also adhere to this assessment (1976, 316, 484).
19 Concerning 'symbolic interactionism' cf., for example, the paper by

H. Joas on G. H. Mead (1978, especially 9 f., 26 ff., 37) as well as the essays referred to (*ibid.*, 512) by R. Paris and M. Wetzel.
20 Here reference should be made to, for example, the essay by Bader *et al.* (*op. cit.*, 100 ff.), the considerations by Berger (1978) and Eder and Rödel (1978) as well as the essays by Polish sociologists (e.g., L. Nowak, 1971b and Bokszański, 1968).
21 The most differentiated and progressive analysis of this problem seems still that of P. Berger and T. Luckman, *The Social Construction of Reality: a Treatise on the Sociology of Knowledge*, Harmondsworth, 1967.
22 Marxist authors who make mention of the 'the theory of social action' throughout portray and criticise T. Parsons as its dominant contemporary representative (cf., e.g., Paciorkovskij, 1975; Kretzschmar, 1978; N. V. Novikov, 1961 and 1964; Bakurkin, 1975). At the same time they certainly do not observe the crucial difference between Weber and Parsons in their definition of the relationship between 'action' and 'system'. The very brief comments made by Naumova (1968, 59 f.) in particular constitute an exception.
23 The reduction of capitalist relations to the interplay of social interactions is the essence of modern sociological ideology. It occurs primarily in US-American sociology, although the sociological models of European theorists, especially those of *Max Weber* and *Pareto* represent crucial preliminary studies. (K. H. Tjaden, 'Introduction' in K. H. Tjaden, *Soziale Systeme*, Neuwied/Berlin 1971, 23)

To lump Weber together with Pareto on this crucial question testifies to a high level of carelessness. This ambiguous argument, which is distorted to accommodate political ideology, is expressed in another work by Tjaden ('Soziale Systeme und gesellschaftliche Totalität', in D. Hülst *et al. Methodenfragen der Gesellschaftsanalyse*, Frankfurt 1973, 49–72). There, for example, Tjaden states: 'Social relations are not given in themselves, but they are essentially realised through regular social activities' (*ibid.*, 69). There is also talk of the 'actors who – however mediated – carry out and develop the constitution of social production through operative and interpretative statements of their lives' (*ibid.*, 71).

5 Special problems of the theoretical and empirical work

1 Assmann and Stollberg (1977, 358) refer to a 'work [by Weber] that seems purely philosophical by its title' and list the title as 'Ascetic Protestantism and the Spirit of Capitalism'. Obviously they know the work of the author under critique only from hearsay.
2 Cf. also Devjatkova (1968, 128). Bel'cer too (1973, 141, 151) justifiably emphasises the key importance of the sociology of religion for Weber's entire work.
3 Karl Marx, 'A Contribution to the Critique of Hegel's Philosophy of Right: Introduction', in *Early Writings*, Harmondsworth, 1974 (243–57), 244.

4 This Engels citation is contained in Engels' letter of 21–22 September 1890 to J. Bloch (Marx and Engels, *Selected Correspondence*, London, 1956, 498).
5 Cf. the overviews, discussions and bibliographies in: Eisenstadt (ed.), 1969; Besnard (ed.), 1970; Seyfarth and Sprondel (eds), 1973.
6 There are several more recent essays (especially those by Birnbaum, Giddens and Sprondel) in the reader edited by Seyfarth and Sprondel (1973) providing a discussion on the many levels of Weberian argumentation and their relationship to a differentiated materialist position.
7 Levina (1972, 4–7) primarily endorses Neusychin's description. Bel'cer's (1973 and 1974) descriptions, for example, are far less adequate. At any rate this author (like Levina, *op. cit.*, 10 ff.) refers to the existence of an extensive non-Marxist critique of Weber's essays on Protestantism (1973, 152 ff.). He also frees the Marxist discussion, at least tendentially in the second essay, from the fixation on the problem of the genesis of capitalism.
8 Naumova (1968, 59) also observes that the theme of *The Protestant Ethic* is the 'elaboration of capitalist norms'. In this context Neusychin notes:

> Weber thinks that this ideology is as relevant to this society as its economic forms. This is how Weber arrived at his concept of the 'spirit of capitalism' and the question regarding the origination of this 'spirit'. This enquiry has as yet nothing to do with philosophical idealism. (*op. cit.*, 445)

A few pages on (448) Neusychin summarises: 'Max Weber is neither an idealist nor materialist.' On the contrary he had consciously distanced himself from philosophical lines of enquiry and concentrated on 'concrete historical-sociological research'. The findings were frequently 'surprisingly close' to those of Marx (*ibid.*, 452).
9 Neusychin (*op. cit.*, 446 f.) cites several pertinent comments made by Marx on the 'capitalist spirit' and its affinity to Protestantism. K. Kautsky (1927, Vol. II, 382 ff.) and L. Kofler give a similar appraisal of Weber's analyses on the 'capitalist spirit'. The latter observes that as a Marxist one could 'simply no longer do without' these analyses by Weber (1966, 289). Kapeljuš (1931, 215 ff.) also provides a fairly detailed and factual discussion on the relationship between the Weberian and Marxian analyses on the genesis of occidental capitalism and the role of the 'capitalist spirit'.

In contrast an interpretation of *The Protestant Ethic* that sees in Weber's argumentation an attempt to 'substitute' the Marxian theory of the 'original accumulation' can be found in, e.g. Braunreuther (1964, 88 f.), Lukács (1962, 525) and Assmann and Stollberg (1977, 358 f.). Borodaj (1979), on the other hand, in turn emphasises that Marx was not in the least concerned with the *explanation* of original accumulation.
10 Bukharin (1926) also repeatedly refers to Weber's 'interesting investigations on the economic ethics of the world religions' (*ibid.*,

197), and notes: 'Very interesting observations are made by Werner Sombart and Max Weber, particularly on the economic psychology of the bourgeoisie and the various stages in its development.' (*ibid.*, 291.)

11 The objection of 'pluralistic agnosticism (Levina, 1972, 6), or an 'eclectic methodology' (Kuznecov, 1975, 12), to Weber's argumentation around *The Protestant Ethic* is obviously connected with this critique.

12 Weber turns against the reductionist programme of both Marxism and Nietzsche in *RS* I, 241 ff., 248. Particularly concerning an empirical science 'explanation' of Christianity, cf. *SWG*, 189.

13 It is therefore not surprising that the anti-enlightenment side was sharply critical of Weber's sociology of religion. O. Spann (*Tote und lebendige Wissenschaft*, 2nd edn, Jena, 1925, 166) in this respect speaks of Weber's 'rare lack of understanding', which dares to approach 'a fundamental area of social life, religiosity, that is beyond his reach' and seeks to 'disintegrate and destroy it as a caustic disease', representing an 'atheistic enlightenment of the most vulgar sort'. Similarly, A. Mettler, *Max Weber und die philosophische Problematik unserer Zeit*, Dissertation, Zurich, 1934, 41. References to this aspect of the Weberian critique are provided by Bel'cer (1973, 154 ff.).

14 With reference to this, see the slightly more detailed considerations in Weiss, 1981a.

15 Marianne Weber (1950) reported that this was the subtitle of Weber's Vienna lectures on 'Economy and Society' in 1918.

16 The observation that this includes 'the negative economic element' too, *de facto* indicates a crucial limitation of this assumption. Engels (Letter to C. Schmidt of 27 October 1890, in Marx and Engels, *Selected Correspondence, op. cit.*, 505) in this respect explicitly speaks of '*only* a negative economic element' (author's emphasis) and explains the meaning of this as follows: 'The low economic development of the pre-historic period is supplemented and also partially conditioned and even caused by the false conceptions of nature.'

17 'The 'so-called "materialist" conception of history' as a *Weltanschauung* or as a formula for the causal explanation of historical reality is to be rejected most emphatically.' (Weber, *MSS*, 68.)

18 On the occasion of his assuming the *Archiv* editorship Weber expressed himself programmatically on this issue in '"Objectivity" in Social Science and Social Policy' (1904). Cf. especially, *MSS*, 63 ff.

19 With regard to the sociology of religion I am only referring to Weber's systematic comments, e.g. in *Economy and Society* (368 ff.) and in the Introduction to 'Wirtschaftsethik der Weltreligionen' (*RS I*, especially 273 ff.).

20 Roth at any rate speaks of the 'pervasive Marxian influence' on Weber (1971, 230) despite the many differences.

21 This obviously applies equally to the essay by Bader *et al.* (1976). The form of contrast used by these authors (particularly in Part D) almost

22 Weber's thesis referred to in Bel'cer (*Economy and Society*, 499) was that in the search for the 'origins' of the 'need for salvation and ethical religion' *side by side* with the 'social condition of the disprivileged and the rationalism of the bourgeoisie, which is shaped by its way of life' one *also* needs to take into account an additional factor, namely 'intellectualism as such'.
23 Thus, for example, Adler, 1964, Vol. III, 35 f.; Braunreuther, 1964, 101 ff.; Herkommer, 1975, 125 f.; Petrov, 1971; Kvesko, 1974, 14; Kon, 1973, 152. Bel'cer (1974), in particular, constitutes the exception, since he developed at least a preliminary approach to an (empirical) discussion of contents.
24 Concerning the general critique of Weber's 'idealistic' or 'subjectivistic' restriction to the 'sphere of distribution' cf. also Kramer (1968, 175, 181) and Cassano (1971, 25 ff.). Crompton and Gubbay (1977, 13) and Giddens (1977, 205 f.) also assert – against Weber – that the class antagonism of capitalist society originated at the level of production, but the latter obviously *without* resort to the Marxian doctrine of labour value.
25 Cf. Marx's observation:

> A definite production thus determines a definite consumption, distribution and exchange as well as *definite relations between these different moments*. Admittedly, however, *in its one-sided form*, production is itself determined by the other moment. (Marx, *Grundrisse: Foundations of the Critique of Political Economy – Rough Draft*, Harmondsworth, 1977b, 99)

26 Cf. Karl Marx (*Grundrisse, ibid.*, 399 ff.). Since there is no analysis of the Marxian theory of value by Weber himself, reference should be made to Marianne Weber's book (1900), which at least hints at Weber's familiarity with the subject matter and is also suggestive of his opinions about it. Cf. also Roth, 1971, 242.
27 This applies, for example, to the fundamental fact that, according to Marx, labour-power distinguishes itself from other modes of production, in that its creation of value is greater than the socially necessary labour for its reproduction.
28 The narrower thesis by Vincent (1968, 89) that to me seems worthy of discussion is that Weber's perspective on the market is directly linked to his leading idea of occidental, particularly modern, history as a process of rationalisation.
29 Cf. the relevant references and comments in I. Fetscher (ed.), *Grundbegriffe des Marxismus*, Hamburg, 1976, 56.
30 Cf. Weber's thesis in summary (*Economy and Society*, 305 f.) referring to the manifold possible interrelationships.
31 The study by Kozyr-Kowalski (1979), which can no longer be considered in this text (for linguistic reasons), but which (like all of this author's essays) would certainly be worth discussing in more

detail. Offe (1969), 166 ff.), Binns (1977), Parkin (1979) and Konrad and Szelényi (1978) suggest the possibility and desirability of integrating the class conceptions of Weber and Marx.
32 1923, citations from the 1974 reprint of the essay.
33 This agreement also extends to Weber's central thesis that the foundation and existence of the city in Antiquity ('at least during the epoch of the independent Polis') were above all determined by political-military interests, in comparison to which the typical city of the Middle Ages was 'a structure oriented immeasurably... towards acquisition through rational economic activity' (*ES*, 1362).
34 There is an entire second section in Neusychin, 1974 (495 ff.) devoted to Max Weber's method ('empirical sociology'). His considerations on this topic are further elaborated in the 1927 essay. The 'continuation' in Stoklickaja-Tereškovič, 1925 (109 ff.) is mainly devoted to these methodological questions.
35 Stoklickaja-Tereškovič thinks that Weber had dealt with the categorial comparison between the antique and medieval city more consistently in the 'Agrarverhältnisse im Altertum'. In *The City* this (accurate) 'antithesis' was very much weakened by the same ideal-type construction of an aristocratic period that was common to both city types.
36 See note 95, Chapter 3, above.
37 Neusychin cites especially Weber's observation that sociology constructs typologies and seeks general rules of history (*ES*, 19).
38 What is meant by this is: in the form of a comparative social and economic historical enquiry (with special reference to the class problem).
39 This applies even more strongly to Wittfogel's analysis of 'Wirtschaft und Gesellschaft in China' (1931). In the essay of 1927, in which Wittfogel describes the bases of his own conception, clearly a central point (3b) of the summarised study programme is: 'Why was there no formation of independent industrial capitalism in China? Form and limits of the development of craft and trade capital. A discussion with *Max Weber*' (*ibid.*, 334). The constitutive role of the problem horizon given in Weber's work is no longer made clear in the study itself. Rather, Weber's comparative enquiries are essentially referred to in evidence among other things. There is no explicit reference even at those points where the influence of Weber's line of enquiry (and even his explanatory approach) is striking. Thus, in the context of urban development and commodity economy Marx is indeed referred to (*ibid.*, 94), whereas Weber is not. In a summary (*ibid.*, 676 ff.), entitled 'early capitalist beginnings – but no natural science', there is no reference to Weber's pertinent considerations, not even where, for explanatory purposes, the lack of 'city authority of the bourgeoisie as in medieval Europe' is specially quoted (*ibid.*, 676; cf. also 718). At another point though there are references to Weber's (514, 418) comments on the role of the medieval guilds in the cities of the European Middle Ages.

40 For further statements by Wittfogel on Weber's 'well-known methodological errors' cf. also his work on China (1931b, 396, 495, 794, 101).
41 Even Kofler does not mention Weber's essays in the relevant parts of his *Geschichte der bürgerlichen Gesellschaft* (1966).
42 Carl Haase (ed.), *Die Stadt des Mittelalters*, three vols, Darmstadt, 1969–73.
43 Article 'Städtische Siedlungen' in Vierkandt's *Handwörterbuch der Soziologie* (1931).
44 One of the few more recent works is the essay by Spencer (1977) which, as it were, rediscovers the examplary interplay between historical and sociological analysis in Weber's essay.
45 In fact another Marxist historian (Töpfer, 1973, 243 and 249) defends Weber's efforts at a clarification and elaboration of the concept of the 'city', particularly from 'bourgeois' researchers.
46 Concerning the fundamentally unavoidable (from Weber's point of view) tense relationships between the 'spheres' of religion, on the one hand, and the economy, politics, aesthetics, eroticism and science, on the other, cf. primarily the 'Zwischenbetrachtung' in *RS I*, 536 ff.
47 This interrelationship plays an even greater role in revolutionary processes than in 'static' social systems. It is particularly applicable to modern revolutions that the 'rationalism' of competing ideologies (i.e. their intellectual persuasive power, radicality and consequences) was of great significance for the relative social and political chances of success enjoyed by participant groups, parties or movements.
48 No doubt Weber's frequently careless and undifferentiated use of the concept of rationality invited this interpretation.
49 Even in Marcuse this observation is not criticised as such (see below in Chapter 5, Section 5). On the other hand, Marxist critiques generally ignore the fact that we can only agree with this observation and, at the same time, reject Weber's thesis of ethical neutrality, if we can contrast the existing modern understanding of science with an alternative (namely 'material') notion of scientific rationality. However, except Marcuse, I cannot find any considerations in this direction in the Marxist critiques of Weber.
50 Cf., particularly, Gajdenko (1971) who offers the most precise portrayal of the various aspects of the modern process of rationalisation from Weber's perspective, due to her conviction of the 'enormous importance' of the Weberian 'doctrine of formal rationality' (*ibid*. 257).
51 A parallel problem in Marxist literature could be shown in the treatment of the role of the 'intelligentsia'. It is obviously a very popular theme in contemporary Soviet sociology. Cf., for example, J. M. Šikin, *Sovremennie buržuaznie koncepcii intelligencii* (Contemporary Bourgeois Conceptions of the Intelligentsia), Dissertation, Leningrad, 1975. The parallelism resides in the fact that the leading role of intellectuals as ideologues of the socialist movement cannot actually be derived (primarily or exclusively) from any

scientific authority. For a less problem-conscious critique of the 'non-Marxist conception of the role of the intelligentsia' in Max Weber and in his successor, C. W. Mills, see Fojtik, 1962 (14 f.).

52 Gajdenko (*op. cit.*, 116) in turn refers to the 'distinguished' Soviet expert on the science of music, B. V. Assaf'ev, who had even worked on a translation into Russian of Weber's treatise, but which 'evidently' remained incomplete. A reference to Weber's enquiry can be found in Assaf'ev's essay of 1976 (76).

53 At this stage it should be mentioned that Lunačarskij's essay is obviously very badly translated. An examination of the original would be necessary, but this could not be done in time.

54 Lunačarskij notes that Weber himself referred to the 'instinctive acknowledgment' (Lunačarskij's formulation) that the fifth was enjoyed as the 'aesthetically positive interval' in all cultures. Cf. the corresponding comments (on the fourth too), on pp. 43 and 45 f. In fact Weber did not refer to an instinctive base in this context (1972, 15).

55 Lunačarskij provides a few references to this relationship (with Weber) on pp. 44 ff. and 50 ff.

56 Concerning this, see the comments made within the framework of the discussion on Weber's sociology of religion (Chapter 5, Section 1).

57 It is impossible to establish whether this 'Preamble' in fact stems from Gajdenko or whether it is, for example, an explanatory introductory comment by the editor. A similar assertion in the actual treatise appears only in a very weak form.

58 The appeal to the supposed facts of nature, as is popularly known, depicts a classical form of rationalisation and justification of highly contingent political or authority requirements.

59 Gajdenko rightly points out that Weber's conception is determined by an epochal, not merely accidental, personal interest.

60 Here I am only referring to Lukács (*Probleme der Aesthetik*, Neuwied/Berlin, 1963) and H. H. Holz (*Vom Kunstwerk zur Ware*, Neuwied/Berlin, 1972). The quality of art is throughout measured by how far it imparts 'true' information on historical-social relations and developments. Even if a specific or, possibly, irreplaceable function in the political process is attached to it, its 'truth' nonetheless still only resides in what can be translated into scientific argumentation.

61 In an important respect the direction of their argumentation is indeed diametrically opposed: whereas Lunačarskij asserts a 'physical substratum' of art as a logical limit to Weber's perspective of rationality, Gajdenko demands an extension of this perspective by the dimension of 'substantive', and therefore historical, rationality.

62 Löwith's (1960) analysis of Weber's work on the leading notion of 'rationalisation' (and in contrast to Marx's leading notion of 'alienation') is still the most subtle.

63 Similar conceptions, although presented in a less stringent style, can be found in Lefèvre, 1971.

64 Cf. concerning this the review and critique of Marcuse's conceptions

in Habermas, 1969, 48 ff. Habermas obviously considers Marcuse's description of the Weberian conception of rationality to be applicable.
65 Čalikova (1970, 15) speaks of Weber's 'emotional', or '*weltanschaulicher*' reference to rationalisation.
66 As far as this goes, Drobnickij (1973, 127) has a point when he observes: 'As a result it follows in Weber that the rationality of sociohistorical thinking consists merely in the rigour of the method and logical operations, rather than in being able to construct the one true picture of history.'
67 This objection could also be raised against Korablev's (1969, 9 and 14) appraisal of the status of formal rationality in Weber's work.
68 Concerning the diverse meanings attached to the Weberian concept of rationality and rationality as 'communicability', cf. the examples and interpretations in Weiss, 1981a. These could also be levelled at the thesis of an irresolvable contradiction in Weber's conception (Fleischer, 1976).
69 Before embarking on the considerations cited above, Marcuse expresses the idea 'that not "pure", formal, technical reason, but the reason of domination erects the "shell of bondage", and that the consummation of technical reason can well become the instrument for the *liberation* of man' (1972a, 223). Marcuse's pertinent arguments in *Soviet Marxism: A Critical Analysis* (1971), particularly in the chapter 'The New Rationality' (68 ff.), are similarly characterised by a lack of clarity and decidedness. This probably stems from the fact that he – unlike, for example, Habermas – failed to undertake a critical discussion of conventional Marxist (and Marxian) conceptions of rationality.
70 Cf. concerning this, for example, Weber's comments in 'Zur Lage der bürgerlichen Demokratie in Russland' (1906), *PS*, 62 ff., also in *PE*, 245. The first detailed study on Weber's stand on this problem has recently been presented by Brugger (1980). Brugger shows that, in starting out from Weber's self-limitations, a broad field of highly rational possibilities of argumentation is opened up within and outside the scope of the empirical sciences.
71 At this point it is worth noting that Weber's concept of charisma has not been subjected to any detailed analysis from Marxist quarters although it is obviously considered controversial. Špakova (1974, 82 f.) – like Lukács (1962, 537 and 547) – sees this concept as an anticipatory description and defence of demagogic leadership, in the sense of fascism and the personality cult surrounding Mao Tse Tung. (Presumably this would also include the cult of Stalin.) Whereas in this instance charisma as 'merely pseudo-revolutionary' is strictly isolated from the 'authority of the proletarian leader', Naumova (1968, 59) notes that Weber's concept of charisma by no means denotes a phenomenon of 'social pathology' or 'disorganisation', but 'a revolutionary force that propels history'. Kautsky (1927, 479 ff.) pleads for a 'disenchantment' of the charisma phenomenon.

72 Bader *et al.* (1976) constitute the only notable exception with regard to the sociology of domination.
73 Here we are not just referring to Trockij's well-known, extremely trenchant, critique (1958, 51 ff., *passim*), but also to the pertinent observations and explanations in Bukharin and Preobrazhensky, *The ABC of Communism: A Popular Explanation of the Program of the Communist Party of Russia*, University of Michigan Press, 1966, 180 ff. A good overview on the views held by leading Soviet theorists on the problem of bureaucratisation is provided by Pethybridge (1974, 261 ff.). Cf. Ahlberg (1976, 15 ff.) and Kofler, *Stalinismus und Bürokratie*, Berlin, 1970, 13 ff.
74 The most important relevant Marxian considerations on bureaucracy are contained in Marx's 'Critique of Hegel's Doctrine of the State', on the one hand, and in his analyses on *The 18th Brumaire of Louis Bonaparte*, *The Civil War in France*, on the other. For a description cf. Schluchter (1972, 34 ff.) and Albrow (1970, 68 ff.).
75 Ahlberg (1976, 111) cites Marx's observation that the societal work under communism would be organised 'in accordance with a common and rational plan' (*MEW*, German edn, Vol. 18, Berlin, 1969, 62).
76 Cf. on this and on the whole context of these considerations, Schluchter, *op. cit.*, 116 ff.
77 Besides this applies much more to the 'official information' of bureaucrats. The latter have the tendency to be transformed into a 'service secret' (*ES*, 1418).
78 Ahlberg (*op. cit.*, 100) too expresses his surprise about this conspicuous gap in critical Marxist research on bureaucracy. For a more recent reference see, for example, Elleinstein, 1977 (207, 28 f.).
79 Concerning this, for example, see Paragraph 54 ('Bureaucracy and the Soviet Power') in Bukharin and Preobrazhensky (*op. cit.*, 188 ff.), in which the party is allocated the task of putting 'the masses' into the place of 'the old official-ridden State' and to make 'the work of State administration a concern of the entire working population' (*ibid.*, 190).
80 Kejzerov and Devjatkova (1971, 53 f., 58 f.) see the logical shortcoming of Weber's conception of power or authority in this.
81 At this point Weber supplies the fundamentally important explanation

> It is not, however, permissible to express this by saying, as is sometimes done, that economic action is a 'psychic' phenomenon. The production of goods, prices, or even the 'subjective valuation' of goods, if they are empirical processes, are far from being merely psychic phenomena. But underlying this misleading phrase is a correct insight. It is a fact that these phenomena have a peculiar type of subjective *meaning*. This alone defines the unity of the corresponding processes, and this alone makes them accessible to subjective interpretation. (*ES*, Vol. 1, 64)

82 Bader et al. (*op. cit.*, 203) think that, with the observation that he did not intend to pursue 'economic theory' (*ES*, Vol. 1, 63), Weber had undertaken a problematic divorce between an economic and a sociological perspective. However, with this observation Weber obviously only meant to say that he did not intend to offer a developed economic *theory*, merely a number of conceptual points and observations about 'certain of the simplest sociological relationships in the economic sphere.'

83 In the context of a Marxist orientation to an economic theory Hofmann (1969) demonstrates a very unbiased approach to concepts from Weber's economic sociology. The explanations by Meurer (1974, 122 ff.) are less productive.

84 The widespread and frequently moralising critique of this definition would be better served if it took Weber's reservation regarding legitimacy seriously and further that if it observed that, according to Weber, physical force represents 'neither the sole, nor even the most usual, method of administration' used by political associations, but the specific method 'is always the last resort when others have failed' (*ES*, Vol. 1, 54).

Note the fact that Weber's political sociology centring attention on the problem of legitimacy is related to his strong consideration for economic preconditions and the functions of political associations (above all those of the modern state). Nixon (1979), for example, demonstrates this in his comparative discussion on Marx's and Weber's conceptions of the state.

85 The key role Poulantzas evidently attributes to Max Weber for the development of political theory as such (1978b, *op. cit.*, 11) unfortunately does not serve as an approach to a discussion on contents.

86 At least it is worth pointing out that Weber establishes almost a (counter-) 'tendency to substantive rationality' in modern mass democracies (*ES*, 226; cf. 893 f.). For further examples, see J. Winckelmann, *Erläuterungsband zu Wirtschaft und Gesellschaft*, 5th edn, 47 f. Another point worth mentioning is that it is precisely the relative success of competing forms of legitimacy (including the 'value-rational' and particularly the one related to natural law) that is considered to be of primary interest to Weber. Evidence for this is provided not only by the conceptual-theoretical or typological, but also by his empirical analyses (not least the essay on the revolutionary events in Russia and his paper on socialism). It would be worth discussing Weber's empirical assumption that value-rational ideas of legitimacy have steadily increasing difficulties in asserting themselves in the face of the dynamic of formal and instrumental rationality, and that there is by no means a historical tendency towards the realisation of democratic ideals.

In any case it is not necessarily a result of the categorial or theoretical fundamental assumptions of his sociology, as Bader *et al.* (*op. cit.*, 433 f.) obviously seem to presume.

87 In this context it is also worth referring to the still unpublished essay

by V. M. Bader (1979) that makes an important contribution to the critical treatment of a series of unclear points on Weber's concept of legitimacy. Bader stresses the empirical usefulness of the concept and observes that Weber's decided empirical orientation in contrast to any blurring or empirical and normative questions has good reasons. Weber's problematic conception of the irrationality of ultimate value orientations is, even according to Bader, not a necessary consequence of this sociological focus on the empirical aspect of the problem of legitimacy. Bader sees the essential shortcoming in the Weberian enquiries to be his restriction to the 'subjective' dimension in the form of a *belief* in legitimacy, which is determined by the action-theory perspective, and the ensuing neglect of the 'objective' (firmly institutionalised) claim to legitimacy of social and political orders, including the possible and momentous conflicts between these two levels.

Another useful reference at this stage is the interesting reception of Weber in the work of F. L. Neumann, who considers the historical change in the relationship between economy, state and law (as well as the problem of fundamental assumptions in the philosophy of history) to be of central importance. Information on Neumann's relationship with the materialist tradition of thought, on the one hand, and with Max Weber, on the other, can be found in G. Schäfer's Epilogue to *Behemoth. Struktur und Praxis des Nationalsozialismus 1933–1944* (Cologne, 1977) and A. Söllner's Introduction to the collection of essays *Wirtschaft, Staat, Demokratie* (Frankfurt, 1978).

6 Social science and political commitment

1 Less convincing or briefer attempts from the Marxist perspective are (or are contained in), for example: Braunreuther, 1958–9 and 1964; Danilov, 1959; Heise, 1962, 1964; Kramer, 1968; Streisand, 1965; Lefèvre, 1971; Kuczynski, 1972; Lewis, 1975. From a fascist perspective: Steding's (1932) 'critique of ideology' analysis of Weberian thinking (as expression of bourgeois decadence).
2 The Epilogue to the second edition (442–77) is particularly important in the present context, since it also contains several references to the relationship between Weber's political conceptions and the 'theoretical work'. Cf. also Mommsen 1974b.
3 Concerning Weber's political conceptions in their historical context cf. further, above all, Bergstraesser, 1957, Roth, 1968 and Schmidt, 1964.
4 Compare the pertinent critique by F. Klein (1961) of Mommsen's book, as well as Mommsen's (1974a, 463 ff.) and Giddens' (1972, 58) anti-critical comments on the common Marxist critique of ideology on Weber.
5 It is common knowledge that Weber himself (as early as his 'inaugural lecture') disputed this possibility or necessity, although in this respect he overestimated the explanatory power of class-

theoretical assumptions and did not harbour the least doubt about his own class membership.

6 Weber also saw a 'catalyst for genuine democracy' in the institution of a strong 'democratically elected president', as long as this did not involve a 'surrender of power to a clique, but subjugation to self-elected leaders' (*PS*, 3rd end, 501). Marxist critics like Lukács (1962, 529) and Streisand (1965, 183) who, to discriminate against the Weberian understanding of democracy, cite a comment by Ludendorff agreeing with a similar formulation by Weber (amended by Marianne Weber), seem to abbreviate unduly the overall context of Weber's considerations on 'radical social democratisation' (*PS*, 3rd edn, 449). They should perhaps also bear in mind a second central Weberian argument for a strong president. Weber comments that it is desirable 'from the standpoint of the tightest socialist organisation possible' (*ibid.*, 469, cf. 498). By now there should be growing evidence for this argument which places emphasis on the efficiency of the executive rather than democratic legitimacy.

Finally, the critique by Marxist-Leninist authors of Weber's supposed merely 'instrumental' understanding of democracy does not seem particularly credible. One cannot seriously assert that Lenin had seen in democracy (particularly parliamentary democracy) a political-ethical 'value in itself'. For example, Lenin's explicit agreement with Plekhanov's totally instrumental treatment of the question of democratic majorities at the Second Congress of the RSDLP 1903 (see D. Shub, *Lenin*, Wiesbaden, 1962, 77), as well as his own political practice in the course of the 1917 revolution, do not lend any support to this.

7 'And for every party opinion there are facts that are extremely inconvenient, for my opinion no less than for others.' (Weber, *FMW*, 147.)

8 Mommsen (1974a, 1) – and with him Giddens (1972, 40 f.) – think that Weber's conception of scientific research can on the whole be interpreted as a 'continual grandiose attempt to secure for himself distance and inner freedom in relation to practical political events'.

9 The 'absurdity' that Weber implies in this concrete case refers to socialisation. Weber considered it a scientifically proven fact that 'the chances of acquisition amongst the broad mass of workers' (*PS*, 3rd edn, 461) would be economically damaging under the given circumstances. Paradoxically the conflicts preceding Weber's nomination as a candidate for the German Democratic Party (DDP) essentially related to the fact that Weber had repeatedly expressed himself to be fundamentally *in favour of* socialisation.

10 Weber's analyses on the problem of the nation, or nationality (*ES*, 921 ff. and *SSP*, 484 ff.) present a particularly important example of this. These sober analyses obviously also influenced Weber's own 'nationalism', and not least determined his criticism of the 'simply hollow and empty, purely animalistic nationalism', which was particularly widespread among the student fraternities, expressing a 'miserable contraction of the intellectual horizon' with respect to

the 'great cultural problems' (Letter of 15 November 1911 to a Freiburg colleague; cited in Mommsen, *op. cit.*, 70). Schmidt (1964, 261 ff.) provides a balanced assessment of Weber's nationalism.

11 Mommsen (*op. cit.*, 71 ff.) refers to Weber's approach to a critique of this hypothesis and notes that its development was probably prevented by Weber's bias in thinking of the power-state (*Machtstaat*).

12 Ritsert (1976) discusses this question in a general form – with absolute comparable results – but starting out from Weber's concept of 'value relevance' and the 'cultural importance' of social science research.

13 Cf. particularly Kretzschmar (1978) for this interpretation.

14 Compare also Mommsen (*op. cit.*, 43) and Baumgarten (1964, 256 f.) on the central importance held by the category of 'conflict'.

15 Cf. similar observations in Rehberg, (*op. cit.*, 219) and Ferber (*op. cit.*, 30).

16 This would also and particularly presuppose that the constitutive characteristics of the Weberian concept of social action are appropriately and absolutely taken as the basis. Thus, for example, Rehberg's observation (*op. cit.*, 211) that affective and traditional action were also structured on the basis of intersubjective meaningful relationships and in so far possess a distinctive understandable 'logic', can by no means be seen as an indication of a logical shortcoming in Weber's conceptual construction.

17 Concerning the relationship between meaningfulness, communicability and the capacity for consciousness cf. the references in Weiss, 1975 (51 ff., 91 f.) and 1981a.

18 This also refers in principle to the characteristics discussed by Ferber. From the fact that we can *also* apprehend an institutionally unattached, person-related and self-assertive action from Weber's concept of social action, one cannot derive that it is restricted to this form of action (or even to a special case of the same exceptional action by any great actors).

19 Cf. Weiss (1975, 97 f.) on the critique of Baumgarten's (1964, 556 f.) overemphasis in interpretation on this category (which in a more special meaning is indeed assimilated with the fundamental sociological categories of *Economy and Society*).

20 'Max Weber and Power-Politics, p. 83, in Stammer (ed.), 1971, 120. The counter-thesis (Korf, 1968a, 17) that Weber's 'political position' also illustrates the determining theme of the entire sociological work ('defence of bourgeois class domination'), only particularly openly and radically, discloses a low capacity for differentiation.

21 Schluchter (1971, 50 f.), Hufnagel (1971, *passim*), Albert (1972, 67 ff.), Kocka (1976, 285 ff.) and Weiss (1981b) particularly tackle the great importance that these considerations, which were largely neglected by the literature on Weber, nonetheless deserve.

22 In this context Weber characteristically speaks of the 'means of *scientific* analysis' (Weber, *FMW*, 145; author's emphasis).

23 Like many other Weber critics who argue at a political level,

Mommsen, (*op. cit.*, 66) also misses the crucial point in his observation that Weber had been able to give 'only more functional answers' to political questions. Since, in the context of empirical science, we cannot in fact give ethical-political answers, different methods for the rational solution of politically evaluative problems need to be developed. The differentiation between (morally) good and bad charismatic leaders, which Mommsen misses in Weber, could be the object of such methods. In Bergstraesser (1957, 217 f.), to whom Mommsen appeals, the differentiating critique suggested here is explicitly practised.

24 We can find comparatively differentiated considerations on the question of the 'partisanship' of the social sciences in Kramer (1968, 84 ff.).

25 Thus Roth (in Bendix and Roth, *Scholarship and Partisanship: Essays on Max Weber*, University of California Press, 1971, 242) with reference to a corresponding comment by Marianne Weber (1900, 1, Note 1) who, according to his sources of information, echoes Max Weber's opinion.

Bibliography

The bibliography is divided into four sections:

I   Works by Weber, including translations into English and Russian.
II Works by Marxist authors (in broader terms).
III Additional works on the relationship between Marx and Weber.
IV General literature referred to.

I have dispensed with a more detailed division by subject matter so as not to complicate the bibliography further. All works are listed only once. For a more comprehensive bibliography on Weber's work I recommend the synopsis by D. Käsler (1978, 424–46). The best bibliography on secondary literature is C. Seyfarth and G. Schmidt, *Max Weber Bibliographie*, Stuttgart, 1977.

Abbreviation used in the bibliography and notes

AR	'*Autoreferat*' ('self-survey' – Summary of Soviet Russian dissertations)
BSE	Bol'šaja Sovjetskaja Enciklopedija
CIS	Cahiers Internationaux de Sociologie
DZPh	Deutsche Zeitschrift für Philosophie
FN	Filosofskie Nauki
KSF	Kratkaja slovar' po filosofii
KZfSS	Kölner Zeitschrift für Soziologie und Sozialpsychologie
MEW	Collected Works/Werke, Marx and Engels
PR	Pečat' i Revol'jucija
PSB	Polish Sociological Bulletin
PZM	Pod Znamenem Marksizma
RIPh	Revue Internationale de Philosophie
SIE	Sovjetskaja Istoričeskaja Enciklopedija
SW	Soziale Welt
UBM	Unter dem Banner des Marxismus
VF	Voprosy Filosofii
ZfS	Zeitschrift für Soziologie

BIBLIOGRAPHY

Phil. *Philosophisches Wörterbuch*, ed. by G. Klaus and K. Buhr,
Wörter- 8th amended edn, Berlin (GDR), 1972.
buch:
Wörter- *Wörterbuch der marxistisch-leninistischen Soziologie*, ed. by
buch: W. Eichhorn et al., 2nd edn, Opladen, 1971.

For abbreviations relating to Weber's works, see below.

1 Works by Weber

1.1 German editions

SSP *Gesammelte Aufsätze zur Soziologie und zur Sozialpolitik*, ed. by Marianne Weber. Tübingen, 1924.

RS *Gesammelte Aufsätze zur Religionssoziologie*, 3 vols. Tübingen, 1920–21.

SWG *Gesammelte Aufsätze zur Sozial- und Wirtschaftgeschichte*, ed. by Marianne Weber. Tübingen, 1923.

WL *Gesammelte Aufsätze zur Wissenschaftslehre* (1922), 3rd edn (extended and improved), ed. by J. Winckelmann, Tübingen, 1968.

PS *Gesammelte Politische Schriften*, 3rd edn, ed. by J. Winckelmann, Tübingen, 1971.

WG *Wirtschaft und Gesellschaft. Grundriss der verstehenden Soziologie*, student edn, ed. by J. Winckelmann, Cologne/Berlin, 1964 (used for quotation). Fifth revised edn with critical commentary, Tübingen, 1976. *Die rationalen und soziologischen Grundlagen der Musik* (1921), Tübingen, 1972.

WGesch *Wirtschaftsgeschichte. Abriss der universalen Sozial- und Wirtschaftsgeschichte. Aus den nachgelassenen Vorlesungen*, ed. by S. Hellmann and M. Palyi, 3rd revised edn, ed. by J. Winckelmann, Berlin, 1958.

PE I *Die Protestantische Ethik. Eine Aufsatzsammlung*, ed. by J. Winckelmann, Munich/Hamburg, 1965.

PE II *Die Protestantische Ethik. Kritiken und Antikritiken*, ed. by J. Winckelmann, Munich/Hamburg, 1968.

'Zur Rechtfertigung Göhres', in *Christliche Welt*, 6/1892, Cols 1104–9.

'Was heisst christlich-sozial?, Zu F. Naumann Gesammelten Aufsätzen', in *Christliche Welt* 8/1894, Cols 472–7.

'Zur Lage der bürgerlichen Demokratie in Russland' in *Archiv für Sozialwissenschaft und Sozialpolitik*, Vol. 22, 1906, No. 1, Supplement, 234–353 (partly reprinted in *PS*).

'Russlands Übergang zum Scheinkonstitutionalismus', in *Archiv für Sozialwissenschaft und Sozialpolitik*, Vol. 23, 1906, No. 1, Supplement, 165–401 (partly reprinted in *PS*).

'Russlands Übergang zur Scheindemokratie', in *Die Hilfe*, Vol. 23, No. 17, 26 April 1917 (reprinted in *PS*, 197–215).

Gutachten *Gutachten zur Werturteilsdiskussion* (1913, printed in manuscript form by the *Verein für Sozialpolitik*). Reprinted in

E. Baumgarten *Max Weber. Werk und Person*, Tübingen, 1964, 102–39.

1.2 Works by Max Weber – English translations (used in quotation)

ES   *Economy and Society: An Outline of Interpretative Sociology*, translated, edited and introduced by G. Roth and C. Wittich, New York, 1968.

FMW   *From Max Weber. Essays in Sociology*, translated, edited and introduced by H. H. Gerth and C. Wright Mills, London/Boston, 1974.

MSS   *The Methodology of the Social Sciences*, translated and edited by E. A. Shils and H. A. Finch, New York, 1949.

PE   *The Protestant Ethic and the Spirit of Capitalism*, translated by T. Parsons, London, 1974.

1.3 Works by Max Weber – Russian translations published in the Soviet Union. (Concerning translations published in other socialist countries cf. the bibliography by Seyfarth and Schmidt, 1977, 12 f., which requires updating.)

Gorod (The City), translated by V. N. Popov, ed. with Foreword by N. I. Kareev, Petrograd, 1923.

Istorija chozjajstva. Očerk vseobščej social'noj i ekonomičeskoj istorii (General Economic History. An Outline of General Social and Economic History), edited with Foreword by I. M. Grevs as well as a contribution by V. D. 'Max Weber as Historian and Sociologist', Petrograd, 1923.

Agrarnaja istorija drevnego mira (Agricultural History of the Ancient World): 3rd version of 'Agrarverhältnisse im Altertum' of 1909), translated, edited and introduced by D. M. Petruševskij; supplemented with the essay 'The Roman Colony' by M. N. Rostovcev, Moscow, 1923.

Chozjajstvennaja etika mirovych religii (Economic Ethics of World Religions; translation of pp. 237–67 in *RS* I), in *Atheist*, 1928, No. 25, 19–39 (with a Foreword by the editor of the journal, 16–18).

Protestanskie sekty i duch kapitalizma (Protestant Sects and the Spirit of Capitalism; translation of pp. 207–36 in *RS* I without comments), in *Athiest*, 1928, No. 26, 19–31.

Protestanskaja etika i duch kapitalizma (The Protestant Ethic and the Spirit of Capitalism; abbreviated version of Part I, 1–3 of Weber's essay – *RS* I, 17–83 – without commentary), in *Atheist*, 1928, No. 30, 43–72.

Protestanskaja etika. Sbornik statej. Čast' pervaja (The Protestant Ethic. A Collection of Essays. First Part; translation of Foreword and Part I of Weber's essay, including Supplementary Notes in the pocket book edn by J. Winckelmann); translated and introduced by M. I. Levina, Moscow (Academy of Sciences of the USSR, Institute for Scientific Information on the Social Sciences), 1972.

II Works with critical discussions on Max Weber's work from a Marxist perspective (in broader terms)

A list of (a) works which refer to Weber's work, although sometimes only very briefly. Among these a few could not be considered in this analysis either for reasons of language or access. Moreover, included are (b) some essays in which Weber is not mentioned by name, but which deal directly with Weber's 'subject matter'.

Adler, Max, 'Politik und Moral', in *Nach dem Weltkrieg. Schriften zur Neuorientierung der auswärtigen Politik*, 5, Leipzig, 1918.

Adler, Max, 'Zum Tode Professor Max Webers', in *Arbeiterzeitung*, 27 June 1920.

Adler, Max, *Lehrbuch der materialistischen Geschichtsauffassung*, 2 vols, Berlin, 1930, 1932. (Now in *Soziologie des Marxismus*, 3 vols, with a contribution by Norbert Leser, Vienna, 1964.)

Anderson, Perry, *Passages from Antiquity to Feudalism*, London, 1978.

Anderson, Perry, *Lineages of the Absolutist State*, London, 1979.

Andreeva, G. M., *Sovremennaja buržuaznaja empiričeskaja sociologija. Kritičeskij očerk* (Contemporary Bourgeois Sociology. A Critical Survey), Moscow, 1965.

Assaf'ev, B. V., *Die musikalische Form als Prozess*, Berlin, 1976.

Assmann, Georg and Stollberg, Rudhard, *Grundlagen der marxistisch-leninistischen Soziologie* (especially 352–60), Frankfurt, 1977.

Bader, Veit-Michael, 'Legitimität und Legalität', unpublished manuscript, 1979.

Bader, Veit-Michael, Berger, Johannes, Ganssmann, Heiner and Knesebeck, Jost v.d., *Einführung in die Gesellschaftstheorie. Gesellschaft, Wirtschaft und Staat bei Marx und Weber*, 2 vols, Frankfurt, 1976 (2nd edn, 1980).

Bakurkin, B. F., 'Koncepcija social'nogo dejstvija M. Vebera – Osnova povedenčeskogo, podchoda v sociologičeskom funkcionalizme' (Max Weber's Theory of Social Action as the Basis of the Leading Approach in Sociological Functionalism), in *Kritika sovremennoj buržuaznoj ideologii*, Moscow, 1975, 18–31.

Bel'cer, L. L., 'O nektorych aspektach sociologii religii Maksa Vebera' (Some Aspects of Max Weber's Sociology of Religion), in *Naučnij ateizm: problemi teorii i praktiki*, Moscow, 1973, 140–57.

Bel'cer, L. L., 'Problema religioznost' social'nych grupp v sociologii Maksa Vebera' (The Problem of the Religiosity of Social Groups in Max Weber's Sociology), in *Vestnik Moskovskogo Universiteta*, No. 3, 1974, 84–93.

Berger, Johannes, 'Die Grenzen des handlungstheoretischen Paradigmas am Beispiel der "soziologischen Grundbegriffe" Max Webers', in K. M. Bolte (ed.), *Materialien aus der soziologischen Forschung*, Darmstadt, 1978, 1081 ff.

Bergner, Dieter et al. (eds), *Die philosophische Lehre von Karl Marx und ihre aktuelle Bedeutung. Philosophischer Kongress DDR 1968*, Berlin, 1968.

Bergner, Dieter and Mocek, Reinhard, *Bürgerliche Gesellschaftstheorien.*

Studien zu den weltanschaulichen Grundlagen und ideologischen Funktionen bürgerlicher Gesellschaftsauffassungen, Berlin, 1976.

Bloch, Ernst, 'Über Freiheit und objektive Gesetzlichkeit, politisch gefasst', in *DZPh* 4, 1954, 824–6.

Bollhagen, Peter, *Soziologie und Geschichte*, Berlin, 1966.

Borodaj, Jurij, 'Genezija kapitalizma u. K. Marksa i M. Vebera' (The Genesis of Capitalism in K. Marx and M. Weber), unpublished manuscript, Moscow, 1979.

Braunreuther, Kurt, 'Bemerkungen über Max Weber und die bürgerliche Soziologie', in *Wissenschaftliche Zeitschrift der Humboldt-Universität Berlin*, Social and Linguistic Science Series VIII, 1958–9, Part 1, 115–23.

Braunreuther, Kurt, 'Ökonomie und Gesellschaft in der deutschen bürgerlichen Soziologie – Wissenschaftsgeschichtliche Studie', in *Fragen der marxistischen Soziologie* (Part II), Berlin, 1964, 75–106. (Both of the above Braunreuther essays are reprinted in Braunreuther, Kurt, *Studien zur Geschichte der politischen Ökonomie und Soziologie*, Berlin, 1978.)

Braunreuther, K. and Steiner, H., 'Zur Situation der bürgerlichen Soziologie in Westdeutschland', in K. Braunreuther (ed.), *Zur Kritik der bürgerlichen Soziologie in Westdeutschland*, Berlin, 1962, 9–85.

Bukharin, N., *Historical Materialism. A System of Sociology*, London, 1926.

Bukharin, N. and Preobrazhensky, E., *The ABC of Communism: A Popular Explanation of the Program of the Communist Party of Russia*, Michigan Press, 1966.

Cacciari, Massimo, *Dopo l'autunno caldo: ristrutturazione e analisi di classe*, Padua, 1973.

Cacciari, Massimo, 'Weber e la critica della ragione socialista', in *Max Weber, Sul socialismo reale*, introduced by M. Ciampa, Rome, 1979, 81–108.

Čalikova, Victorija A., 'Koncepcija rational'noj organizacii v sociologii Maksa Vebera i v sovremennych buržuaznych teorijach bjurokratii. Kritičeskijj analiz' (The Conception of Rational Organisation in Max Weber's Sociology and Contemporary Bourgeois Theories of Bureaucracy. A Critical Analysis), *AR* of candidate's dissertation, Faculty of Philosophy at the Academy of Sciences, Moscow, 1970.

Čalikova, Victorija A., 'Idej Maksa Vebera v sovremennoj, amerikanskoj sociologii. Teoretičeskij obzor' (Max Weber's Ideas in Contemporary American Sociology. Theoretical Overview), unpublished manuscript, Moscow, undated.

Cantimori, Delio, *Studi di storia*, 1959 (especially 86–110: 'Nota introduttiva a Max Weber'; 111–17: 'Weber e la vita politica tedesca'; 118–36: 'Studi sulle origini e lo spirito del capitalismo').

Cassano, F., *Autocritica della sociologia contemporanea*, Bari, 1971, 25–70.

Cerroni, U., *La Libertá dei moderni*, Bari, 1968.

Colletti, Lucio, *From Rousseau to Lenin. Studies in Ideology and Society*, London, 1972.

Crompton, Rosemary and Gubbay, Jon, *Economy and Class Structure*, London, 1977.
Danilov, A. I., *Problemy agrarnoj istorii rannego srednevekov'ja v nemeckoj istorigrafii konca XIX – načala XX v.* (Problems of Agricultural History in German Historiography at the End of the 19th and Beginning of the 20th Century), Moscow, 1958.
Danilov, A. I., 'Die deutschen Historiker der "liberalen Schule" während des 1. Weltkrieges und der Revolution 1918–19, in *Sowjetwissenschaft*, 1959, 300–17. (Originally in Russian, in *Novja Novejšaja Istorija* 1958, No. 5, 111–24).
Danilov, A. I., 'Max Weber', in *SIE*, Vol. 3, Cols 17–18, Moscow, 1963.
Devjatkova, Rimma P., 'Max Weber und Karl Marx', in *DZPh*, 16, 1968a, 1356–61.
Devjatkova, Rimma P., 'Maks Veber i problema "zapadnoj racional nosti"' (Max Weber and the Problem of 'Occidental Rationality'), in *Vestnik Leningrad Universiteta*, Serija ekononomiki, filosofii i prava, Vol. 17, No. 3, 1968b, 127–9.
Devjatkova, Rimma P., 'Nekotorye aspekty sociologii M. Vebera, Kritičeskij analiz' (Some Aspects of Max Weber's Sociology. A Critical Analysis), *AR* of candidate's philosophical dissertation, Leningrad, 1969.
Devjatkova, Rimma P., 'Problema vlasti v nemeckoj sociologii konca XIX – načala XX v.' (The Problem of Power in German Sociology at the End of the 19th and Beginning of the 20th Century), in *Vestnik Leningrad Universiteta*, Serija ekonomiki, filosofii i prava, Vol. 23, 1970, 75–85.
Devjatkova, Rimma P., 'Kritica principa "svobody nauki ot cennostej" v sociologii M. Vebera' (Critique of the Principle of 'Ethical Neutrality in the Sciences' in Max Weber's Sociology), in *Učen. zap. kafedr obščestvenn. nauk vuzov Leningrada*, Filosofija, 1971, No. 12, 187–98.
Devjatkova, Rimma P., 'Max Weber', in *BSE*, 3rd edn, 1970 ff., Vol. 17, Col. 1031 f. Also in the English edn, *Great Soviet Encyclopedia*, New York/London, 1974, Vol. 4, 680 f.
Devjatkova, R. and Štoff, V. A., 'Problemy ideal'noj tipologii i modelej v istoriko-social'nych naukach' (Problems of Ideal Typology and Models in the Historical Sciences), in *Problemy methodologii social'nogo issledovanija*, Leningrad, 1970.
Dmitriev, A. V., *Političeskaja sociologija SSA. Ocerki* (Political Sociology of the United States. Studies), Leningrad, 1971.
Döbert, Rainer, 'Zur Logik des Übergangs von archäischen zu hochkulturellen Religionssystemen', in K. Eder (ed.), *Seminar: Die Entzauberung von Klassengesellschaften*, Frankfurt, 1973a, 330–63.
Döbert, Rainer, 'Die evolutionäre Bedeutung der Reformation', in Seyfarth and Sprondel (ed.), 1973b, 303–12.
Döbert, Rainer, 'Methodologische und forschungsstrategische Implikationen von evolutionstheoretischen Stadienmodellen', in Jaeggi and Honneth (eds), 1977, 524–60.
Domin, G., Lanfermann, H. H., Mocek, R. and Pälicke, D., *Bürgerliche Wissenschaftstheorie und ideologischer Klassenkampf* (especially

148–51), Berlin, 1973.
Drobnickij, O. G., 'Buržuaznaja socioligija i social'naja filosofija prošlogo' (The Bourgeois Sociology and Social Philosophy of the Past), in *VF*, 1973, No. 1, 120–32 (especially 125 ff.).
Eder, Klaus, *Die Entstehung staatlich organisierter Gesellschaften*, Frankfurt, 1976.
Eder, Klaus, 'Zum Problem der logischen Periodisierung von Produktionsweisen. Ein Beitrag zu einer evolutionstheoretischen Rekonstruktion des Historischen Materialismus', in Jaeggi and Honneth (eds), 1977, 501–23.
Eder, Klaus, 'Die Entwicklung von Begründungsstrukuren des modernen Rechts', in Seyfarth and Sprondel (eds), *Max Weber und die Rationalisierung sozialen Handelns*, Stuttgart, 1981.
Eder, Klaus and Rödel, Ulrich, 'Handlungstheoretische Implikationen des Historischen Materialismus, in K. M. Bolte (ed.), *Materialien aus der soziologischen Forschung*, Darmstadt, 1978, 1092 ff.
Filipec, J., 'Max Weber a současná sociologia' (Max Weber and Sociology Today – Report to the 15th German Sociology Conference 1964), in *Sociologicky Časopis*, 1965 (Prague), 72–4.
Fleischer, Julia, 'Max Weber und das Problem der Rationalität, in *Annales Universitatis Scientiarum Budapestinensis de Rolando Eötvös Nominatae*, Sectio Philosophica et Sociologica, Tomus X, 1976, 115–27 (originally in Hungarian, in *Világosság*, 1973).
Fojtik, I., 'Kritica sub'ektivizma sociologii Maksa Vebera i jego posledovatelej' (Critique of the Subjectivism of Max Weber's and Weberian Sociology), *AR* of candidate's dissertation, Academy of the Social Sciences at the Central Committee of The Soviet Communist Party, Moscow, 1962.
Gabel, Joseph, 'Une Lecture Marxiste de la Sociologie Religieuse de Max Weber', in *CIS*, 46, 1969, 51–66.
Gajdenko, P. P., 'Sociologičeskie akspekty analiza nauki' (Sociological Aspects of Scientific Analysis), in *Učenye o nauke i jego razvitii*, Moscow, 1971, 232–58.
Gajdenko, P. P., 'Ideja racional'nosti v sociologii muzyki M. Vebera' (The Idea of Rationality in Max Weber's Sociology of Music), in *Sovjetskaja Muzyka* 9, 1975, 114–22.
Gisselbrecht, A., 'Vorbemerkungen und Anmerkungen zu Lukács', (Preamble and Notes to Lukács), 1955.
Goldmann, Lucien, *Gesellschaftwissenschaften und Philosophie*, Frankfurt, 1971.
Gulyga, A. V., 'Ponjatie i obraz v istoričeskoj nauke' (Conceptualisation and Perspective of the Historical Sciences), in *VF*, 1965, No. 9, 3–14.
Gvišiani, D. M., *Management* (especially 296 ff.), Frankfurt, 1974. (Originally published in Russian under the title *Organizacija i upravlenie. Sociologičeskij analiz buržuasnych teorii* – Organisation and Administration. Sociological Analysis of Bourgeois Theories, Moscow, 1970.)
Habermas, Jürgen, *Wissenschaft und Technik als 'Ideologie'*, Frankfurt, 1969.

Habermas, Jürgen, *Zur Logik der Sozialwissenschaften Materialien*, Frankfurt, 1970.
Habermas, Jürgen, *Legitimation Crisis*, London, 1976a.
Habermas, Jürgen, *Zur Rekonstruktion des Historischen Materialismus*, Frankfurt, 1976b.
Hahn, Erich, *Historischer Materialismus und marxistische Soziologie*, Berlin, 1968.
Havelka, Miloš, 'Kritické poznámky ke koncepci rationality a svobody u Maxe Webera' (Critical Notes on M. Weber's Conceptions of Rationality and Freedom), in *Sociologicky Časopis*, Prague, 1976 (12), 300–12.
Heise, Wolfgang, *Die deutsche Philosophie von 1895 bis 1917*, Berlin, 1962.
Heise, Wolfgang, *Aufbruch in die Illusion. Zur Kritik der bürgerlichen Philosophie in Deutschland*, Berlin, 1964.
Herkommer, Sebastian, 'Soziologie der Sozialstruktur. Historisch-materialistische Kritikpunkte zu "Klasse" und "Schicht"', in H. J. Krysmanski and P. Marwedel (eds), *Die Krise in der Soziologie*, Cologne, 1975, 122–39.
Hilferding, Rudolf, 'Das historische Problem', in *Zeitschrift für Politik*, 1/1954, 295–324.
Hofmann, Werner, *Gesellschaftslehre als Ordnungsmacht. Die Werturteilsfrage – heute*, Berlin, 1961.
Hofmann, Werner, *Grundelemente der Wirtschaftsgesellschaft*, Reinbek, 1969.
Hofmann, Werner, *Ideengeschichte der sozialen Bewegung des 19. und 20. Jahrhunderts*, 3rd revised edn, Berlin, 1970.
Horn, Johannes Heinz, 'Religion und Gesellschaft. Kritik herrschender Auffassungen in der bürgerlichen Religionssoziologie', in R. Schulz (ed.), *Beiträge zur Kritik der gegenwärtigen bürgerlichen Geschichtsphilosophie*, pp. 53–165, Berlin, 1958.
Ionin, L. G., 'Koncepii "ponimanija" v amerikanskoj sociologii. Kritika mirovozzrenčeskich osnovanii' (Conception of 'Verstehen' in American Sociology. Critique of 'Weltanschaulicher' Bases), *AR* of candidate's dissertation, Moscow, 1974.
Kapeljuš, F., *Religija rannego kapitalizma* (The Religion of Early Capitalism), Moscow, 1931.
Kautsky, Karl, *Die materialistische Geschichtsauffassung, Vol. II: Der Staat und die Entwicklung der Menschheit*, Berlin, 1927.
Kejzerov, N. M., and Devjatkova, R. P., 'Kritika concepcii vlasti M. Vebera i R. Arona' (Critique of the Concept of Power in M. Weber and R. Aron), in *Problemy borby protiv buržuaznoj ideologii* (Problems of the Struggle against Bourgeois Ideology), No. 1, Leningrad, 1971, 47–68.
Kissel, M. A., *Idealizm protiv Nauki* (Idealism against Science), Leningrad, 1969, 229–37.
Kittsteiner, Heinz-Dieter, 'Theorie und Geschichte. Zur Konzeption der modernen westdeutschen Sozialgeschichte', in *Das Argument*, No. 75, Berlin, 1972, 18–32.
Kittsteiner, Heinz-Dieter, 'Objektivität und Totalität. Vier Thesen zur

Geschichtstheorie von Karl Marx', in R. Koselleck, W. J. Mommsen and J. Rüsen (eds), *Objektivität und Parteilichkeit in der Geschichtswissenschaft*, Munich, 1977, 159–70.

Klein, Fritz, Review of W. Mommsen, 'Max Weber und die deutsche Politik 1890–1920', Tübingen, 1959, in *Deutsche Literaturzeitung*, Vol. 82, Cols 827–31.

Klügl, Johann, 'Die bürgerliche Religionssoziologie und ihre Funktion im ideologischen System des staatsmonopolistischen Kapitalismus', in *DZPh*, 15, 1967, 671–90.

Klügl, Johann, 'Die protestantische Ethik und die Entstehung des Kapitalismus. Zur Kritik der Religionssoziologie Max Webers', in *Wissenschaftliche Zeitschrift der Friedrich-Schiller-Universität Jena*, Social and Linguistic Science Series, 19/1970, 591–5.

Kmita, Jerzy and Nowak, Leszek, 'Studia nad teoretycznymi podstawami humanistyki' (Studies on the Theoretical Bases of the Human Sciences), Poznan, 1968 (cf. the review in *PSB*, 1969, No. 2.

Kmita, Jerzy and Nowak, Leszek, 'The Rationality Assumption in Human Sciences', in *PSB*, 1970, 43–68.

Koch, Gisela, '"Soziales Handeln" kontra Praxis – Zur soziologischen Konzeption Ralf Dahrendorfs', in *DZPh*, 7, 1965, 789–805.

Kofler, Leo, *Zur Geschichte der bürgerlichen Gesellschaft*, 3rd edn, Neuwied/Berlin, 1966.

Kofler, Leo, *Die Wissenschaft von der Gesellschaft*, Cologne, 1971.

Kon, Igor S., *O sovremennoj buržuaznoj filosofii istorii* (Contemporary Bourgeois Philosophy of History), Leningrad, 1957.

Kon, Igor S., *Filosofskij idealizm i krizis buržuaznoj istoričeskoj mysli* (Philosophical Idealism and the Crisis in Bourgeois Historical Thinking) (especially 87–95), Moscow, 1959.

Kon, Igor, S., *Die Geschichtsphilosophie des 20. Jahrhunderts*, 2 vols, Berlin, 1964 (2nd edn, 1966).

Kon, Igor S., *Der Positivismus in der Soziologie. Geschichtlicher Abriss*, Berlin, 1973.

Konya, I., 'A Kalvinismus – a Kapitalista társadalom vallasi felé pitiméne' (Calvinism as a Religious Superstructure of Capitalist Society), in *Acta Universitatis Debreciensis de Ludovico Kossuth nominatae*, Serial Marxistica-Leninistica et pedagogica 8 (1), Budapest, 1962, 7–29.

Korablev, L. V., 'Die marxistische Methode der Ausarbeitung der Typen der sozialen Erscheinungen und ihr prinzipieller Gegensatz zur Konzeption "konkreter Typen"', *Wissenschaftliche Zeitschrift der Technischen Hochschule Otto von Guericke*, Magdeburg, 12, 1968a, 525–8.

Korablev, L. V., 'Osnovnye čerty tipologii M. Vebera' (Basic Features of M. Weber's Typology), in *Vestnik MGU*, No. 4, Serija filosofija, Moscow, 1968b.

Korablev, L. V., 'V. I. Lenin o goseologičeskoj kategorii "tip"' (V. I. Lenin concerning the Gnoseological Category 'Type'), in *Nektoroye voprosy Leninskogo filosofskogo nasledstvo*, Moscow, 1968c.

Korablev, L. V., 'M. Veber i sovremennaja koncepcija "konstruirovannych tipov"' (Max Weber and the Current Conception of 'Constructive Types'), in *Iz istorii buržuaznoj sociologii XIX-XX VV.* (ed. by G. M. Andreev), Moscow, 1968d, 48–69.

Korablev, L. V., 'Koncepcija "ideal'nych tipov" "social'nogo dejstivija" Maksa Vebera i jego teoretičeskaja nesostojatelnost'" (The Conception of Max Weber's 'Ideal Types' of 'Social Action' and Their Scientific Untenability), *AR* of the candidate's dissertation, Moscow, 1969.

Korf, Gertraud, 'Der Idealtypus Max Webers und die historisch-gesellschaftlichen Gesetzmässigkeiten', in *DZPh* 11, 1964, 1328–43.

Korf, Gertraud, 'Die Kategorien "kausale Zurechnung" und "Idealtypus" in der Methodologie Max Webers. Darstellung und Kritik', philosophical dissertation, Berlin, 1968a.

Korf, Gertraud, 'Die Marxismus-Kritik in der Methodologie Max Webers' in D. Bergner *et al.* (eds), *Die philosophische Lehre von Karl Marx und ihre aktuelle Bedeutung*, Berlin, 1968b, 253–61.

Korf, Gertraud, *Ausbruch aus dem 'Gehäuse der Hörigkeit'? Kritik der Kulturtheorien Max Webers und Herbert Marcuses*, Frankfurt, 1971.

Kozyr-Kowalski, Stanislaw, 'Krytyka Teorii Nauki Maxa Webera szkic Marksistowskiego Modelu Nauki', in *Studia Socjologiczno-polityczne*, 17, 1964, 127–64.

Kozyr-Kowalski, Stanislaw, 'Max Weber (1894–1920)', in *Euhemer*, 6, 1965, 25–34.

Kozyr-Kowalski, Stanislaw, 'Miejsce wartości w poznaniu humanistycznym w ujeciu M. Webera i K. Marksa. Studium z socjologii wiedzy' (The Position of Value in Humanist Knowledge from the Perspectives of M. Weber and Karl Marx. An Enquiry in the Sociology of Knowledge), Post-Doctoral Thesis, Torun, 1968a.

Kozyr-Kowalski, Stanislaw, in *PSB*, 1968b, 5–17 (part of Chapter 3 of the book: *Max Weber a Karol Marks. Socjologia Maxa Webera jako 'pozytywna krytyka materializmu historycznego'* – Max Weber and Karl Marx. Max Weber's Sociology as 'Positive Critique of Historical Materialism', Warsaw, 1967).

Kozyr-Kowalski, Stanislaw, 'Krytyka modelu biurokracje Maksa Webera' (Critique of Max Weber's Model of Bureaucracy), in *Państwo i Pravo*, 23, 1968c, 446–54.

Kozyr-Kowalski, Stanislaw, 'Wlasnosc jako zjawisko ekonomiczno – spoleczne w swietle badan Karola Marksa i Maxa Webera', in S. Kozyr-Kowalski (ed.), *Wlasnosc: gospodarka a prawo*, Warsaw, 1977, 47–157.

Kozyr-Kowalski, Stanislaw, *Max Weber a wspolczesne teorie stratyfikaji spolecznej*, Warsaw, 1979.

Kozyr-Kowalski, Stanislaw, 'Weberowska socjologia religii a teoria spoteczeństwa jako calości' in *Max Weber, Szkice z socjologii religii*, Warsaw, 1984, pp. 7–68.

Kramer, Horst, 'Philosophische Aspekte der Soziologie Max Webers', philosophical dissertation, Karl-Marx-Universität, Leipzig, 1968.

Kretzschmar, Ute, *Theorien des sozialen Handelns im Dienste der Monopole* (especially 10–50), Berlin, 1978.

Krzemiński, Irenusz, 'Marx's Methodological Ideas' (Debate article on L. Nowak, U podstaw . . . 1971), in *PSB*, 1972, 128–30.

Kuczynski, Jürgen, *Die politökonomische Apologetik des Monopolkapitals in der Periode der allgemeinen Krise des Kapitalismus*, Berlin, 1952.

Kuczynski, Jürgen, *Studien zur Wissenschaft von den Gesellschaftswissenschaften* (especially 189 ff.), Berlin, 1972.

Kuznecov, Anatolij Aleksandrovič, 'Problema voznikovenija sovremennoj zapadnojevropejsko kultury v sociologii religii M. Vebera' (The Problem of the Emergence of Modern West European Culture in Max Weber's Sociology of Religion), in *Kritika antinaučnych koncepcii o prirode, obščestve i poznanii* (Critique of Anti-Scientific Conceptions of Nature, Society and Knowledge), Sovjet molodych učenych LGU, State University of Leningrad, 1974a, 93–8. (Chapter 2 of the author's dissertation.)

Kuznecov, Anatolij Aleksandrovič, 'Kritika sociologija religii M. Vebera' (Critique of Max Weber's Sociology of Religion), *AR* of the candidate's dissertation, Leningrad, 1974b.

Kuznecov, Anatolij Aleksandrovič, 'Predmet i zadači sociologii religii v trudach M. Vebera' (Object and Tasks of the Sociology of Religion in the Works of Max Weber), unpublished manuscript, Soviet Academy of Sciences (Moscow), 1978.

Kvesko, Raisa Bronislarovna, 'Kritika koncepcija "ideal'nych tipov" Maksa Vebera v svete marksistskoy teorii poznanija' (Critique of the Max Weber's Conception of Ideal Types in the Light of the Marxist Theory of Knowledge), in *F. Engel's i obščestvennye nauki*, Tomsk, 1971a.

Kvesko, Raisa Bronislarovna, 'Maks Veber o predmete sociologii' (Max Weber on the Objective of Sociology), in *Voprosy metodologii nauki*, No. 1, Tomsk, 1971b.

Kvesko, Raisa Bronslarovna, 'K voprosu o principe "ob'jectivnost" v sociologii Maksa Vebera, (o sootnošenii ob' jektivnosti i pertiinosti) (Concerning the Question of the Principle of 'Objectivity' in Max Weber's Sociology – On the Relationship between Objectivity and Partisanship), in *Voprosy metodologii nauki*, No. 2, Tomsk, 1972.

Kvesko, Raisa Bronslarovna, 'Sociologičeskaja koncepcija Maksa Vebera i sovremennaja ideologičeskaja bor'ba' (The Sociological Conception of Max Weber and the Contemporary Ideological Struggle), *AR* of the philosophy-candidate's dissertation, Tomsk, 1974.

Lefèvre, Wolfgang, *Zum historischen Charakter und zur historischen Funktion der Methode bürgerlicher Soziologie, Untersuchungen am Werk Max Webers*, Frankfurt, 1971.

Lenin, V. I., 'Lecture on the 1905 Revolution', in V. I. Lenin, *Works*, Vol. 23, London, 1964.

Levada, I. A., 'Osnovnie napravlenija buržuaznoj sociologii religii' (Basic Directions of the Bourgeois Sociology of Religion), in *Filosofskie problemy ateizma*, Moscow, 1963, 63 ff. (on Weber, see particularly, 68–74).

Levada, I. A., 'Sociologija i religija' (Sociology and Religion), in *Marksistskaja i buržuaznaja sociologija segodnja* (ed. by the Academy of the Sciences of the USSR), Moscow, 1964, 432–8.

Levina, M. I., Introduction to Max Weber, *The Protestant Ethic* (In Russian), Moscow, 1972, 1–15.

Lewis, John, *Max Weber and Value-Free Sociology: A Marxist Critique*, London, 1975.

Lukács, Georg, *History and Class Consciousness: Studies in Marxist Dialectics*, Second edn, London, 1968.

Lukács, Georg, 'Značenie "Materializma i Empiriokriticizma" dlja bolševizacii kommunističeskich partii' (The Importance of 'Materialism and Empirio-Criticism' for the Bolshevisation of the Communist Parties), in *PZM*, 1934, 143–8 (extracts in Watnik, 1965, 195 ff.).

Lukács, Georg, 'Marx und das Problem des ideologischen Verfalls', in *Einheit*, I/1946a, 108–17.

Lukács, Georg, 'Die deutsche Soziologie von dem ersten Weltkrieg', in *Aufbau*, I/1946b, 476–89.

Lukács, Georg, 'Die deutsche Soziologie zwischen dem 1. und dem 2. Weltkrieg', in *Aufbau* I/1946c, 585–600. (Both of the articles from the journal *Aufbau* correspond with Chapters IV and V in Lukács, 1962).

Lukács, Georg, 'Max Weber et la Sociologie Allemande', in *La Nouvelle Critique*, 1955 (Paris), 75–91 (corresponds essentially with Chapter IV in Lukács, 1962).

Lukács, Georg, 'Die Zerstörung der Vernunft', *Werke*, Vol. 9, Neuwied, 1962, 521–37.

Lukács, Georg, *Zur Ontologie des gesellschaftlichen Seins. Die ontologischen Grundprinzipien von Marx*, Darmstadt/Neuwied, 1972.

Lukáš, P., 'Tři studie o Maxu Weberovi' (in Czech), philosophical dissertation, University of Brünn, 1972.

Lunačarskij, Anatolij, 'Über die soziologische Methode in der Musiktheorie und Musikgeschichte. Zu Max Webers Musikbuch (1925), in A. Lunačarskij, *Die Revolution und die Kunst. Essays-Reden-Notizen*, Dresden, 1962, 32–54.

Mägdefrau, Werner, 'Spätmittelalterliche Klassenkämpfe und frühbürgerliche Revolution. Grundfragen der Entwicklung der Städte und des Bürgertums im Mittelalter', in *Wissenschaftliche Zeitschrift der Friedrich-Schiller-Universität Jena*, Social and Linguistic Science Series, Vol 26, No. 3, 1977, 377–404.

Marcuse, Herbert, 'Zur Auseinandersetzung mit Hans Freyers "Soziologie als Wirklichkeitswissenschaft"', in *Philosophische Hefte* 3, Berlin, 1931-2, 83–91.

Marcuse, Herbert 'Industrialisation and Capitalism in the Work of Max Weber', in H. Marcuse, *Negations: Essays in Critical Theory*, Harmondsworth, 1972a.

Marcuse, Herbert, *One Dimensional Man*, London, 1972b.

Markarjan, E. S., 'O značenii sravnitel'nogo metoda v kul'turnoističeskom poznanii' (The Importance of the Comparative Method in Cultural-Historical Knowledge), in *Vestnik istorii mirovoj kul'tury*, 1957, No. 4, 23–39.

Markarjan, E. S., 'Metodologičeskie problemy sistemnogo issledovanija obščetvennoj žizni (Methodological Problems of the System Theory Approach to Social Life), Ph.D. Dissertation, Moscow, 1967.

Markiewicz, Wladyslaw, 'Marx or Weber: A Genuine or an Imaginary Dilemma? in *Dialectics and Humanism. The Polish Philosophical Quarterly*, Vol. 8, No. 3, 1983, pp. 5–21.
Maschkin, N. A., *Römische Geschichte*, Berlin, 1953.
Merleau-Ponty, Maurice, *Les Aventures de la Dialectique*, Paris, 1955.
Merleau-Ponty, Maurice, *Adventures of the Dialectic*, Illinois, 1973.
Meurer, Bärbel, *Mensch und Kapitalismus bei Max Weber. Zum Verhältnis von Soziologie und Wirklichkeit*, Berlin/Munich, 1974.
Miksic, Dragutin, Debate article on M. Weber, The Protestant Ethic ... (in Serbo-Croat; Sarajevo, 1968), in *Naše teme* 13/1969, 837–41.
Miliband, R., 'The Capitalist State – Reply to Nicos Poulantzas', *New Left Review*, 59, 1970, 53–60.
Miliband, R., 'Poulantzas and the Capitalist State', *New Left Review*, 82, 1973, 83–92.
Mills, C. Wright, *The Sociological Imagination*, Oxford, 1959.
Moskvičev, L. N., *The End of Ideology Theory: Illusions and Reality*, Moscow, 1974 (originally in Russian, 1971).
Muhić, Fuad, Debate article on M. Weber, The Protestant Ethic ... (in Serbo-Croat; Sarajevo, 1968), in *Pregled*, No. 59, 1968, 572–7.
Musil, J., 'Metodologické problémy u Maxe Webera' (Methodological Problems in Max Weber), philosophical dissertation, Karls-University, Prague, 1952.
Naumann, Robert, *Theorie und Praxis des Neoliberalismus*. Berlin, 1957.
Naumova, N. F., 'Nekotorye uroki razvitija zapadnoj sociologii' (Some Lessons from the Development of West-German Sociology), in *VF*, 12, 1968, 54–65.
Neusychin, Aleksandr I., 'K voprosu ob elementach kapitalizma v srednevekovom obščestve' (V svjazi s polemikoj A. Dopša protiv V. Sombarta)' (Concerning the Question of Elements of Capitalism in Medieval Society – in Connection with A. Dopsch's Polemic against W. Sombart), in *Pěcat'i Revoljucija*, 1923a, No. 5, 21–37.
Neusychin, Aleksandr, I. 'Sociologičeskoe issledovanie Maksa Vebera o gorode' (Max Weber's Sociological Enquiry into The City), in *PZM*, 1923b, No. 6, 219–50.
Neusychin, Aleksandr I., 'Novij opyt postrojenija sistematičeskoj istorii chozjajstva (Po povodu knigi: M. Weber, Wirtschaftsgeschichte etc. 1923)' (A New Attempt to Construct Systematic Economic History – On the Occasion of the Book: M. Weber, General Economic History etc.), in *Archiv Marksa i Engel'sa*, 1924. Vol. I, 425–35.
Neusychin, Aleksandr I., Review of S. G. Lozinskij, 'Klassovskaja bor'ba v srednevekovom gorode' (The Class Struggle in the Medieval City), in *Pěcat' i Revoljucija*, 1926a, No. 1, 180–2.
Neusychin, Aleksandr I., Review of W. Sombart 'Soziologie' (in Russian), in *Pěcat' i Revoljucija*, 1926b, No. 5, 175.
Neusychin, Aleksandr I., '"Empiričeskaja sociologija" Maksa Vebera i logika istoričeskoj nauki' (Max Weber's 'Empirical Sociology' and the Logic of the Historical Sciences), in *PZM*, 1927, No. 9, 113–43 and No. 12, 111–37.
Neusychin, Aleksandr I., *Die Entstehung der abhängigen Bauernschaft als*

Klasse der früh-feudalen Gesellschaft in Westeuropa vom 6. bis zum 8. Jahrhundert, Berlin, 1961.
Neusychin, Aleksandr I., *Problemy jevropejskogo feodolizma. Izbranie trudy* (Problems of European Feudalism. Selected Essays), Moscow, 1974. Contains, among others, the essays 'Sociologičeskie issledovanie . . .' (472–500) and 'Empiričeskaja Sociologija . . .' (413–71).
Novikov, N. S., 'O tendencijach i problemach buržuaznoj sociologii pervogo tridcatiletija 20 veka' (Tendencies and Problems of Bourgeois Sociology in the First Third of the 20th Century), in *Vestnik istorii mirovoj kul'tury*, No. 5, Moscow, 1959, 123–9.
Novikov, N. V., 'Ideologičeskij smysl "teorii social'nogo dejstvija"' (The Ideological Importance of the 'Theory of Social Action'), in *FN*, 1961, No. 4, 54–61.
Novikov, N. V., 'Ob ischodnych posylkach i glavnych čertach buržuaznoj teorii "social'nogo dejstvija"' (The Initial Prerequisites and the Central Characteristics of the Bourgeois Theory of 'Social Action'), in *Marksistskaja i buržuaznaja sociologija segodnja* (ed. by the Academy of Sciences of the USSR), Moscow, 1964, 351–74.
Novikov, N. V., *Kritika sovremennoj buržuaznoj nauki o social'noj povedenii* (Critique of the Modern Bourgeois Science of Social Behaviour), Moscow, 1966.
Nowak, Leszek, 'Historical Generalizations and Problems of Historicism and Idiographism', *PSB*, 1969, No. 2, 48–55.
Nowak, Leszek, 'Social Action versus Individual Action', in *PSB*, 1971a, No. 1, 84–93.
Nowak, Leszek, Debate acticle on E. Mokrzycki, Zacozenia etc., 1970, in *PSB*, 1971b, No. 1, 144–7.
Nowak, Leszek, 'Karol Marks contra Max Weber', in *Nurt*, No. 3, 1971c (Posen), 46–8.
Nowak, Leszek, *U podstaw marksistowskiej metodologii nauk* (The Bases of Marx's Scientific Methodology), Warsaw, 1971d. (Cf. the debate article by I. Krzemiński in *PSB*, 1972, Nos 1–2, 128–30.)
Nowak, Leszek, 'Das Problem der Erklärung in Marx' Kapital', in J. Ritsert (ed.), *Zur Wissenschaftslogik einer kritischen Soziologie*, Frankfurt, 1976, 13–45.
Offe, Claus, 'Politische Herrschaft und Klassenstrukturen – Zur Analyse spät-kapitalistischer Gesellschaften', in G. Kress and D. Senghaas (eds), *Politikwissenschaft*, Frankfurt, 1969, 155 ff.
Offe, Claus, 'Rationalitätskriterien und Funktionsprobleme politisch-administrativen Handelns', in *Leviathan*, 2/1974, 333–45.
Osipov, G. V., *Sovremennaja buržuaznaja sociologija* (Modern Bourgeois Sociology), Moscow, 1964.
Osipova, E. V., 'The Problem of Ideology in M. Weber', unpublished Manuscript, Moscow. 1979.
Ossowska, Marie, 'Value-Judgements in our Conceptual Apparatus', in *PSB*, 1968, No. 2, 22–3.
Paciorkovskij, V. V., 'Kritičeskij analiz koncepcii social'nogo dejstvija' (Critical Analysis of the Conception of Social Action), in *Sociologičeskie issledovanija*, No. 2, 1975, 197–206.

Petrov, I. I., 'O nekotorych ponjatijach teorii social'noj stratifickacii M. Vebera' (Some Concepts of Max Weber's Theory of Social Stratification), in *Istoriko-filosofskij sbornik. Materialy teoretičeskoj konferencii aspirantov filosofskogo facul'teta*, Moscow, 1971, 161–71.

Petrov, I. I., 'Ponjatie gospodstva u K. Marksa i M. Vebera' (The Concept of Domination in Karl Marx and Max Weber), unpublished manuscript, Moscow, 1979.

Petruševskij, D. M., *Očerki iz ekonomičeskoj istorii srednevekoj Evropy* (Studies on the Economic History of Medieval Europe), Moscow, 1928.

Philosophisches Wörterbuch, ed. by G. Klaus and M. Buhr, revised edn, Berlin, 1972.

Pokrovskij, M. N., *Istoričeskaja nauka i bor'ba klassov. Istorio-grafičeskie očerki, kritičeskie stat'i zametki* (Historical Science and the Class Struggle. Historigraphical Studies, Critical Article and Notes), 2 vols, Moscow/Leningrad, 1933. (See particularly, 'New' Tendencies in Russian Historical Literature; Vol. 1, 305–24.)

Poulantzas, Nicos, 'The Problem of the Capitalist State', *New Left Review*, 58, 1969, 67–78.

Poulantzas, Nicos, 'The Capitalist State: A Reply to Miliband and Laclau', *New Left Review*, 95, 1976, 63–83.

Poulantzas, Nicos, *Political Power and Social Classes*, London, 1978a.

Poulantzas, Nicos, *State, Power, Socialism*, London, 1978b.

Ritsert, Jürgen, 'Praktische Implikationen in Theorien', in J. Ritsert (ed.), *Zur Wissenschaftslogik einer kritischen Soziologie*, Frankfurt, 1976, 46–83.

Ritsert, Jürgen and Rolshausen, Claus, *Der Konservatismus der Kritischen Theorie*, Frankfurt, 1971.

Schuon, Karl Theodor, 'Typologie und kritische Theorie', in *Das Argument*, No. 50 (Kritik der bürgerlichen Wissenschaften), 1974, 93–124.

Seregin, A. S., *Kratkaja slovar' po filosofii* (The Little Philosophical Dictionary), Moscow, 1966.

Seregin, A. S., 'Veberovskaja "koncepcija racional'nosti" na službe buržuaznoj ideologii' (The Weberian 'Conception of Rationality' as a Function of Bourgeois Ideology), in *Voprosy effektivnosti part. propagandy i polit. informacii*, Moscow, No. 2, 1974, 88–101.

Seregin, A. S., 'Metodologičeskaja "nesostojateilnost" i social "naja suščnost" buržuaznoj koncepii racional'nosti' (The Methodological Untenability and the Social Essence of the Bourgeois Conception of Rationality), in *Kritika sovremennoj buržuaznoj i revizionistkoj ideologii*, Moscow, 1975, 68–83.

Sorg, Richard, *Marxismus und Protestantismus in Deutschland. Eine religions-soziologisch-sozialgeschichtliche Studie zur Marxismus-Rezeption in der evangelischen Kirche 1848–1948*, Cologne, 1974 (see 41 ff.).

Špakova, R. P., Dmitriev, A. V., and Lebedev, P. N., 'Maks Veber i sovremennaja buržuaznaja sociologija (racionalističeskie koncepcii upravlenija)' (Max Weber and Current Sociology – Rationalist Conceptions of Administration), in *Vestnik Leningradskogo Universiteta*, No. 11, 1973, 76–87.

Špakova, R. P., 'Kritika teorii charizmatičeskogo liderstva', (Critique of the Theory of Charismatic Leadership), in *Vestnik Leningradskogo Universiteta*, No. 23, 1974, 75–84.
Stoklickaja-Tereškovič, V., 'Gorod c istoriko-sociologičeskoj tocki zrenija' (The City from a Historical-Sociological Perspective), in *Pečat' i Revol'jucija*, 1925, No. 1, 62–78 and No. 3, 109–18.
Streisand, Joachim, 'Max Weber: Politik, Soziologie und Geschichtsschreibung', in J. Streisand (ed.), *Studien über die deutsche Geschichtswissenschaft*, Vol. 2, Berlin, 1965, 179–89.
Streisand, Joachim, 'Max Weber', in *Biographisches Lexikon zur deutschen Geschichte. Von den Anfängen bis 1945*, 2nd (revised) edn, Berlin, 1970, 722–3.
Szczepánski, Jan, '"Socijologia Rzumiejaca" Maxa Webera', in *Socjologia Rozwój Problematyki i Metod*, Warsaw, 1967, 334–5.
Tadić, Lubomir, 'Sozialismus und Bürokratie', in Ossip K. Flechtheim and E. Grassi (eds), *Marxistische Praxis. Selbstverwirklichung und Selbstorganisation des Menschen in der Gesellschaft*, Munich, 1973.
Therbon, Göran, *Science, Class and Society. On the Formation of Sociology and Historical Materialism*, London, 1976.
Tokarew, S. A., 'Entstehung und Frühformen der Religion', in *Sowjetwissenschaft. Gesellschaftswissenschaftliche Beiträge*, No. 7, Berlin, 1957.
Töpfer, Bernhard, 'Neue Publikationen zur Stadtgeschichte der Feudalepoche', in *Jahrbuch für Wirtschaftsgeschichte*, 26, 1973, 235–49.
Ugrinovič, D. M., *Religija i obščestvo* (Religion and Society), Moscow, 1971.
Ugrinovič, D. M., *Vvedenie v teoretičeskoe religiovedenie* (Introduction to the Theoretical Science of Religion), Moscow, 1973, 72 ff.
Vincent, Jean-Marie, 'Weber, Max', in *BSE*, Vol. 7, 81, 2nd edn, Moscow, 1951.
Vincent, Jean-Marie, 'La methodologie de Max Weber', in *Les Temps Modernes*, 1967a, 1826–49 (No. 251, also in Vincent, 1973, 171–96).
Vincent, Jean-Marie, 'Aux sources de la pensée de Max Weber', in *L'homme et la société*, 1967b, No. 6, 49–66 (also in Vincent, 1973, 145–70).
Vincent, Jean-Marie, 'Weber ou Marx', in *L'homme et la société*, 1968, No. 10, 87–102 (also in Vincent, 1973, 197–216).
Vincent, Jean-Marie, *Fétichisme et société*, Paris, 1973. Apart from the abovementioned articles, it also contains the following chapters on Weber's work: 'Le capitalisme selon Weber' (Chapter 6, 145–70); 'Remarques sur Marx et Weber comme théoriciens du droit et de l'Etat' (Chapter 3, 75–90).
Weights, A., 'Weber on "Legitimate Domination": A Theoretical Critique of Weber's Conceptualization of "Relations of Domination"', in *Economy and Society*, 7, 1978, 56–73.
Wittfogel, Karl August, *Die Wissenschaft der bürgerlichen Gesellschaft. Eine marxistische Untersuchung*, Berlin, 1922.
Wittfogel, Karl August, *Geschichte der bürgerlichen Gesellschaft*, Vienna, 1924.

Wittfogel, Karl August, 'Probleme der chinesischen Wirtschaftsgeschichte', in *Archiv für Sozialwissenschaft und Sozialpolitik*, Vol. 57, 1927.
Wittfogel, Karl August, 'Wissen und Gesellschaft. Neuere deutsche Literatur zur "Wissenssoziologie"', in *UBM*, 5, 1931a, 83–102.
Wittfogel, Karl August, *Wirtschaft und Gesellschaft Chinas. Versuch der Wissenschaftlichen Analyse einer grossen asiatischen Agrargesellschaft (Part 1: Produktivkräfte, Produktions – und Zirkulationsprozess)*. Leipzig, 1931b.
Wörterbuch der maxistisch-leninistischen Soziologie, ed. by W. E. Hahn *et al.*, 2nd edn, Opladen, 1971.
Zdravomyslov, A. G., 'Max Weber and his "Overcoming" of Marxism', unpublished manuscript, Moscow, 1979.

III Additional works on the relationship between Marx and Weber

Antonio, Robert J. and Glassman, Ronald H. (eds), *A Weber-Marx-Dialogue*, University Press of Kansas, Lawrence, 1985.
Ashcroft, Richard, 'Marx and Weber on Liberalism as Bourgeois Ideology', in *Comparative Studies in Sociology and History*, 14, 1972 (The Hague), 130–68.
Bedeschi, Giuseppe, 'Da Marx a Weber', in Max Weber, *Sul socialismo reale*, with an introduction by M. Ciampa, Rome, 1979, 111–21.
Below, Georg von, *Die deutsche Geschichtsschreibung*, Leipzig, 1916.
Bendix, Reinhard, 'Inequality and Social Structure. A Comparison of Marx and Weber', in *ASR*, 39, 1974, 149–61.
Birnbaum, Norman, 'Conflicting Interpretations of the Rise of Capitalism: Marx und Weber', in *British Journal of Sociology*, Vol. IV, 1953, 125–41.
Buhler, Antoine, 'Production de sens et légitimation sociale. Karl Marx et Max Weber', in *Social Compass*, XXIII, 1976, 317–44.
Ferrarotti, Franco, *Max Weber and the Destiny of Reason*, London and New York, 1982.
Giddens, Anthony, *Capitalism and Modern Social Theory. An Analysis of the Writings of Marx, Durkheim and Weber*, Cambridge, 1971.
Giddens, Anthony, *The Class Structure of the Advanced Societies*, London, 1973a.
Giddens, Anthony, 'Marx, Weber und die Entwicklung des Kapitalismus', in Seyfarth and Sprondel (eds), 1973b, 65–96.
Giddens, Anthony, *Studies in Social and Political Theory*, London, 1977.
Hennen, Manfred, *Krise der Rationalität – Dilemma der Soziologie. Zur kritischen Rezeption Max Webers*, Stuttgart, 1976.
Houtart, François, 'Geneviève Lemercinier, Weberian Theory and the Ideological Function of Religion', in *Social Compass* XXIII, 1976, 345–54.
Kocka, Jürgen, 'Karl Marx und Max Weber im Vergleich. Sozialwissenschaften zwischen Dogmatismus und Dezisionismus', in H.-U. Wehler (ed.), *Geschichte und Ökonomie*, Cologne, 1973, 54–84. (An extended version is reprinted in J. Kocka, *Sozialgeschichte. Begriff – Entwicklung – Problem*, Göttingen, 1977, 9–47.)

Kocka, Jürgen, 'Kontroversen über Max Weber', in *Neue Politische Literatur*, XXI, 1976, 281–301.
Landshut, Siegfried, *Kritik der Soziologie und andere Schriften zur Politik*, Neuwied/Berlin, 1969.
Lenhardt, Gero, 'Theorie der Rationalisierung und Sozialismuskritik bei M. Weber', in *Leviathan*, 3, 1980, 295–319.
Löwith, Karl, 'Max Weber und Karl Marx (1932)', in *Gesammelte Abhandlungen*, Stuttgart, 1960, 1–67.
Löwith, Karl, *Max Weber and Karl Marx*, edited with an introduction by Tom Bottomore and William Outhwaite, London, 1982.
Lowy, Michael, 'Weber et Marx', in *L'homme et la société*, 1971, No. 20, 85–110.
Marshall, Gordon, *In Search of the Spirit of Capitalism. An Essay on Max Weber's Protestant Ethic Thesis*, London, 1982.
Martin, Alfred von, 'Zum Verhältnis von Mensch und Gesellschaft, Karl Marx – Carl Schmitt – Max Weber', in A. Martin, *Ordnung und Freiheit*, Frankfurt, 1956, 186 ff.
Mayer, Carl, 'Die Marx-Interpretationen von Max Weber', in *SW*, 25, 1974, 265–77.
Mommsen, Wolfgang, 'Kapitalismus und Sozialismus. Die Auseinandersetzung mit Karl Marx', in W. Mommsen, *Max Weber*, Frankfurt, 1974, 144–81.
Nixon, Charles R., 'The Relations between States and Economies in Marx and Weber', unpublished manuscript, 1979.
Roth, Guenther, 'Introduction' to Max Weber, *Economy and Society*, ed. by G. Roth and C. W. Wittich, New York, 1968.
Roth, Guenther, 'The Historical Relationship to Marxism', in R. Bendix and G. Roth, *Scholarship and Partisanship: Essays on Max Weber*, Berkeley, 1971, 227–52.
Roth, Guenther, 'Political Critiques of Max Weber: Some Implications for Political Sociology', in Bendix and Roth, *op. cit.*, 55–69.
Roth, Guenther, 'Max Weber: A Bibliographical Essay', in *ZfS*, 6, 1977, 91–118.
Roth, Guenther, Essay on J. Kocka, Sozialgeschichte, in *Soziologische Revue*, 2, 1979, 3–8.
Steinvorth, Ulrich, 'Wertfreiheit der Wissenschaften bei Marx, Weber und Adorno', in *Zeitschrift für allgemeine Wissenschaftstheorie*, 9, 1978, 293–306.
Therborn, Goeran, *Science, Class and Society*, London, 1976.
Turner, Bryan S., *Weber and Islam. A Critical Study*, London, 1974 (particularly Chapter 11: 'Marx, Weber and Islam').
Weiss, Johannes, 'On the Marxist Reception and Critique of Max Weber in Eastern Europe' in R. J. Antonio and R. M. Glassman (eds), *op. cit.*, pp. 117–31.
Weiss, Johannes (ed.), 'Die aktuelle Bedeutung des Werks von Karl Marx und Max Weber. Beiträge zi einer internationalen Konferenz', forthcoming.
Zander, Jürgen, *Das Problem der Beziehung Max Webers zu Karl Marx*, Frankfurt, 1978.

Zeitlin, Irving, *Rethinking Sociology: A Critique of Contemporary Theory*, New York, 1973, 123–36.

IV General literature

Ahlberg, René, *'Dialektische Philosophie' und Gesellschaft in der Sowjetunion*, Berlin, 1960.
Ahlberg, René, 'Der vergessene Philosoph. Abraham Moissevitsch Deborin', in L. Labedz (ed.), 1965, 162–86.
Ahlberg, René, *Entwicklungsprobleme der empirischen Sozialforschung in der UdSSR (1917–1966). Eine wissenschaftsgeschichtliche Analyse*, Wiesbaden, 1968.
Ahlberg, René (ed.), *Soziologie in der Sowjetunion. Ausgewählte sowjetische Abhandlungen zu Problemen der sozialistischen Gesellschaft*, Freiburg, 1969.
Ahlberg, René, *Die sozialistische Bürokratie. Die marxistische Kritik am etablierten Sozialismus*, Stuttgart, 1976.
Albert, Hans, *Konstruktion und Kritik. Aufsätze zur Philosophie des kritischen Rationalismus*, Hamburg, 1972.
Albrow, Martin, *Bureaucracy*, London, 1970.
Aleksandrov, G. F., *Istorija sociologičeskich učenii* (History of the Sociological Doctrines), Vol. 1, Moscow, 1959.
Bab, Julius, 'Max Weber', in *Die Weltbühne. Der Schaubühne XIV. Jahr*, Vol. 16, Manuals 1 and 2, 1920, 101–4.
Baechler, Jean, 'Die Entstehung des kaptialistischen Systems', in Seyfarth and Sprondel (eds), 1973, 135–61.
Balla, Balint, *Kaderverwaltung. Versuch zu einer Idealtypisierung der 'Bürokratie' sowjetisch-volksdemokratischen Typs*, Stuttgart, 1972.
Baumgarten, Eduard, *Max Weber. Werk und Person, Dokumente*, selected and annotated by Eduard Baumgarten, Tübingen, 1964.
Bergstraesser, A., 'Max Webers Antrittsvorlesung in zeitgeschichtlicher Perspektive', in *Vierteljahreshefte für Zeitgeschichte*, 5, 1957, 209–19.
Besnard, Philippe (ed.), *Protestantisme et Capitalisme – La Controverse Post-Weberienne*, Paris, 1970.
Binns, David, *Beyond the Sociology of Conflict*, London, 1977.
Bokszański, Zbigniew, 'Florian Znanieckie's Concept of Social Action and the Theory of Action in Sociology', in *PSB*, 1968, No. 1, 18–29.
Boring, G. and Taubert, H., (eds), *Sociological Research in the German Democratic Republic*, Berlin, 1970.
Bosse, Hans, *Marx-Weber-Troeltsch. Religionssoziologie und marxistische Ideologiekritik*, Munich and Mainz, 1970.
Breuer, Stefan, 'Die Evolution der Disziplin. Zum Verhältnis von Rationalität und Herrschaft in Max Webers Theorie der vorrationalen Welt', in *KZfSS*, 30, 1978, 409–37.
Brinkmann, Heinrich, *Stalin, Theoretiker der Bürokratie. Eine Streitschrift gegen den offenen Stalinismus und gegen die verlegenen Entstalinisierer*, Erlangen, 1971.
Brokmeier, Peter, 'Uber die Bedeutung Sohn-Rethels für eine materialistische Theorie der Übergangsgesellschaften in Osteuropa', in Peter

W. Schulze (ed.) *Übergangsgesellschaft: Herrschaftsform und Praxis am Beispiel der Sowjetunion*, Frankfurt, 1974, 115–48.

Brugger, Winfried, *Menschenrechtsethos und Verantwortungspolitik. Max Webers Beitrag zur Analyse und Begründung der Menschenrechte*, Freiburg, 1980.

Bruun, H. H., *Science, Values and Politics in Max Webers Methodology*, Copenhagen, 1972.

Bryant, Christopher G. A., *Sociology in Action. A Critique of Selected Conceptions of the Social Role of the Sociologist*, London, 1976.

Buchholz, A., *Ideologie und Forschung in der sowjetischen Naturwissenschaft*, Stuttgart, 1953.

Bukharin, Nikolai and Deborin, Abram, *Kontroversen über dialektischen und mechanistischen Materialismus*, Frankfurt, 1974.

Čagin, B. A., 'Razvitie sociologičeskoj mysli v SSR v 20-e gody' (The Development of Sociological Thought in the USSR in the 1920s), in *FN*, 1967, No. 5, 100–9.

Čagin, B. A., *Očerk istorii sociologičeskoj mysli v SSSR* (Sketch of the History of Sociological Thought in the USSR), Leningrad, 1971.

Cavalli, Luciano, *Max Weber. Religione e societá*, Bologna, 1968.

Coniavitis, Thomas, *Irrationalitet – rationalitet. Max Weber – Georg Lukács – en uppgörelse* (with English summary), Stockholm, 1977.

Costea, Stefan and Ungureanu, Ion, *A Concise History of Romanian Sociology*, Bucharest, 1981.

Dux, Günther, 'Religion, Geschichte und sozialer Wandel in Max Webers Religionssoziologie', in Seyfarth and Sprondel (eds), 1973, 313–37.

Eisenstadt, S. N. (ed.), *The Protestant Ethic and Modernization*, New York/London, 1969.

Elleinstein, Jean, *Geschichite des 'Stalinismus'*, Berlin, 1977.

Ferber, Christian von, 'Der Werturteilsstreit 1909/1959. Versuch einer wissenschaftsgeschichtlichen Interpretation', in Ernst Topitsch (ed.), *Logik der Sozialwissenschaften*, 2nd edn, Cologne/Berlin, 1965, 165–80.

Ferber, Christian von, *Die Gewalt in der Politik. Auseinandersetzung mit Max Weber*, Stuttgart, 1970.

Fetscher, Iring, 'Zum Begriff der "objektiven Möglichkeit" bei Max Weber und G. Lukács', in *RIPh*, 27, 1973, 501–25.

Giddens, Anthony, *Politics and Sociology in the Thought of Max Weber*, London, 1972.

Graham, Loren R., *Dialektischer Materialismus und Naturwissenschaften in der UdSSR*, Frankfurt, 1974.

Grušin, B. A., 'Sociology and the Sociologist', in *Current Digest of the Soviet Press*, Vol. 17, No. 40, 1965, 15–16.

Hahn, Erich, *Theoretische Probleme der marxistischen Soziologie*, Cologne, 1974.

Hahn, Jeffrey, W., 'The Role of Soviet Sociologists in the Making of Social Policy', in R. B. Remnek (ed.), 1977, 34–58.

Hanak, T., *Die marxistische Philosophie und Soziologie*. Stuttgart, 1976.

Henrich, Dieter, *Die Einheit der Wissenschaftslehre Max Webers*, Tübingen, 1952.

Hofmann, Werner, *Stalinismus und Antikommunismus. Zur Soziologie des Ost-West-Konflikts*, 2nd revised edn, Frankfurt, 1968.

Hufnagel, Gerhard, *Kritik als Beruf. Der kritische Gehalt im Werk Max Webers*, Frankfurt/Berlin/Vienna, 1971.

Jaeggi, Urs and Honneth, Axel (eds), *Theorien des Historischen Materialismus*, Frankfurt, 1977.

Jakovlev, W. M., 'Social'naja priroda bjurokratii v sovremmenoj buržuaznoj sociologii' (The Social Nature of Bureaucracy in Contemporary Bourgeois Sociology), dissertation, Leningrad, 1975.

Joas, H. 'G. H. Mead', in D. Käsler (ed.), *Klassiker des soziologischen Denkens*, Vol. II, Munich, 1978, 7–39.

Käsler, Dirk, 'Max Weber', in D. Käsler, *Klassiker des soziologischen Denkens*, Vol. II, Munich, 1978, 40–177.

Kiss, Gabor, *Marxismus als Soziologie: Theorie und Empirie in den Sozialwissenschaften der DDR, UdSSR, Polens, der CSSR, Ungarns, Bulgariens und Rumäniens*, Reinbek, 1971.

Klaus, G. and Schulze, H., *Sinn, Gesetz und Fortschritt in der Geschichte*, Berlin, 1967.

Klušin, V. I., 'Sociologija v Petrogradskom Universitete (1920–1924)', in *Vestnik LGU*, 1964, No. 5.

Kon, Igor S., 'Zur Frage des Gegenstandes der Soziologie – kurzer geschichtlicher Abriss', in *DZPh*, 1, 1961, 46–65.

König, René, 'Soziologie in der Sowjetunion', in *KZfSS*, 11, 1959, 345–7.

Konrad, György and Szelényi, Ivan, *Die Intelligenz auf dem Weg zur Klassenmacht*, Frankfurt, 1978.

Koschwitz, Hans Jürgen, 'Zur Entwicklung der soziologischen Forschung und Wissenschaft in der Sowjetunion', in *KZfSS*, 22, 1970, 501–19.

Kozlovskij, V. E. and Sychev, J. A., 'Discussion of J. A. Levada's Course of Lectures on Sociology', in *Soviet Sociology*, 9, No. 3, 1970–1, 475–94.

Krahl, Hans-Jürgen, *Konstitution und Klassenkampf. Zur historischen Dialektik von bürgerlicher Emanzipation und proletarischer Revolution*, Frankfurt, 1971.

Krysmanski, Hans-Jürgen and Marwedel, Peter (eds), *Die Krise in der Soziologie*, Cologne, 1975.

Kuczynski, Jurgen, 'Sociologičeskie zakony' (Sociological Laws), in *VF*, 1957, 95–100.

Labedz, Leopold (ed.), *Der Revisionismus*, Cologne/Berlin, 1965.

Lecourt, Dominique, *Proletarische Wissenschaft? Der 'Fall Lyssenko' und der Lyssenkismus* (Foreword by L. Althusser), Berlin, 1976.

Lenin, V. I., 'Materialism and Empiro-Criticism: Critical Comments on a Reactionary Philosophy', in V. I. Lenin, *Collected Works*, Vol. 14, London, 1962.

Lenin, V. I., *Collected Works*, London, 1964.

Levada, J. A., 'Lekcii po sociologii' (Lectures on Sociology), in *Informationnij bjulleten*, published by the Scientific Council for the Problems of Concrete Sociological Research, Academy of Sciences of the USSR, Moscow, 1967.

Lewytzkyj, Borys, *Politische Opposition in der Sowjetunion 1960–1972*,

Munich, 1972.
Lewytzkyj, Borys, *Die linke Opposition in der Sowjetunion*, Hamburg, 1974.
Loeser, Franz, 'A Measuring Unit for the Social Value of Social Processes', in J. W. Davis (ed.), *Value and Valuation. Axiological Studies in Honor of R. S. Hartman*, Knoxville, 1972, 233–8.
Löwenstein, Karl, *Max Webers staatspolitische Auffassungen in der Sicht unserer Zeit*, Frankfurt, 1965.
Marcuse, Herbert, *Soviet Marxism – A Critical Analysis*, Harmondsworth, 1971.
Markiewicz, Wladyslaw, 'Poland', in J. J. Wiatr (ed.), 1971, 97–135.
Marx, Karl, *Capital: A Critique of Political Economy*, 3 vols, London, 1977a.
Marx, Karl, *Grundrisse: Foundations of the Critique of Political Economy – Rough Draft*, Harmondsworth, 1977b.
Marx, Karl and Engels, Friedrich, *Werke (MEW)*, Berlin (East), 1956a ff.
Marx, Karl and Engels, Friedrich, *Selected Correspondence*, London, 1956b.
Marx, Karl and Engels, Friedrich, *Collected Works (MEW)*, London, 1975 ff.
Medvedev, Roy A., *Die Wahrheit ist unsere Stärke. Geschichte und Folgen des Stalinismus*, Frankfurt, 1973.
Medvedev, Zhores A., *Der Fall Lyssenko. Eine Wissenschaft kapituliert*, Munich, 1974.
Medvedev, Zhores A., *The Medvedev Papers. The Plight of Soviet Science Today*, London, 1971.
Mokrzycki, Edmund, 'Two Concepts of Humanistic Sociology', in *PSB*, 1969, No. 2, 32–47.
Mokrzycki, Edmund, 'The Operation of "Verstehen"', in *PSB*, 1970a, No. 2, 5–14.
Mokrzycki, Edmund, *Zacożenia socjologii humanistyczej* (The Presuppositions of Humanistic Sociology), Warsaw, 1970b. (Cf. the debate by L. Nowak and the reply of the author in *PSB*, 1971, No. 1, 144–9.)
Mommsen, Wolfgang J., *Max Weber und die deutsche Politik 1890–1920* (1959), 2nd revised and extended edn, Tübingen, 1974a.
Mommsen, Wolfgang J., *The Age of Bureaucracy. Perspectives on the Political Sociology of Max Weber*, Oxford, 1974b.
Mtschedlow, M. and Rutkewitsch, M., 'Der Kampf der Ideen in der gegenwärtigen Soziologie', in *Sowjetwissenschaft. Gesellschaftswissenschaftliche Beiträge*, 1975, No. 3, 269 ff.
Negt, Oskar, 'Marxismus als Legitimationswissenschaft. Zur Genese der stalinistischen Philosophie', in N. Bukharin and A. Deborin, 1974, 7–48.
Nowak, Leszek, 'Historical Momentums and Historical Epochs. An Attempt at a Non-Marxian Historical Materialism', in *Analyse und Kritik*, 1, 1979.
Osipov, G. and Rutkevich, M. N., 'Sociology in the USSR 1965–1975', *Current Sociology*, Vol. 26, No. 2, 1978.
Osipova, Elena V., 'The Soviet Union', in Wiatr (ed.), 1971, 177–98.

Parkin, Frank, *Marxism and Class Theory*, London, 1979.
Parsons, Talcott, 'Max Weber's Sociological Analysis of Capitalism and Modern Institutions', in Harry Elmer Barnes (ed.), *An Introduction to the History of Sociology*, Chicago, 1948.
Pawlowski, Tadeusz, *Methodologische Probleme in den Geistes- und sozialwissenschaften*, Warsaw, 1975.
Pethybridge, Roger William, *A Key to Soviet Politics. The June Cricis of 1957*, Geneva, 1962.
Pethybridge, Roger William, *The Social Prelude to Stalinism*, London, 1974.
Popov, S. I., *Kritika sovremennoj buržuaznoj sociologii*, Moscow, 1970.
Rehberg, Karl-Siegbert, 'Rationales Handeln als Grossbürgerliches Aktionsmodell bei Max Weber. Thesen zu einigen handlungstheoretischen Implikationen der "soziologischen Grundbegriffe" Max Webers', in *KZfSS*, 31, 1979, 199–236.
Remnek, Richard B. (ed.), *Social Scientists and Policy Making in the USSR*, New York, 1977.
Rex, John, *Discovering Sociology. Studies in Sociological Theory and Method*, London/Boston, 1973.
Sandkühler, Hans Jörg, 'Zur Begründung einer materialistischen Hermeneutik durch die materialistische Dialektik', in *Das Argument*, No. 77, 1972, 977–1005.
Sandkühler, Hans Jörg, *Praxis und Geschichtsbewusstsein. Studie zur materialistischen Dialektik, Erkenntnisteorie und Hermeneutik*, Frankfurt, 1973.
Ščeglov, A. V., 'Filosofskie diskussi v SSR v 20-ch i načale 30-ch godov' (The Philosophical Discussions in the USSR in the 1920s and beginning of 1930s), in *FN*, 1967, No. 5.
Schluchter, Wolfgang, *Wertfreiheit und Verantwortungsethik. Zum Verhältnis von Wissenschaft und Politik bei Max Weber*, Tübingen, 1971.
Schluchter, Wolfgang, *Aspekte bürokratischer Herrschaft; Studien zur Interpretation der fortschreitenden Industriegesellschaft*, Munich, 1972.
Schluchter, Wolfgang, *Die Entwicklung des okzidentalen Rationalismus. Eine Analyse von M. Webers Gesellschaftsgeschichte*, Tübingen, 1979.
Schmidt, Gustav, *Deutscher Historismus und der Übergang zur parlamentarischen Demokratie. Untersuchungen zu den politischen Gedanken von Meinecke – Troeltsch – Max Weber*, Lübeck, 1964.
Schulze, P. W., *Herrschaft und Klassen in der Sowjetgesellschaft. Die historischen Bedingungen des Stalinismus*, Frankfurt, 1977 (2nd edn, 1978).
Seyfarth, Constans, 'Protestantismus und gesellschaftliche Entwicklung: Zur Reformulierung eines Problems', in Seyfarth and Sprondel (eds), 1973, 338–66.
Seyfarth, Constans and Sprondel, W. M. (eds), *Religion und gesellschaftliche Entwicklung. Studien zur Protestantismus-Kapitalismus-These Max Webers*, Frankfurt, 1973.
Siemek, Marek J., 'Marxismus und hermeneutische Tradition', in B. Waldenfels *et al.* (eds), *Phänomenologie und Marxismus*, Vol. 1,

Frankfurt, 1977, 45–70. (In English, *Phenomenology and Marxism*, London, 1984.)

Sociologija v SSSR, 2 vols, Moscow, 1965.

Sorokin, P., 'Soziologie in Russland', in *Kölner Vierteiljahreshefte für Soziologie*, Vol. 3, 1923–4, 92–3.

Sorokin, P., 'Die russische Soziologie im 20. Jahrhundert', in *Jahrbuch für Soziologie. Eine internationale Sammlung*, ed. by G. Salomon, 2 vols, Karlsruhe, 1926, 462–83.

Spencer, Martin E., 'History and Sociology: An Analysis of Weber's "The City"', in *Sociology*, 11, 1977, 507–25.

Sprenkel, Otto B. van der, 'Weber on China', in *History and Theory*, 1964, 348–70.

Sprondel, Walter M., 'Sozialer Wandel, Ideen und Interessen: Systematisierungen zu Max Webers Protestantischer Ethik', in Seyfarth and Sprondel (eds), 1973, 206–24.

Stammer, Otto (ed.), *Max Weber and Sociology Today*, Oxford, 1971.

Steding, Christoph, *Politik und Wissenschaft bei Max Weber*, Breslau, 1932.

Tenbruck, Friedrich H., '"Science as a Vocation" – Revisited', in E. Forsthoff and R. Hörstel (eds), *Standorte im Zeitstrom. Festschrift für A. Gehlen*, Frankfurt, 1974.

Trotsky, Leo, *The Revolution Betrayed: What is the Soviet Union – Where is it going?*, New York, 1973.

Tuchscheerer, Walter, *Bevor das 'Kapital' entstand. Die Herausbildung und Entwicklung der ökonomischen Theorie von K. Marx in der Zeit von 1843 bis 1858*, Berlin, 1973.

Watnik, Morris, 'Relativismus und Klassenbewusstsein: Georg Lukács', in L. Labedz (ed.), 1965, 189–221.

Webb, Sidney and Webb, Beatrice, *Soviet Communism: A New Civilization*, 2 vols, 2nd edn, London, 1936.

Weber, Marianne, *Fichtes Sozialismus und sein Verhältnis zur Marxschen Doktrin*, Tübingen, 1900.

Weber, Marianne, *Max Weber. Ein Lebensbild*, Heidelberg, 1950.

Weinberg, Elizabeth Ann, *The Development of Sociology in the Soviet Union*, London, 1974.

Weiss, Johannes, *Max Webers Grundlegung der Soziologie. Eine Einführung*, Munich, 1975.

Weiss, Johannes, 'Review Essay on V. M. Bader et al., 1976, in *Soziologische Revue*, 1, 1978, 119–26. (Cf. the reply of the authors and the reply to the reply of the reviewer in *Soziologische Revue*, 2, 1979.)

Weiss, Johannes, 'Rationalität als Kommunikabilität. Überlegungen zur Rolle von Rationalitätsunterstellungen in der Soziologie', in Seyfarth and Sprondel (eds), *Max Weber und die Rationalisierung sozialen Handelns*, Stuttgart, 1981a.

Weiss, Johannes, 'Max Weber: Die Entzauberung der Welt', in *Grundprobleme der grossen Philosophen. Philosophie der Gegenwart IV*, ed. by J. Speck, Göttingen, 1981b.

Weyembergh, M., *Le volontarisme rationel de Max Weber*, Brussels, 1972.

Weyembergh, M., 'M. Weber et G. Lukács', in *RIPh*, 27, 1973, 474–580.
Wiatr, Jerzy J., 'Political Sociology in Eastern Europe: A Trend Report and Bibliography', in *Current Sociology*, 8, 1964.
Wiatr, Jerzy J. (ed.), *The State of Sociology in Eastern Europe Today*, Carbondale, 1971.
Wiatr, Jerzy J., 'Status and Prospects of Sociology in Eastern Europe', in J. J. Wiatr (ed.), 1971, 1–19.
Zingerle, Arnold, *Max Webers historische Soziologie. Aspekte und Materialien zur Wirkungsgeschichte*, Darmstadt, 1981.

Name index

Adler, Max, 17, 90, 158, 164
Adorno, T., 105
Ahlberg, René, 12, 169
Albert, Hans, 158, 173
Albrow, Martin, 169
Althusser, Louis, 145
Anderson, Perry, 95
Aron, Raymond, 100, 127, 134, 143
Assaf'ev, B. V., 167
Assmann, Georg, 153, 156, 161, 162

Bab, Julius, 147
Bader, Veit-Michael, 55, 111, 117, 118, 120, 156, 159, 160, 161, 163, 169, 170, 171
Bahro, Rudolf, 115
Bakurkin, B. F., 160, 161
Baumgarten, Eduard, 147, 173
Bedeschi, Giuseppe, 144
Bel'cer, L. L., 19, 88, 91, 155, 156, 161–4
Berger, Peter L., 161
Bergner, Dieter, 150
Bergstraesser, Arnold, 171, 173
Besnard, Phillipe, 162
Beyer, W. R., 159
Binns, David, 165
Birnbaum, Norman, 162
Boese, Franz, 151
Bogdanov, A., 20
Bokszański, Zbigniew, 148, 161

Bollhagen, Peter, 69
Boring, G., 13
Borodaj, Jurij, 162
Bosse, Hans, 89
Braunreuther, Kurt, 19, 25, 68, 92, 150, 151, 153, 155, 156, 159, 162, 164, 171
Brugger, Winfried, 168
Bryant, Christopher G. A., 151
Bukharin, Nikolaj, 17, 90, 114, 146, 162, 169

Cacciari, Massimo, 144
Čagin, B. A., 12, 146, 148
Čalikova, Victorija A., 111, 168
Cantimori, Delio, 124
Cassano, F., 156, 164
Colletti, Lucio, 69
Coniavitis, Thomas, 157
Cooley, C. H., 158
Crompton, Rosemary, 164

Danilov, A. I., 45, 143, 148, 149, 156, 171
Deborin, 146
Devjatkova, Rimma P., 111, 115, 147, 149, 151, 154, 155, 156, 157, 158, 161, 169
Döbert, Rainer, 122
Drobnickij, O. G., 168
Durkheim, Emile, 74, 88, 148, 153

Eder, Klaus, 122, 161

INDEX

Einstein, Albert, 145
Eisenstadt, S. N., 162
Elleinstein, Jean, 115, 169
Engels, Friedrich, 3, 9, 64, 65, 75, 76, 81, 85, 93, 120, 127, 144, 147, 148, 150, 151, 160, 162, 163

Ferber, Christian von, 124, 129, 130, 133, 151, 173
Fetscher, Iring, 57, 59, 157, 164
Feuerbach, Ludwig, 22, 76, 88
Fleischer, Julia, 168
Fojtik, J., 65, 143, 148, 149, 155, 166
Freud, Sigmund, 88
Freyer, Hans, 151
Fromm, Erich, 159

Gajdenko, P. P., 19, 101, 103, 105, 106, 149, 166, 167
Gedö, András, 159
Giddens, Anthony, 124, 139, 143, 162, 164, 171, 172
Glezerman, G. E., 74
Graham, Loren A., 145
Grušin, B. A., 12, 13
Gubbay, Jon, 164
Gvišiani, D. M., 158

Haase, Carl, 166
Habermas, Jürgen, 40, 100, 119, 122, 141, 168
Hahn, Erich, 12, 73, 78, 159, 160
Hegel, G. W. F., 21, 28, 39, 49, 53, 55, 60, 107, 157, 169
Heise, Wolfgang, 149, 171
Heller, Agnes, 159
Hempel, C. G., 62
Henrich, Dieter, 149, 155
Herkommer, Sebastian, 52, 91, 164
Hofmann, Werner, 33, 146, 149, 151, 152, 170
Holz, Hans Heinz, 167
Horn, Johannes-Heinz, 85, 86, 88
Hufnagel, Gerhard, 173

Ionin, L. G., 158

Jaeggi, Urs, 144

Jaspers, Karl, 143
Joas, Hans, 161

Kant, Immanuel, 19, 21, 22, 24, 44, 53, 149, 150, 154, 157
Kapelju š, F., 95, 147, 162
Kareev, N. I., 95
Kautsky, Karl, 17, 90, 95, 97, 162, 168
Kejzerov, N. M., 169
Kempski, Jürgen von, 158
Kiss, Gabor, 12, 15, 73, 146, 159, 160
Klaus, Georg, 153
Klein, Fritz, 171
Klügl, Johann, 85, 159
Klušin, V. I., 146
Kmita, Jerzy, 68, 144, 158, 159
Koch, Gisela, 78, 79, 159, 160
Kocka, Jürgen, 149, 150, 173
Kofler, Leo, 17, 162, 166, 169
Kolakowski, Leszek, 15
Kon, Igor, S., 19, 33, 147, 149, 151, 153, 155, 159, 164
Konrad, György, 165
Korablev, L. V., 62, 156, 168
Korf, Gertraud, 45, 49, 50, 53, 55, 61, 62, 111, 147, 148, 149, 150, 154, 155, 157, 160, 173
Kosik, Karel, 159
Kozlovskij, V. E., 74
Kozyr-Kowalski, Stanislaw, 101, 144, 154, 164
Krahl, Hans-Jürgen, 59, 157
Kramer, Horst, 113, 149, 164, 171, 173
Kretzschmar, Ute, 75, 76, 158, 160, 161, 173
Krysmanski, Hans-Jürgen, 145
Kuczynski, Jürgen, 33, 35, 36, 151–3, 155, 171
Kuznecov, Anatolij A., 19, 85, 87, 88, 111, 163
Kvesko, Raisa B., 100, 114, 143, 159, 164

Lecourt, Dominique, 145
Lefebvre, Henri, 159
Lefèvre, Wolfgang, 150, 167, 171

Leithäuser, Thomas, 159
Lenhardt, Gero, 144
Lenin, V. I., 11, 14, 16, 20-2, 49, 64, 65, 69, 114, 119, 127, 145, 146, 148, 149, 151, 153, 155, 159, 160, 172
Levada, J., 73, 74, 159
Levina, M. I., 147, 156, 162, 163
Lewis, John, 151, 153, 171
Lewytzkyj, Boris, 145
Loeser, Franz, 154
Löwith, Karl, 167
Luckmann, Thomas, 161
Luhmann, Niklas, 83
Lukács, Georg, 17, 19, 56-61, 94, 124, 137, 146, 148, 151, 153, 154, 157, 162, 167, 168, 172
Lunačarskij, Anatolij, 20, 101-5, 167

Mach, Ernst, 20, 149
Mägdefrau, Werner, 98
Mannheim, Karl, 143
Marcuse, Herbert, 17, 109-11, 124, 144, 148, 151, 166, 168
Markarjan, E. S., 148, 158
Markiewicz, Wladyslaw, 148
Marwedel, Peter, 145
Marx, Karl, 1, 3, 5, 9, 21-3, 33, 39, 52, 55, 62, 64, 65, 67, 69, 75-9, 81, 85, 89, 93, 104, 110, 112, 114, 115, 117, 127, 131, 141, 143, 144, 147, 149-53, 156, 160-5, 167, 169, 170
Maschkin, N. A., 147
Matthes, Joachim, 148
Mayer, Carl, 143
Mead, George Herbert, 158, 160
Medvedev, Roj A., 146, 148
Medvedev, Zhores A., 145
Merleau-Ponty, Maurice, 57
Mettler, A., 163
Meurer, Bärbel, 170
Michels, Robert, 152
Miliband, Ralph, 120
Mills, C. W., 143, 166
Milskaja, L. T., 143
Mocek, Reinhard, 150
Mokrzycki, Edmund, 148

Momdjian, K. N., 74
Mommsen, Wolfgang J., 124, 126, 127, 129-33, 143, 147, 171-4
Moskvičev, L. N., 151
Mtschedlow, M., 153

Naumova, N. F., 158, 161, 162, 168
Neumann, Franz L., 171
Neumann, T., 156
Neusychin, Alexander I., 2, 7, 17, 48, 87, 88, 90, 95-7, 143, 147-9, 155, 158, 162, 165
Nietzsche, Friedrich, 88, 163
Nixon, Charles R., 170
Novikov, N. V., 161
Nowak, Leszek, 62, 63, 68, 144, 158, 159, 161

Offe, Claus, 119, 121, 165
Osipov, G. V., 13, 19, 156
Osipova, E. V., 13, 148
Ossowska, Marie, 152

Paciorkovskij, V. V., 19, 160, 161
Pareto, V., 161
Paris, R., 161
Parkin, F., 165
Parsons, Talcott, 83, 161
Pethybridge, Roger W., 169
Petrov, Igor I., 164
Petruševskij, D. M., 148
Plekhanov, Georgij V., 172
Pokrovskij, M. N., 148, 155
Poulantzas, Nicos, 120, 170
Preobrazhensky, E. A., 114, 169

Rachfahl, Friedrich, 155
Rehberg, Karl-Siegbert, 124, 129, 130, 133, 173
Rickert, Heinrich, 21, 50, 108, 149, 158
Ritsert, Jürgen, 173
Rödel, U., 122, 161
Roth, Guenther, 90, 95, 143, 152, 157, 163, 164, 171, 174
Rutkevitsch, M., 13, 153

Sandkühler, H. J., 70, 71, 150, 159
Sartre, Jean-Paul, 71

INDEX

Ščeglov, A. V., 148
Schäfer, G., 171
Schluchter, Wolfgang, 100, 121, 169, 173
Schmidt, Gustav, 171, 173
Schulze, H., 153
Schulze, P. W., 146
Schütz, Alfred, 158
Seregin, A. S., 114
Seyfarth, Constans, 162
Shub, D., 172
Siemek, Marek J., 64, 159
Šikin, J. M., 166
Simmel, Georg, 148, 156
Smith, Adam, 76
Söllner, A., 171
Sombart, Werner, 98, 152, 163
Sorokin, Pitirim, 146
Špakova, R. P., 114, 157, 168
Spann, Otmar, 163
Spencer, Martin E., 166
Sprondel, Walter M., 162
Stalin, J. V., 5, 10, 13, 14, 146, 168
Stammer, Otto, 127, 173
Steding, Christoph, 171
Steinvorth, Ulrich, 152
Stetsky, A. J., 145
Štoff, V. A., 158
Stoklickaja-Tereškovič, V., 95–7, 158, 165
Stollberg, Rudhard, 153, 156, 161, 162
Streisand, Joachim, 171, 172
Suvorov, S. A., 20
Sychev, J., 74

Szczepánski, Jan, 144
Szelényi, Ivan, 165

Tadić, Lubomir, 115
Tarde, Gabriel, 149
Taubert, H., 13
Thomas, W. I., 158
Tjaden, Karl Heinz, 161
Töpfer, Bernhard, 166
Trotzky, L., 15
Tuchscheerer, Walter, 160

Vincent, Jean-Marie, 67, 95, 111, 164

Webb, Beatrice, 145
Webb, Sidney, 145
Weber, Marianne, 147, 163, 164, 172, 174
Weinberg, Elizabeth Ann, 12, 73, 146
Weiss, Johannes, 134, 149, 155, 156, 158, 163, 168, 173
Wetter, Gustav A., 146
Wetzel, M., 161
Weyembergh, M., 157
Wiatr, Jerzy J., 73, 148, 159
Winch, Peter, 159
Winckelmann, Johannes, 121, 147, 170
Wittfogel, Karl August, 17, 19, 95, 97, 145, 149, 165, 166

Zander, Jürgen, 143
Znaniecki, Florian, 18

Subject index

Action: social, 5, 6, 48, 49, 54, 55, 57, 72, 74, 76, 77, 79–83, 99, 100, 116, 117, 124, 128–30, 133, 134, 160, 161, 173; theory, 7, 74, 79–84, 120, 132, 158, 160, 171
Agnosticism, 19, 25, 44, 45, 48, 140, 163
Alienation, 6, 67, 79, 80, 117, 131, 167
Art, 7, 98, 100, 101, 103–7, 167
Authority, 7, 103, 108, 111, 112, 119–21, 139, 140, 145, 167–9

Base/Superstructure, 54, 55, 85, 87, 96, 98, 104, 118, 131, 156
Bourgeoisie, 16, 20, 25, 27, 58, 65, 97, 109, 110, 112, 115, 123, 125, 129, 145, 147, 163–5, 173
Bureaucracy, 67, 108, 109, 112–15, 119, 121, 127, 157, 169; socialist, 113
Bureaucratism, 113, 114

Capitalism, 16, 25, 79, 85, 87, 88, 92, 93, 95, 109–11, 118, 119, 125, 128, 131, 150, 151, 154, 160, 162, 165; the spirit of, 87, 162
Causal explanation, 23, 30, 34, 44, 63, 66, 68, 86, 159, 163
Chance, 49, 62
Charisma, 111, 129, 134, 168, 174
Christianity, 95, 163
City, 7, 94–8, 158, 165, 166
Class, 6, 7, 25–7, 35, 36, 38, 51, 52, 59, 66, 80, 90–5, 108, 114, 120, 123–5, 129, 131, 137, 147, 150, 164, 165, 171–3; conflict/struggle, 37, 93, 95, 97, 120, 153; consciousness, 57–9, 69, 94, 157; interests, 25, 36, 37, 41, 94, 118, 123–5, 157
Communicability, 47, 104, 110, 133, 134, 155, 159, 168, 173
Conflict/struggle, 27, 134, 137–9, 173
Culture, 98–109, 127, 173

Decisionism, 31, 42, 58, 141
Democracy, 113, 115, 119, 120, 126, 128, 133, 134, 140, 147, 170, 172; plebiscitary leader-democracy, 127
Depersonalisation (*Verunpersönlichung*), 80, 111, 113, 134, 154
Determinism, 39, 49, 61, 120, 124, 146, 153, 157
Dialectic, 5, 8, 22, 39, 52, 53, 56, 65, 70, 96, 137, 144, 153, 157
Dictatorship of the proletariat, 11, 112
Disenchantment (*Entzauberung*), 89, 108, 168
Domination, 108–10, 112–15, 118, 120, 122, 129, 150, 168, 169, 173

Economism, 120
Economy, 7, 22, 85, 87–92, 95, 96, 102, 110, 111, 114, 116–18, 127, 135, 144–6, 163, 165, 166, 170, 171
Elective affinity, 26, 27

Empirical research, 3, 13, 25, 26, 31, 48, 60, 66, 69, 73, 89, 93
Epistemology, 5, 19–28, 45, 46, 50, 52, 61, 64, 67, 69, 125, 128, 133, 143, 145, 150, 154
Ethical neutrality, 5, 20, 25, 28–33, 44, 63, 106, 125, 135–40, 149–54, 166
Ethics, 32, 35, 39, 87, 115, 123, 127, 132, 133, 135, 136, 139, 141, 150, 174; economic, 87, 162
Evolution, 56, 122, 153

Fatalism, 111
Formalism, 21, 25, 26, 33, 52, 105, 106, 109, 110

Hermeneutics, 30, 33, 42, 68–70, 136, 159
Historicity, 23, 36, 52, 53, 55, 63, 157, 168
History, 7, 36, 37, 39, 44–8, 50–6, 59, 70, 76, 88, 90, 91, 95–9, 103–6, 119, 122, 140, 144, 153, 158, 163–5
Human rights, 111, 115
Humanism, 18, 20, 115, 129, 132, 148

Ideal type, 5, 20, 25, 43, 46–9, 51–4, 56, 59–64, 66, 68, 96, 125, 149, 151, 155–8, 165
Idealisation, 48–51, 54, 56, 62, 63
Idealism, 6, 19, 20–2, 24, 25, 39, 44, 47, 48, 51, 53–6, 67, 68, 74, 76, 78, 80, 85, 90, 92, 93, 95, 98, 107, 125, 140, 149, 155, 156, 162, 164
Ideas, 54, 67, 78, 85, 88, 89, 102, 135, 146, 150, 153, 156, 170
Ideology, 26, 27, 45, 70, 80, 81, 85, 87, 88, 101, 104, 109, 110, 112, 114, 115, 118–20, 123–5, 128, 133, 134, 144, 147, 148, 150, 151, 161, 166; critique of, 15, 19, 20, 26–8, 70, 83, 99, 107, 123, 124, 130, 132, 135, 150, 171
Individualism, 6, 74, 76–8, 80, 128–30, 132, 134, 160

Intelligentsia, 146, 166
Interactionism, 81, 160
Interpretative: sociology, 100; understanding (*Verstehen*), 44, 63, 64, 66–71, 156
Irrationalism, 21, 25, 37, 40–2, 111, 115, 141, 154
Irrationality, 111, 115, 119, 139, 140, 154, 171

Labour value, 164
Law, the (*Recht*), 7, 116, 121, 122, 171
Laws/lawfulness, 14, 20, 21, 34, 37–9, 45, 48–52, 56, 61–3, 69, 75, 78–80, 93, 96, 97, 110, 116, 117, 119, 125, 140, 143, 155; natural, 78, 79, 117, 153, 170
Legitimacy, 12, 36, 40, 80, 88, 99, 112, 115, 116, 119–21, 126, 152, 170–2
Life world (*Lebenswelt*), 69
Logic, 26, 29–33, 35–40, 47, 48, 50–2, 54, 55, 57, 59, 70, 78, 91, 101, 104, 107, 109–11, 122, 129, 130–2, 136, 137, 140, 141, 146, 151, 152, 158, 168, 173

Machtstaat, 173
Materiality, 21, 63, 64, 78, 79, 80, 117, 156, 159
Meaning, 5, 6, 47, 48, 50, 51, 54, 61, 63, 67, 68, 70, 78, 83, 88, 99, 104, 106, 107, 117, 124, 133, 134, 136, 139, 169, 173; cultural, 42, 149, 173
Meaningful adequacy, 47–50, 54, 56, 60, 62, 155
Model, 62, 158
Music, 101–6, 167

Nation, 127, 172
Nationalism, 126, 172, 173
Nature, 36, 39, 69, 79, 87, 89, 104, 105, 109, 117, 163, 167
Neo-Kantianism, 19–21, 39, 149, 150, 155
Nihilism, 19, 25, 97

INDEX

Objective possibility, 48, 55–61, 63, 137, 155, 157
Objectivism, 25, 38, 120
Objectivity, 17, 20, 28, 33, 38, 45, 53, 56, 61, 63, 69, 70, 74, 78–80, 98, 117, 122, 156
Original accumulation, 88, 162

Party, 14, 58, 59, 115, 137, 146, 157, 166, 169
Personality cult, 13, 14, 168
Philosophy, 10, 11, 12, 20, 25, 40, 65, 73, 139, 149, 154, 162; of history, 7, 95, 131, 159, 171; of science, 7, 13, 19, 20, 63, 91; transcendental, 21, 45, 48, 150
Pluralism, 11, 31, 97, 145, 163
Positivism, 19, 20, 61, 90, 145, 149
Power, 11, 97, 109, 112, 115, 116, 120–2, 127, 133, 138, 145, 146, 169
Practice (*Praxis*), 39, 43, 44, 47, 51, 52, 54, 56, 58, 60, 61, 63, 65, 66, 71, 77, 78, 91, 94, 100, 115, 119, 123, 131, 134, 137, 152, 154, 157
Pragmatism, 20
Production: forces of, 50, 55, 67, 77, 96, 101, 110, 116, 117, 122, 153; relations of, 50, 55, 67, 69, 74, 75, 96, 118
Progress, 12, 23, 24, 34–7, 41, 61, 107, 152, 153
Protestantism, 7, 85, 162
Psychology, 50, 67, 88, 102, 118, 146, 163

Rationalism, 21, 105, 164, 166
Rationality, 8, 40, 42, 56, 66, 85, 100–9, 115, 116, 120–2, 133, 134, 137–41, 150, 166, 167, 168, 170; economic, 110; formal, 100, 110; instrumental, 109, 110; material, 109, 110, 115; technical; 100, 109, 110, 116; scientific, 100–2
Realism, 20, 53, 105
Reification, 61, 67, 79, 80
Relativism, 21, 143
Religion, 85–90, 91, 96, 103, 106, 110, 122, 150, 164, 166; sociology of, 85, 87, 89–91, 95, 99, 121, 161, 163, 167

Science, 7, 10, 21, 31, 40, 43, 46, 53, 96–8, 110, 123, 124, 135, 137–41, 145, 151, 152, 154, 166; natural, 1, 20, 46, 49, 50, 62–4, 78, 145, 150, 158, 165; of social reality, 21, 149
Scientific: critique, 15, 16, 136, 137, 144; method, 6, 26, 28, 31, 36, 41, 67
Social totality, 56–8, 60, 74, 80
Socialism, 9, 12, 16, 27, 86, 87, 100, 101, 110–15, 118, 127, 141, 143, 145, 150, 154, 166, 170, 172; rational, 112, 115
Society, 35, 36, 56, 74–6, 85, 90, 95, 103, 105, 109, 110, 116–18, 131, 134, 144, 145, 159
Stalinism, 10–17, 120, 146
State, 7, 75, 95, 115–21, 169–71
Statism, 120
Subjectivism, 19, 20, 21, 23–5, 44, 47, 93, 105, 118, 143, 150, 160, 164
System, 5, 82, 83, 88, 100, 103, 134, 161, 166

Technology, 24, 35, 78, 79, 100, 101, 106, 109, 145, 146, 153
Theory, 3, 13, 15, 22, 39, 44, 47–9, 51, 54–6, 64, 65, 72, 78, 82–4, 94, 95; critical, 4, 65, 122; of knowledge, 22, 34, 54, 64; of value, 93, 118, 164

Value: judgements, 30–3, 40–2, 151–4; relevance, 21, 23–5, 40–4, 50, 63, 64, 106, 108, 121, 126, 133, 135, 138, 149, 152, 173
Verein für Sozialpolitik, 28, 151
Volkswohlstand, 150

Work, 77, 131
World view (*Weltanschauung*), 11, 31, 65, 90, 134, 147, 154, 163, 168